REASONABLE DISAGREEMENT

This book examines the ways in which reasonable people can disagree about the requirements of political morality. Christopher McMahon argues that there will be a "zone of reasonable disagreement" surrounding most questions of political morality. Moral notions of right and wrong evolve over time as new zones of reasonable disagreement emerge out of old ones; thus political morality is both different in different societies with varying histories, and different now from what it was in the past. McMahon explores the phenomenon of reasonable disagreement in detail and traces its implications for the possibility of making moral judgments about other polities, past or present. His study sheds light on an important and often overlooked aspect of political life, and will be of interest to a wide range of readers in moral and political philosophy and in political theory.

CHRISTOPHER MCMAHON is Professor of Philosophy at the University of California, Santa Barbara. His publications include *Collective Rationality and Collective Reasoning* (2001).

REASONABLE DISAGREEMENT

A Theory of Political Morality

CHRISTOPHER McMAHON

CAMBRIDGE
UNIVERSITY PRESS

CAMBRIDGE UNIVERSITY PRESS
Cambridge, New York, Melbourne, Madrid, Cape Town, Singapore, São Paulo, Delhi

Cambridge University Press
The Edinburgh Building, Cambridge CB2 8RU, UK

Published in the United States of America by Cambridge University Press, New York

www.cambridge.org
Information on this title: www.cambridge.org/9780521762885

First published 2009

Printed in the United Kingdom at the University Press, Cambridge

A catalogue record for this publication is available from the British Library

Library of Congress Cataloguing in Publication data
McMahon, Christopher, 1945–
Reasonable disagreement : a theory of political morality / Christopher McMahon.
p.   cm.
ISBN 978-0-521-76288-5
1. Reasoning.   2. Political ethics.   I. Title.
BC177.M39   2009
172–dc22
2009008945

ISBN 978-0-521-76288-5 hardback

For Janine

Contents

Introduction

Talk of reasonable disagreement is a staple of political discourse. We often hear that a political issue admits of reasonable disagreement or is one about which reasonable people can disagree. But there has been little philosophical discussion of reasonable disagreement, and it is not clear how the phenomenon is to be understood.[1] Wherever we find political disagreement, the parties will typically be prepared to offer reasons for the positions they take. The different positions will, in this sense, be reasoned. But to assert that disagreement in a particular case is reasonable is to do more than acknowledge that the parties have reasons for the positions they take. It is to imply that at least two of the opposing positions could be supported by reasoning that is fully competent.

In many contexts, competent reasoning within a group can be expected to produce a convergence of opinion. When the exchange of arguments is carried out in good faith, it eliminates mistakes in reasoning, and we usually suppose that if everyone's reasoning has been purged of mistakes, there will be agreement. To offer and receive arguments in good faith is to respond only to the force of reason, ignoring the possibility that the options being considered will impinge positively or negatively on one's personal interests or the interests of a group with which one is affiliated. If there is to be such a thing as reasonable disagreement, however, it must sometimes be the case that competent reasoning within a group fails to produce a convergence of opinion.

---

[1] Charles Larmore discusses reasonable disagreement in "Pluralism and Reasonable Disagreement," in his *The Morals of Modernity* (Cambridge: Cambridge University Press, 1996), pp. 152–174. Larmore argues that reasonable disagreement, not pluralism, is the defining feature of a liberal society. He says, "The insight that has proven so significant for liberal thought is that reasonableness has ceased to seem a guarantee of ultimate agreement about deep questions concerning how we should live" (p. 168). On the view I shall propose, there is nothing peculiarly modern about reasonable disagreement, although it may be true that the possibility of reasonable disagreement has only recently been recognized.

Reasonable disagreement is disagreement that survives the best efforts of a group of reasoners to answer a particular question – that is, to find a unique answer that is required by reason. In political contexts, the question will concern how some aspect of political cooperation ought to be organized. In describing what he calls communicative action, "action oriented to reaching an understanding," Jürgen Habermas asserts that it proceeds on the assumption that agreement can be reached if discussion is carried on openly enough and continued long enough.[2] But when disagreement is reasonable, it will persist no matter how open discussion is or how long it continues. "Discussion," here, means the collective examination of the force of a given body of rational considerations. The considerations available to the group are such that no matter how competently they are examined, or for how long, agreement will not be produced. So understood, reasonable disagreement with respect to a particular issue need not be a permanent condition. Disagreement which has been reasonable may cease to possess this character if new considerations capable of guiding all competent reasoners to a definite conclusion become available. In general, disagreement among competent reasoners is marked by a continual search for considerations that will have this effect. Sometimes, however, the effort fails.

The principal challenge we face in providing an account of reasonable disagreement in politics is capturing both aspects of the phenomenon, the reasonableness and the disagreement. We usually suppose that competently reasoned views will agree, so part of what is involved in meeting the challenge is explaining why this need not always be the case. But in addition, the parties to political disputes often view at least some of those with whom they disagree as seriously mistaken about the appropriate way of organizing political cooperation. An adequate account of reasonable disagreement in politics must preserve this feature. It must explain not only how reasonable people can reach different conclusions, but also how they can fail to recognize other reasonable conclusions as reasonable.

This book connects with three main discussions in philosophy. In the first place, there has been much discussion in political philosophy of deliberative democracy. As has been mentioned, reasonable disagreement in politics can be understood as disagreement that survives, or would survive, shared deliberation conducted in good faith over an extended period of time. Thus if we accept the existence of reasonable political disagreement, we must acknowledge that there is more to political decision-

---

[2] Jürgen Habermas, *The Theory of Communicative Action*, vol. I, trans. Thomas McCarthy (Boston: Beacon, 1984), p. 42.

making, even under ideal conditions, than shared deliberation. This is not particularly controversial. Most deliberative democrats would be prepared to give a role to voting, for example. But I believe that a stronger claim is warranted. Consideration of the way political disagreement evolves over time makes it plausible that shared deliberation is not the sole engine of reasonable opinion formation in politics.

Second, reasonable political disagreement, as I understand it, has an important moral element. It is, in the first instance, disagreement about issues of political morality. An account of reasonable political disagreement must, then, explain how people reasoning competently about moral questions can nevertheless fail to agree. This requires an excursion into meta-ethics, the branch of philosophy that studies whether there is a legitimate place for truth and knowledge in connection with moral judgments. The two most familiar positions are realist and anti-realist. Realists suppose that we confront a domain of moral facts, and that moral judgments are true if they correctly represent these facts. Similarly, we have moral knowledge if we are justified in making moral judgments that are true. Anti-realists deny that moral judgments play a fact-stating role. I argue that neither view can provide an adequate account of reasonable moral disagreement. I thus develop an intermediate position that I call moral nominalism. I use it to explain how judgments of political morality that are competently reasoned can nevertheless disagree, but I believe that it has some appeal as a general meta-ethical position.

Third, the book makes contact with important issues in the philosophy of history. On the nominalist view that I propose, moral judgments employ socially available normative and evaluative concepts to construct moral worlds. But the available concepts of political morality vary somewhat from place to place, and they were also different in the past than they are today. A number of philosophical theories provide for the evolution of moral concepts. But some regard the moral thinking of past periods, and perhaps the present period as well, as determined by contingent social forces. The moral nominalism that I propose is different. It views the evolution of moral and political concepts as normatively guided. What evolves is the zone of reasonable disagreement, the set of positions that competent reasoners can hold. This means that the requirements of morality – the genuine requirements – were different in the past than they are now.

These themes are explored in six chapters. Chapter 1 begins with a discussion of reasonable disagreement about matters of empirical fact. It then proceeds to the political case. On the view of reasonable disagreement in politics that I present, the concept of reasonableness is employed in two

different ways. Reasonable disagreement is disagreement about the pattern of concessions that ought to characterize political cooperation, and the reasonableness of the different positions is manifested in two different ways. The positions display a willingness to make concessions, and it is possible to support the positions with competent reasoning. I believe that these two senses of reasonableness also underlie T. M. Scanlon's proposal that moral wrongness can be understood as the violation of a rule that no one can reasonably reject.[3] Scanlon's formula gives us a way of describing reasonable disagreement in politics. Where there is reasonable disagreement about how political cooperation morally ought to be organized, every proposal can be reasonably rejected by somebody.

Chapter 2 develops the theory of moral nominalism. As I understand it, the role of reason in politics is not limited to establishing efficient or effective means to the satisfaction of desires that people simply happen to have. Reason can criticize desires and establish ends. It can, as I put it, set targets. Given this, providing an account of reasonable disagreement involves developing a meta-ethics capable of explaining how competent reasoning about ultimate ends can fail to produce agreement. As I have said, the moral nominalism that I propose steers a middle course between anti-realist views according to which ends are set by desires that are, ultimately, beyond rational criticism, and realist views that posit mind-independent moral facts to which competent reasoners can gain epistemic access. In describing his own nominalism, Nelson Goodman speaks of "worldmaking," and according to the moral nominalism that I shall propose, in making moral judgments, we make the moral worlds we live in.[4] We can distinguish between moral judgments that are competently made and moral judgments that are incompetently made, but competent judgments will sometimes disagree.

Having developed, in chapter 2, a meta-ethical theory capable of providing for reasonable moral disagreement, I proceed in chapter 3 to examine agreement and disagreement in politics. The members of a particular political society, or polity, will typically have available a set of normative and evaluative concepts that can be employed to express claims, or more broadly, to advance reasons for or against particular ways of organizing political cooperation. Reasonable disagreement within a polity can be grounded in the fact that different people draw on different subsets of these concepts in making political judgments, in the fact that they interpret

---

[3] T. M. Scanlon, *What We Owe to Each Other* (Cambridge, MA: Harvard University Press, 1998), p. 153.
[4] Nelson Goodman, *Ways of Worldmaking* (Indianapolis: Hackett, 1978), esp. ch. 1.

the resulting reasons differently, or in the fact that they resolve in different ways conflicts among these reasons.

Reasonable disagreement survives open debate carried out over a long period of time. There are, however, other ways of resolving political disagreements, of settling on a way of organizing political cooperation when the members of a polity reasonably disagree. These are explored in chapter 4. One important point is that where we find reasonable disagreement about how some aspect of political cooperation ought to be organized, people will often have opportunities to act unilaterally on the judgments of political morality that they regard as correct. These actions can, in turn, create a social environment in which other people feel compelled, as competent reasoners, to modify their moral concepts. The ultimate result may be the resolution of disagreement by a force that is not the force of the better argument. Yet this outcome is not merely caused. The conceptual changes come about because people find that their former judgments no longer make sense in the evolving social situation.

Different communities can operate with different moral concepts. Chapter 5 discusses the implications of this fact. Traditionally, moral relativism holds that what is morally right in a particular community is relative to the social norms in place there. Moral nominalism does not have this consequence, but it does have a related one. No one can actually employ in moral reasoning all of the normative and evaluative concepts associated with the various cultures of the world. Each person operates with a subset. As has been noted, this can be a source of reasonable disagreement within a given polity. But the phenomenon is more pronounced when the parties to a disagreement are members of different polities, and especially when their concepts are provided by different cultural traditions. Thus on the view I am proposing, the differences in moral judgment that some writers regard as supporting moral relativism are instead explained as manifestations of a particularly deep form of reasonable disagreement.

I call the alternative to relativism that I sketch in chapter 5 "localism." The final chapter discusses its historical implications. Just as the people comprising different contemporary polities can reasonably reach different conclusions about how political cooperation should be structured, so can people living at earlier and later times. Given moral nominalism, this means that earlier people lived in a different moral world. Moral nominalism can make a place for a few requirements of political morality that all competent reasoners will acknowledge, and with respect to these, we can tell a story of the emergence over time of the moral truth. But most requirements of political morality are constituted by competent judgments employing

socially available normative or evaluative concepts, and if the concepts were different in an earlier era, so were the requirements. Chapter 6 develops this picture and explores its implications for the enterprise of making moral judgments about the past.

Despite the familiarity of the phrase, some might wish to deny that there is such a thing as reasonable moral disagreement in politics. They may be willing to concede that there can be political disagreements in which all the positions taken are unreasonable. But, they will insist, where we find genuine disagreement, at most one of the positions can claim the support of reason. In this book, I do not argue directly for the existence of reasonable moral disagreement in politics. I proceed on the assumption that some questions concerning how political cooperation morally ought to be organized admit of reasonable disagreement. I propose a way of understanding such disagreement and explore what it implies for political life and political morality. Presumably, a study of this sort must be undertaken before we can decide whether to acknowledge the existence of reasonable political disagreement.

I have tried, in writing this book, to make the argument accessible to readers who are not philosophers by training. For such readers, the parts of the book that set out the meta-ethical theory of moral nominalism, the final section of chapter 1 and the whole of chapter 2, are likely to present the greatest difficulty. The discussion there is somewhat removed from the social phenomenon of political disagreement. I urge readers who find these parts of the book heavy going to skip to chapter 3, possibly returning to them later.

The writing of this book has been a solitary project, but I have received helpful comments on chapter 2 from my colleague, Aaron Zimmerman, and on the whole manuscript from two anonymous referees for Cambridge University Press. I have also received helpful comments from the Cambridge philosophy editor, Hilary Gaskin.

The structure of reasonable disagreement

In this initial chapter I consider the characteristic features of reasonable disagreement. I have said that one of the marks of reasonable disagreement is that shared deliberation about what is justified by a given body of evidence, or set of reasons, does not produce convergence on a single answer, no matter how openly it is conducted or for how long. As I have indicated, my primary concern is reasonable disagreement in politics, disagreement concerning how political cooperation is to be organized. The focus of the book is normative and evaluative disagreement as it pertains to the organization of political cooperation. But decisions about how to organize political cooperation often turn on the answers to questions of empirical fact. So after an initial section explaining why the phenomenon of reasonable disagreement is puzzling, I briefly consider whether questions of empirical fact admit of reasonable disagreement. This topic is of interest in its own right, and discussing it will help us to see, in the fourth section, what is distinctive about reasonable normative and evaluative disagreement. The chapter concludes with some material on meta-ethics that sets the stage for chapter 2.

THE PROBLEM

It is difficult, in providing an account of reasonable disagreement in politics, to keep both aspects of the phenomenon firmly in view. Disagreement in politics concerns how political cooperation ought to be organized. It is disagreement concerning the actions that are to be taken collectively by the members of a polity. Collective action requires coordination, which in turn requires agreement on a cooperative scheme. This may be produced by a political decision procedure, such as voting, on the employment of which there is widespread agreement. If we emphasize the reasonableness of the different views about the way the polity should proceed in a given case, it can seem that not much is at stake in such decisions. The views are more or

less equivalent in overall acceptability, so it is appropriate for each party to acquiesce in the adoption of any of them, or at least to make some sort of accommodating move toward the views advanced by the other parties. Emphasizing the reasonableness of reasonable disagreement thus risks losing the element of disagreement.

This is especially problematic if we want to use the concept of reasonable disagreement to characterize actual political controversies. In practice, the contending parties are often convinced that the opposing views reflect deep moral errors and are thus pernicious. Consider, for example, the disagreement between Thomas Jefferson and Alexander Hamilton about how political cooperation was to be organized in the early United States. Hamilton was a supporter of a strong central government and of mercantile interests, while Jefferson was deeply suspicious of centralized government and envisaged an agrarian republic of independent farmers. As Jefferson saw it, Hamilton's aim was to establish in the United States institutions of the sort found in Britain, which would have constituted a betrayal of the revolution. If, however, we emphasize the element of disagreement, it becomes unclear what can be meant by saying that the contending positions all share the attribute of reasonableness. It seems to be characteristic of genuine disagreement in politics that the partisans of each view regard those advancing opposing views, and thus the opposing views themselves, as unreasonable.

We can restate the issue here by clarifying the connection between reasonableness and competence. Let us say that the position taken by a party to a disagreement is reasonable if and only if it is or could be the product of competent reasoning. Reasoning is competent when it is carried out in awareness of all the relevant considerations, the cognitive capacities exercised in extracting conclusions from the relevant considerations are appropriate, and these capacities are functioning properly. Given this, the last point in the previous paragraph might elicit the response that what matters is not what the parties to the disagreement think, but what is actually the case. The parties to a political disagreement may regard the opposing positions as incompetently reasoned, but they can be mistaken. This simply returns us to the first point, however. If the opposing positions are grounded in competent reasoning, or could be, why does it matter which is adopted? Also, if the reasoning is competent, how can it produce opposing conclusions?

An account of reasonable political disagreement that provides both for reasonableness and for disagreement must, then, accomplish several tasks. It must explain how it is sometimes possible for competent reasoners,

reasoning competently, to obtain different answers to a question germane to the organization of political cooperation. It must also make clear why this can happen even when the parties take advantage of all the available epistemic resources, including, importantly, the exchange of arguments in shared deliberation. Finally, it must explain how, despite the fact that all the positions are, or could be, supported by competent reasoning, each party can competently conclude that those taking opposing positions are reasoning incompetently.

This last point has an important methodological implication that should be noted at the outset. It will not usually be possible, using the kind of reasoning characteristic of applied ethics, to present examples of reasonable political disagreement, cases that seem, intuitively, to involve reasonable disagreement. To the extent that it can be made intuitively plausible that both of two competing political positions are reasonable, it will seem that either would be acceptable, and thus that the choice between them should be made by some device like flipping a coin. But as I have said, one of the defining features of reasonable disagreement in politics is that the contending positions do not seem equally reasonable to the parties, despite the fact that all are reasoning competently. Opposing views seem mistaken. This means that the contending positions will not seem equally reasonable to the reader, or at least to a reader who is engaged with the issue. An engaged reader will be engaged on one of the competing sides, and regard the reasoning supporting opposing positions as mistaken. As I explain more fully later, the principal way we have of determining that a particular disagreement is reasonable is by noticing that it has survived shared deliberation conducted in good faith over an extended period of time.

DISAGREEMENT ABOUT MATTERS OF EMPIRICAL FACT

We can begin by considering disagreement about questions of empirical fact that are germane to the organization of political cooperation. One such question concerns the policy that will produce the highest rate of economic growth. Can disagreements of this sort be reasonable, in the sense I have identified? Can competent reasoners continue, after shared deliberation conducted in good faith, to hold opposing views concerning the policy that will produce the highest rate of economic growth? To be a competent reasoner in this case, one must have had suitable training in economics. So what we are considering is the possibility of reasonable disagreement among experts of a certain kind. Whether fostering economic growth is an appropriate goal for a polity might itself admit of reasonable disagreement. Moral

disagreements of this sort are the principal focus of the present study. But for those who regard economic growth as an appropriate goal, the question of how to achieve it may still admit of disagreement. So we need to know whether such disagreements can be regarded as reasonable.

Let us suppose that there is a single correct answer to any question of empirical fact. It follows that where there is disagreement about the answer to such a question, at most one position can be correct. That is, it follows that some members of the group, and perhaps all, are making a mistake. It need not be the case, however, that some and perhaps all are reasoning incompetently. The available evidence may be inconclusive. It may not force the acceptance of just one answer to the question being considered. This situation seems typical of the empirical questions that arise in connection with the organization of political cooperation. These questions concern the consequences that different candidate policies will have if adopted, and the evidence that is available prior to the adoption of a particular policy may be compatible with different conclusions about this.

It can be argued that a competent reasoner confronted with inconclusive evidence will not draw a conclusion, but will rather suspend judgment. In the political case, however, this is not always possible. A polity may face a situation in which it must adopt some policy or other (which can include the policy of maintaining the status quo), despite the fact that the available evidence is compatible with different conclusions concerning the consequences of the candidate policies. Indeed, it may be that the only way to determine conclusively what the consequences of adopting a particular policy would be is to perform the experiment of adopting it. When this is the case, there is a sense in which a definitive answer to the question of which policy would produce a given outcome is epistemically inaccessible, since there is no possibility of adopting all of the candidate policies (at the same time and in the same circumstances) and comparing the results.

In such situations, we typically find disagreement among the experts. Can this disagreement be regarded as reasonable? Can we suppose that the experts are displaying competent reasoning in reaching opposing conclusions, instead of suspending judgment? Let us focus on the question of the economic policy that would produce the highest rate of economic growth. To reach a conclusion about this, one must bring to bear an economic theory. This gives us two main ways of modeling the inconclusiveness of the evidence. Within the framework of a particular theory, the evidence germane to the question of growth may be such that there is no basis for making a choice among the policies in a particular set, no basis for judging one to be productive of a higher rate of economic growth. Alternatively,

each theory may yield a definite answer to the question of which policy would produce the highest rate of economic growth, but the evidence germane to the question of which theory is correct may not warrant a definite conclusion about that.

In the first case, where the theory is held constant, it is less clear that the disagreement can be reasonable in the sense described in the previous section. If a given economic theory does not provide any basis for choosing among the candidate policies, it can plausibly be maintained that the adherents of the theory should be willing to assent to the adoption of any of them. That is, the political requirement that some policy or other be adopted should be taken by them as a reason to employ a tie-breaking procedure, and then to unite in advocating the adoption of whatever policy is produced by the procedure.

In the second case, however, there may be warrant for regarding the disagreement about which policy would produce the highest rate of economic growth as reasonable in the sense specified. The evidence germane to the choice among theories is, we are supposing, inconclusive. But this is not all that experts have to go on. They will have acquired, through long experience in economic problem solving, an educated sense of how things tend to work in the economic domain, which can be, so to speak, added to the available evidence for and against the different theories. Or perhaps the process of theory formation involves not just the extraction of conclusions from evidence by some sort of neutral logic, but the bringing to bear of an educated sense of how the things tend to work in the economic domain, so that the theory a given individual accepts gives expression to such a sense. The experience in economic problem solving that each expert acquires in the course of achieving expertise will be somewhat different for each, with the result that the educated sense that each has of how things work in the economic domain will be somewhat different as well. The ability to bring to bear such an intuitive sense of how things work in the economic domain is, however, plausibly regarded as an aspect of competence in economic thinking. Thus different experts, reasoning competently, can reach different conclusions about which economic theory is correct. And the different theories may yield different answers to the question of how best to promote economic growth.

Since a sense of how things work in the domain under investigation, acquired through experience in problem solving, is a feature of expertise of all sorts, we can expect to find reasonable disagreement of the kind just described wherever expertise is brought to bear. If, for example, the evidence concerning the choice among astrophysical theories is inconclusive, there can be reasonable disagreement among astrophysicists grounded in

the fact that their problem solving experience has given each a somewhat different sense of how things tend to work in the astrophysical domain. In natural sciences such as physics, reasonable disagreement is characteristic of work at the frontier of the discipline. As the evidence germane to the tenability of a particular hypothesis, or the appropriateness of a particular theory, accumulates, it may lose the character of inconclusiveness, with the result that all competent reasoners reach the same conclusion. A question that once admitted of reasonable disagreement may no longer do so.

In the social sciences, this situation is less common. It is less often the case that the evidence forces even investigators with different histories of problem solving to agree that a particular hypothesis or theory is correct. Part of the explanation may be that the social sciences are interpretive in a way that the natural sciences are not. Theory construction involves finding a way to understand the possession by behavior in the relevant domain of a normative attribute, rationality. The exercise of an educated sense of how the social world works will play a role, but it will not be constrained by evidence in the way the educated sense of a natural scientist is. If a person or group behaves in an unexpected way, the advocate of a particular hypothesis or theory may be able to avoid judging it false by attributing what is happening to irrationality. This point applies to disagreement concerning the economic policy that will produce the highest rate of economic growth. The different theories may be based on different expectations about how rational economic actors will respond to moves by the government, with the result that these theories are less constrained by hard evidence.

For present purposes, however, the important point is that there seems to be a place for the idea that questions of empirical fact germane to the organization of political cooperation can admit of reasonable disagreement. I have taken as an example the question of the policy that will produce the highest rate of economic growth, but questions in the natural sciences can be relevant as well, for example, the question whether human activity is contributing to global warming. The accumulation of evidence germane to this question has recently removed it from the list of politically relevant empirical questions admitting of reasonable disagreement. As I have suggested, this sort of transition may take place with less frequency in the social sciences. In both cases, however, where there is reasonable disagreement, it is to be understood in the same way. The competence of experts includes an educated sense of how things tend to work in the domain of their expertise, a sense created by a personal history of problem solving in that domain. But since personal histories of problem solving differ, competently reasoning experts can disagree.

It should be emphasized that we are discussing disagreement among competent reasoners. Experts, like other people, have personal interests, including interests created by membership in various groups, and different policies may affect the interests of experts differently. This will give an expert a reason to examine carefully any reasoning favoring policies that would threaten her interests, policies that would reduce the value of her investments, for example. By itself, adopting such a posture is not incompatible with competent reasoning. But it is a familiar fact that the examination of evidence favoring policies that would threaten one's interests can be subtly corrupted by bias, with the result that good reasoning in support of these policies is not recognized as good. Similarly, bad reasoning supporting policies that would favor one's interests may not be recognized as bad. In suggesting that there can be reasonable disagreement about matters of empirical fact germane to the organization of political cooperation, I am not denying that much actual disagreement, even among experts, reflects such errors. I am merely affirming the possibility that genuinely competent reasoning among experts can produce different answers to politically relevant questions of empirical fact.

DISAGREEMENT AMONG EPISTEMIC PEERS

I have suggested that experts can reasonably disagree about the answer to a question of empirical fact if the evidence is inconclusive and each has a somewhat different educated sense of how the domain they are investigating works. What about the case where the evidence is conclusive? Given that the question being investigated has a unique right answer, where the evidence is conclusive, disagreement means that someone is reasoning incompetently. This is compatible with the assumption that the parties to the disagreement are experts, because humans are fallible, and even an expert can fall into error. Although the parties can be regarded as possessing equal competence in matters of the kind being addressed, some are not reasoning competently in the case at hand. Indeed, they all may be reasoning incompetently. The important point, however, is that the advocates of at most one position can actually be displaying competent reasoning.

Epistemologists have begun to discuss this case, or a somewhat more general version of it, under the heading of disagreement among epistemic peers. The disagreements described in the previous section can be regarded as disagreements among epistemic peers, because the parties have access to the same evidence and are equally competent in extracting conclusions from this evidence. But because each party brings to bear a different educated

sense of how things work in the domain of investigation, we do not need to conclude that some are reasoning incompetently in the case at hand. At most one of the positions taken can be right, but the advocates of the opposing positions can all be reasoning competently. By assuming that the evidence is conclusive, we remove this possibility. There is only one conclusion that a competent reasoner can reach. In a situation of this sort, disagreement entails that someone's reasoning is faulty. The epistemological issue that is starting to receive discussion concerns a particular question raised by such cases. Can a competent reasoner – that is, someone whose reasoning in matters of the relevant kind is generally competent – legitimately retain his personal view of the force of the evidence, or should he rather move toward the views of the other members of the group (who should at the same time be moving toward his view)?

In a noteworthy recent paper, Thomas Kelly holds that it is appropriate to retain one's personal view in cases of disagreement with epistemic peers.[1] It is clear that somebody is reasoning incorrectly, but one has no reason to ascribe error to oneself rather than the others, so it would be inappropriate to change one's mind. In another noteworthy recent paper, David Christensen takes the opposite view, holding that one has no reason to ascribe the mistake to others rather than to oneself.[2] Thus one should be prepared to give up one's own view of the force of the evidence. One should opt for an intermediate position when the disagreement, such as one concerning the probability of rain, admits of this. Some adjustment may also be required when the question being addressed does not admit of an intermediate position. The fact that all are competent reasoners, even though some are reasoning incorrectly on this occasion, means that the opinion of each group member constitutes some evidence as to where the truth lies. So, it can be argued, when no intermediate position is available, one should adopt the view held by the majority, or a plurality, of investigators.

This is not the place to enter into a detailed discussion of the subtle arguments made by the participants in this debate. But I would like to suggest a reason, not to my knowledge generally recognized, why the parties to a dispute of this sort should retain their personal views. Christensen makes his case in two steps. First, the fact of disagreement provides a reason

---

[1] Thomas Kelly, "The Epistemic Significance of Disagreement," in T. Gendler and J. Hawthorne, eds., *Oxford Studies in Epistemology*, vol. I (New York: Oxford University Press, 2006), pp. 167–196.
[2] David Christensen, "Epistemology of Disagreement: The Good News," *The Philosophical Review* 116 (2007), pp. 187–217.

to suppose that someone is making a mistake. Second, given that there is just as much reason to ascribe the mistake to oneself as to the other parties, one should be prepared to surrender one's own view, moving toward the view, or views, of the others.[3] I agree that the fact of disagreement provides a reason to suppose that someone is making a mistake, and in particular, a reason to doubt that one's own view is correct. But I do not agree that one should therefore move toward the view or views of one's epistemic peers. Rather, the appropriate response to disagreement is reexamination of what might be called the first-order evidence. This consists of all the available evidence, excluding the evidence provided by the judgments of others. Whether a change of mind is appropriate depends on the result of this reexamination.

The reason for adopting this posture is, in a way, moral rather than epistemic. One will be behaving irresponsibly, as a member of the group of investigators, if one changes one's mind simply because others have reached different conclusions. In particular, one will be acting in a way that distorts the reason, provided by the fact of disagreement, for each group member to suspect that his or her view is incorrect.[4]

To regard the judgment of another as a reason to change one's mind is to deem it appropriate to add that judgment to the first-order evidence. Suppose that the question is whether a certain human trait has a genetic basis. The first-order evidence germane to this question consists of some considerations that support the conclusion that the trait has such a basis and some that it does not. This evidence is conclusive, we are assuming, but there is nevertheless disagreement among the biologists investigating the question. Thus someone is reasoning incorrectly. A particular member of the group, Smith, may regard the evidence that there is a genetic basis as stronger, and so make this judgment. If, however, the contrary judgments of epistemic peers constitute a reason not just to believe one may be mistaken but also to change one's mind, Smith must add the fact that others have reached the opposite conclusion to the available first-order evidence. This may have the effect, for her, of tipping the total balance of evidence toward the conclusion that there is no genetic basis.

We can begin to see the problem this presents by considering a simple two-person case involving Smith and another researcher, Jones, who has reached the opposite conclusion. Smith believes that there is a genetic basis

---

[3] Ibid., p. 198.
[4] I first made this argument in *Collective Rationality and Collective Reasoning* (New York: Cambridge University Press, 2001), pp. 115–118.

for the trait and Jones believes that there is not. The situation is symmetrical. So if it is true that Jones's judgment gives Smith a reason to change her mind, it is also true that Smith's judgment gives Jones a reason to change his mind. Suppose that each judges a change of mind to be appropriate. The distribution of opinion will simply be reversed. Alternatively, if Smith learns of Jones's assessment of the first-order evidence and is prompted as a result to change her mind, while Jones learns of Smith's judgment only after she has made this change, Jones will have no reason to change his mind and the group will converge on the conclusion that the trait lacks a genetic basis. But this result is completely arbitrary. Had the order of discovery been reversed, the opposite outcome would have been produced.

The problem becomes clearer if we consider a group of 100 researchers, 49 of whom have concluded that the trait possesses a genetic basis and 51 of whom have concluded that it does not. Let us assume further that, although they all feel justified in reaching a conclusion, each has a slightly different view of the force of the first-order evidence, the strength with which it supports the presence or the absence of a genetic basis for the trait. Since we are supposing that incorrect reasoning in a particular case is compatible with general competence in matters of the kind being considered, we can make the additional assumption that differential assessment of the strength of the evidence is compatible with general competence.

In the situation described, the additional evidence provided by the judgments made by the members of the group points slightly against the conclusion that the trait has a genetic basis. This might make no difference to any member of the group. If member A, for example, regards the first-order evidence for a genetic basis as significantly stronger than the evidence for the contrary conclusion, the addition to the mix of a further, relatively weak reason for believing that there is no genetic basis may not lead her to change her mind.[5]

But it is conceivable that within the group, there is someone who judges that there is a genetic basis for the trait, but finds the first-order evidence for

---

[5] We are assuming that all 100 are competent reasoners, although some are not manifesting this competence in the case at hand. It might be suggested that the assumption that all are competent reasoners can support a categorization of all as more likely to be right than not, thus allowing the Condorcet jury theorem to be brought to bear, and strengthening the reason to suppose that the majority view is correct. This would make little difference with such a small group, however, and it is doubtful that we could plausibly regard all the members of a group of say, one million, as epistemic peers in the sense we are now employing. It is doubtful that we could plausibly regard them all as competent reasoners in possession of conclusive evidence. The bearing of the Condorcet jury theorem on the question of deference to epistemic peers is discussed by Philip Pettit in "When to Defer to Majority Testimony – and When Not to," *Analysis* 66 (2007), pp. 179–187.

this only slightly stronger than the evidence for the contrary conclusion, and is thus led to change his mind by the fact that more investigators judge the first-order evidence to support the absence of a genetic basis. That is, the fact that only 49 members of the group judge the evidence to support the presence of a genetic basis while 51 judge it to support the absence of such a basis tips the balance, for him, in favor of the conclusion that there is no genetic basis. We then have a situation in which 52 believe that there is no genetic basis and 48 believe there is. Given the new distribution of opinion, all the remaining members who believe that there is a genetic basis for the trait must consider whether they now have a reason to change their minds. And someone may conclude that she does. When it was 51 to 49, she regarded the first-order evidence for a genetic basis as strong enough to defeat the combination of the first-order evidence to the contrary and the additional reason for accepting the absence of a genetic basis provided by the distribution of opinion within the group, but she now finds the first-order evidence for a genetic basis defeated by the evidence provided by the distribution of opinion. The first-order evidence against a genetic basis, supplemented by the additional support provided by the fact that 52 people accept this conclusion while 48 do not, is judged sufficient to tip the balance.

Again, the remaining partisans of a genetic basis will need to revisit the question whether there is warrant for this conclusion. And now that it is 53 to 47, a further member of this group may conclude that a change of mind is warranted. This process could, in theory, continue until it produces a consensus that there is no genetic basis for the trait in question, until all 100 members of the group accept that there is no genetic basis. But clearly something will have gone wrong. No further first-order evidence has been introduced, and shared deliberation has changed no minds about what the first-order evidence requires. Rather the evidence provided by the judgments of others has undergone a misleading inflation. The real force of this evidence is that which obtained initially, that which obtained when the judgment of each member of the group was determined solely by her reading of the available first-order evidence.

If the members of the group are to preserve the integrity of the reason their judgments collectively provide for supposing that one of the contending positions is mistaken, if they are to ensure that the apparent force of this reason corresponds to its real force, each must take the disagreement of others as warranting only a reexamination of the first-order evidence, not a change of mind. I said above that the reason for taking the disagreement of others as warranting only a reexamination of the first-order evidence is, in a way, a

moral reason. We can now see why. The preservation of a true impression of the strength of the reason for believing that someone is mistaken which is created by the existence of disagreement requires a collective effort within the group as a whole. By changing one's mind simply because others disagree, one fails to do one's part in this collective effort.

It should be mentioned that this result does not establish the reasonableness of the initial disagreement. By hypothesis, the first-order evidence was conclusive, so some members of the group were reasoning incorrectly. They were displaying incompetence as reasoners in the case at hand. But the result provides indirect support for one salient feature of reasonable disagreement, the retention of one's position despite the fact that others disagree. Indeed, it suggests that when, after reexamination of the first-order evidence, one finds that one remains in disagreement with other investigators, one should publicize one's disagreement. Agreement is agreeable, but disagreement can be morally, as well as epistemically, required.

REASONABLE DISAGREEMENT AND POLITICAL MORALITY

Political decision-making determines how political cooperation is to be organized. Questions of empirical fact are germane to organization of political cooperation, and as we have seen, they can admit of reasonable disagreement. This alone suffices to establish that political decisions can be, and probably often are, made in the face of reasonable disagreement. But when we think about disagreement in politics, we more often have in mind normative and evaluative questions, and in particular, moral questions. The parties to the disagreement disagree about the moral acceptability of the different ways that political cooperation might be organized, the moral acceptability of a particular tax policy, for example. It seems, if anything, more plausible that questions of political morality admit of reasonable disagreement than that empirical questions do. We must, then, consider how reasonable disagreement is to be understood in this case. Some of the remarks that follow apply as well to disagreement about matters of empirical fact germane to political decision-making.

A useful first step is to distinguish two senses of "reasonable." I have said that a reasonable view is one that is competently reasoned. An unreasonable view thus becomes one that is incompetently reasoned. The competence in question is exercised in the identification of the considerations relevant in a given context and in the assignment of relative weights to them. This is the sense of "reasonable" employed in the standard of proof in a criminal trial, which requires that guilt be established beyond a reasonable doubt. The

evidence presented must be such that no competent reasoner, confronted with that evidence, could doubt the defendant's guilt. Disagreement is reasonable when the relevant considerations are such that competent engagement with them is compatible with the reaching of different conclusions.

The second thing that can be meant by labeling a view as reasonable is restricted to cooperative contexts. A reasonable person, in a cooperative context, is someone who is prepared to make concessions to the other cooperators if they are similarly prepared to make concessions to him. To put it another way, a reasonable person is one who accepts that the way cooperation is organized should reflect concessions by all the cooperators. A reasonable view then becomes a view of the appropriate pattern of concessions that a person who is reasonable, in the specified sense, could hold. An unreasonable view lacks this feature.

The concessions at issue are concessions from some initially favored way of organizing political cooperation. One might initially favor a way of organizing political cooperation because it would satisfy a personal interest, perhaps by increasing one's income. In this case, concession would involve accepting a somewhat lower income. But as I interpret the idea of appropriate concession, it does not presuppose any particular way of understanding the positions initially taken. This will be context-dependent. Thus in certain circumstances a reasonable person might find it appropriate to make a concession from a moral concern, to accept the diminished realization of certain moral values to which she is committed, for example, environmental values. Indeed, as we shall see, there can be such a thing as higher-order concession from a first-order view of the appropriate pattern of concessions.

To make a place for reasonable disagreement in connection with this second conception of reasonableness, we must combine it with the first. Let us call the second conception "reasonableness as fairness" and the first "reasonableness as competence."[6] In disagreeing about the appropriate pattern of concessions, people are disagreeing about what is fair. Such disagreement will be reasonable in the first sense if the reasoning germane to the fairness of a cooperative enterprise is such that its competent performance does not guarantee convergence on a single understanding of what is fair. Political justice is also a matter of appropriate concession, so we can provide in the same way for reasonable disagreement about justice. In

---

[6] I distinguish these two senses of reasonableness in *Collective Rationality and Collective Reasoning*, pp. 92–93. Jeremy Waldron makes a similar distinction in "Justice Revisited," *The Times Literary Supplement*, no. 4707, June 18, 1993, pp. 5–6.

general, I will not be making a sharp distinction between fairness in the political case and justice.

A bit more should be said about reasoning that addresses the justice or fairness of political cooperation. Such reasoning will often involve weighing claims that can be made by the members of a polity. Certain features of the situation are regarded as grounding claims that can be made by some members against others, or against the polity as a whole. For example, the fact that a new drug treating a particularly vicious disease has become available may be thought to create a claim to the public provision of that drug. An appropriate pattern of concessions is then one that appropriately reconciles all the legitimate claims. Disagreement can concern either the legitimacy of particular claims or the way they should be reconciled. Disagreements of both sorts will be reasonable if competent reasoners could reach different conclusions.

Lying behind this picture is the assumption that a distinctive capacity is engaged when competent reasoners think about the pattern of concessions that ought to mark political cooperation. Competent reasoning about the appropriate pattern of concessions is not competent participation in a bargaining process. It is a kind of thinking that presupposes the general appropriateness of concession to the other participants in a cooperative endeavor, regardless of their bargaining power, and that attempts to determine the particular pattern of concessions required in the case at hand. In mature humans, this capacity to make, and also to seek, concessions is structured by concepts that identify different kinds of claims that can be made, and also by social values that can justify concession. This receives further discussion in the next chapter. For present purposes, the important point is that the reasoning about fairness or justice associated with the exercise of the capacity for making concessions typically involves first identifying features of the situation that, given the available concepts, can be regarded as justifying concession, and then considering how these considerations should be reconciled.

John Rawls has proposed that we attribute reasonable political disagreement to the operation of what he calls the "burdens of judgment." These are "hazards involved in the correct (and conscientious) exercise of our powers of reason and judgment in the ordinary course of political life."[7] Among the burdens that Rawls mentions, the most important for political purposes is that "the way we assess evidence and weigh moral and political values is

---

[7] John Rawls, *Political Liberalism* (New York: Columbia University Press, 1993), pp. 56–57.

shaped by our total experience, our whole course of life up to now, and our total experiences must always differ." The observation in the second section to the effect that an expert's personal history of problem solving will produce a distinctive sense of how things tend to work in the domain of her expertise can be regarded as pointing toward this phenomenon. I say more about how total experience affects moral judgment in the following chapters.

Bias is especially likely to distort judgments of the fairness of a cooperative scheme. One of the marks of competent reasoning about fairness is that bias is neutralized. Reasoning which takes the form of shared deliberation is especially important here. In accepting the possibility of reasonable disagreement in politics, however, we are accepting that disagreement about what would be fair cannot always be attributed to bias. This point is germane to the interpretation of Rawls's burdens of judgment. They are not to be understood as sources of bias. Rather they are deep features of the human situation which have the consequence that the competent exercise of our powers of reason and judgment will not always yield agreement.

As Jeremy Waldron has pointed out, although Rawls envisages reasonable disagreement about comprehensive moral doctrines, he does not appear to envisage reasonable disagreement about justice.[8] In a Rawlsian well-ordered society, there will be an overlapping consensus of reasonable comprehensive doctrines. A comprehensive doctrine counts as reasonable to the extent that it authorizes concessions to those holding other comprehensive doctrines sufficient to enable them to participate in the overall scheme of political cooperation. The concessions the doctrines authorize, however, are in each case the same, those specified by the political conception of justice that is the subject of the overlapping consensus. This is provided by Rawls's theory of justice as fairness. So although comprehensive doctrines can reflect different views about what constitutes a good human life, there will be no disagreement about justice. Waldron argues that this makes the disagreement characteristic of a Rawlsian well-ordered society unsuitable as a model for actual political disagreement. The most important political disagreements are precisely disagreements about justice or fairness. We can, then, follow Rawls in attributing reasonable disagreement to the burdens of judgment. But if we are to see reasonable disagreement as playing a role in the most important political controversies, we must

---

[8] Jeremy Waldron, "Rawls's *Political Liberalism*," in his *Law and Disagreement* (Oxford: Oxford University Press, 1999), pp. 149–163.

suppose that these burdens can affect competent reasoning about what justice or fairness requires.

How, exactly, is reasonable disagreement about questions of political morality to be understood? Some prominent current discussions of the democratic resolution of disagreement propose that respect for the moral seriousness of the people advancing opposing political views requires accommodating these views, at least to some extent. Thus Amy Gutmann and Dennis Thompson advocate what they call "economizing on moral disagreement." When a number of different justifications for the view that one advocates are available, one should choose the justification that minimizes the disagreement with opposing views.[9] Another writer who has given an important place to accommodation grounded in mutual respect is Henry Richardson. Richardson advocates "deep compromise." This is a process by which political actors reformulate ends so as to make agreement possible, but do so in response not to the force of opposing arguments, or to bargaining power, but to the normative pressure exerted by the requirement to respect other people as self-originating sources of claims.[10] The "democratic deliberation within" advocated by Robert Goodin as a way of compensating for the inefficiencies of actual shared deliberation also seems to involve an element of mutual accommodation. Goodin suggests that by imaginatively occupying the positions of others, "each of us might be able to conduct a wide ranging debate within our own heads among all the contending perspectives."[11] But he does not envisage the achievement of an internal consensus. Rather, internalizing the perspectives of others

---

[9] "Mutual respect among those who reasonably disagree is a value in itself, and in turn it has further beneficial effects for democracy. One of the most important effects is what we call the economy of moral disagreement. When political opponents seek to economize on their disagreements, they continue to search for fair terms of social cooperation even in the face of their fundamental (and often foundational) disagreements. They do so by justifying the policies that they find most morally defensible in a way that minimizes the rejection of the reasonable positions they nonetheless oppose on moral grounds." (Amy Gutmann and Dennis Thompson, *Why Deliberative Democracy?* [Princeton: Princeton University Press, 2004], p. 134. See also their *Democracy and Disagreement* [Cambridge, MA: Harvard University Press, 1996], pp. 84–85.)

   Economizing on disagreement, so characterized, seems to presuppose that a number of different moral justifications are available, and that they are all equally good. It may often be the case, however, that the best justification – the one that, in the judgment of the person holding a view, provides the strongest support for it – is one that exacerbates disagreement. In this case, choosing the justification that minimizes disagreement would seem not show respect for those with whom one disagrees, at least in their capacity as rational agents. Alan Wertheimer's "Internal Disagreements: Deliberation and Abortion" (in Stephen Macedo, ed., *Deliberative Politics: Essays on Democracy and Disagreement* [New York: Oxford University Press, 1999], pp. 170–183), contains a useful discussion of the connections between deliberation, accommodation, and respect.

[10] Henry S. Richardson, *Democratic Autonomy* (Oxford: Oxford University Press, 2002).

[11] Robert Goodin, *Reflective Democracy* (Oxford: Oxford University Press, 2003), p. 183.

involves "balancing them with [one's] own."[12] This seems to mean effecting in one's thinking some kind of mutual accommodation.

The overall strategy of these proposals can be explained using the distinction I have made between two kinds of reasonableness. When there are conflicts concerning how a cooperative venture is to be organized, reasonable-as-fair people will make concessions. They will thus advocate cooperative schemes that embody such concessions. The proposals just examined can be understood as suggesting that when reasonable-as-fair people find themselves disagreeing about the appropriate pattern of concessions, they will reinstitute the process of concession at a higher level, seeking a compromise among their competing views.

But it can also be argued that confronted with such a situation, reasonable-as-fair people will resist accommodation. Each initial judgment will embody an understanding, taken to be competently generated, of the pattern of concessions appropriate to the cooperative venture in question. So moving in the direction of opposing judgments can appear to be unreasonable. The pattern of concessions produced by mutual accommodation can seem unfair in light of the prior understanding of the appropriate pattern of concessions.[13] When the situation is viewed in this way, mutual accommodation comes at the cost of detachment from what each regards as the correct understanding of what would be fair.

It is not obvious, then, that accommodation is the reasonable response to reasonable disagreement. What does this imply about how we should view reasonable disagreement? It is useful to consider how reasonable disagreement is to be distinguished from disagreement in which some of the contending positions are unreasonable in the dual sense. They display incompetent reasoning about what would be fair, or incompetently disregard considerations of fairness entirely. Gutmann and Thompson

---

[12] Ibid., p. 10. Goodin describes this balancing as an internal analogue of aggregative procedures like voting. One important justification for such procedures is that they express respect for the each citizen as an individual with a particular perspective on the issue to be decided. The word "balancing," however, suggests more accommodation of opposing views than is provided by a shared willingness to abide by the results of a vote.

Cass Sunstein's "incompletely theorized agreements" constitute another mechanism of accommodation grounded in respect for the diversity of moral and political opinion. See his *Legal Reasoning and Political Conflict* (New York: Oxford University Press, 1996), ch. 2. In the most important case, an incompletely theorized agreement is one that resolves a relatively concrete issue in a way that can be endorsed from a number of different theoretical perspectives, and thus does not require a choice among these perspectives. However, Sunstein regards incompletely theorized agreements as more appropriate to the resolution of legal disputes than to democratic decision-making, where the ascent to higher-level principle has a legitimate place.

[13] I discuss this phenomenon in *Collective Rationality and Collective Reasoning*, chs. 2 and 4.

distinguish the rejection of manifest injustice from what they call "deliberative disagreement." A deliberative disagreement, they say, should not be resolved – a social choice among the contending positions should not be made – because these positions are all reasonable. The parties should simply economize on disagreement, as described above.[14] Employing T. M. Scanlon's formula, they cite as the mark of deliberative disagreement the fact that none of the contending positions can be reasonably rejected.[15] Manifest injustice, by contrast, can be reasonably rejected. However, this proposal also seems to blunt the seriousness of political disagreement. If one cannot reasonably reject an opposing view, shouldn't one regard it as an acceptable substitute for one's own?

We can provide for reasonable disagreement that is also serious by giving the Scanlonian formula a different employment. A reasonable political disagreement is not a disagreement in which none of the contending views of what would constitute an appropriate pattern of concessions can be reasonably rejected. Rather it is a disagreement in which *each* of the contending views can be reasonably rejected by at least one of the parties. This leaves us with the problem of distinguishing the sort of rejection of opposing views that is characteristic of reasonable disagreement from the sort that constitutes a response to manifest injustice. But a solution is available. We can introduce the concept of the reasonable rejection of a reasonable rejection. Where there is reasonable disagreement, the reasonable rejection of a particular position can itself be reasonably rejected by those holding that position. The defining feature of manifest injustice, by contrast, is that its rejection cannot be reasonably rejected by anyone.

If we could identify a representative subset of the population whose members were always reasonable in the dual sense, we could extract a criterion of reasonable disagreement from the observations just made. Where all the members of this group reject a particular way of organizing political cooperation, we have manifest injustice, and where they differ concerning the rejectability of a particular way of organizing political cooperation – where the rejections of some are rejected by others – we

---

[14] *Why Deliberative Democracy?*, p. 28.

[15] Ibid., p. 28. Scanlon says, "[A]n act is wrong if its performance under the circumstances would be disallowed by any system of rules for the general regulation of behavior that no one could reasonably reject as a basis for informed, unforced, general agreement" (T. M. Scanlon, *What We Owe to Each Other* [Cambridge, MA: Harvard University Press, 1998], p. 153). Scanlon seems to be employing the notion of reasonableness in the dual sense I have proposed. What one can reasonably reject as a basis for agreement is what one can competently reject as demanding excessive concessions from one, or as not demanding sufficient concessions from others.

have reasonable disagreement. But it is doubtful that there is such a subset. Everyone sometimes displays unreasonableness in the dual sense.

Explicability by Rawls's burdens of judgment gives us some epistemic access to reasonable disagreement. Disagreement about what is just or fair can be regarded as reasonable when it is explicable by the burdens. This creates the possibility of my identifying as reasonable (as competently reasoned) a view about what would be fair that I myself can reasonably, in the sense of competently, reject. There may be situations in which I can recognize that an opposing position is explicable by the burdens, in particular, that it is explicable by a given individual's total experience up to the present, and thus that it is compatible with the competent exercise of human powers of reason and judgment.

More needs to be said, however, about what is involved in recognizing explicability by the burdens. The burdens of judgment are to be distinguished from sources of bias. They can be understood as features of each individual's experience that give him or her a distinctive perspective on the relevant reasons, on the reasons relevant to the fairness or justice of some way of structuring political cooperation. To recognize that an opposing position is explicable by the burdens of judgment is thus to see how the total experience of a particular individual or group could, consistent with competent reasoning, produce a distinctive perspective on these reasons – a distinctive understanding of what the relevant reasons are, of how they are to be interpreted, or of their relative weights.[16] Manifest injustice, by contrast, when it is the product of a perspective on the relevant reasons, is the product of a distorted perspective. This perspective may be explicable by the total experience of an individual or group, but it cannot be regarded as a manifestation of competent reasoning carried out within the framework of that experience.

Because each competent moral agent operates from a perspective shaped by her own experiences, it may not always be easy for such an agent to determine whether an opposing view is a manifestation of competent

---

[16] Jürgen Habermas, who argues that moral disagreements should be resolved by the force of the better argument, describes the deliberation that accomplishes this as a process of mutual perspective taking. Shared deliberation makes the perspective of each person on the relevant reasons available to the rest. If the different perspectives are understood as grounded in different configurations of the burdens of judgment, however, it cannot be expected that mutual perspective taking will actually produce agreement. To the extent that shared deliberation creates an appreciation of the perspective of each participant, it will make explicit the associated burdens. But it need not result in a sharing of these burdens. One can understand why someone says what he does without accepting it as correct. I discuss Habermasian mutual perspective taking (without, however, connecting perspectives with the burdens of judgment) in "Why There is No Issue Between Habermas and Rawls," *The Journal of Philosophy* 99 (2002), pp. 111–129.

reasoning carried out within the framework of different experiences. But more can be done when we introduce a historical dimension. Reflection on the history of a dispute can facilitate the identification of the underlying disagreement as reasonable. Disagreement grounded in conflicting perceptions of the nature and force of the available reasons gives rise to argument. Moreover, the clash of opposing arguments promotes sound reasoning. It exposes bias and other sources of incompetence in reasoning. But when disagreement is reasonable, argument will not produce agreement. So if a particular form of political disagreement arises in a number of different contexts, and generally survives extended debate, conducted in good faith, in the contexts where it arises, we will have some basis for confidence that the disagreement is reasonable. We will have some basis for supposing that the disagreement is grounded in competent reasoning carried out within the framework of different life experiences. Or to be more precise, we will have some basis for confidence that contained in the actual dispute, as it has evolved over time, is a core of reasonable disagreement that may itself have evolved over time. An example, which receives further discussion in the later chapters, is provided by the disagreement between advocates of capitalist economic arrangements and advocates of socialist economic arrangements.

MORAL REALISM AND REASONABLE POLITICAL DISAGREEMENT

The previous section described the structure of reasonable disagreement in politics, which I understand as disagreement about the pattern of concessions that ought to characterize political cooperation. As I have said, I wish to focus particularly on moral, in contrast to factual, disagreement in politics. I have suggested that disagreement is reasonable when competent reasoners can reach different conclusions about the answer to a given question. In the case of moral disagreement, the question is moral. Moral disagreement must be distinguished from practical conflict. The question each reasoner seeks to answer might be, "Which course of action, of those available, would most fully satisfy my concerns?" The answers obtained could give rise to practical conflict, to a situation in which the members of a group seek incompatible ends. But there need be no disagreement. All may agree about what would most fully satisfy the concerns of each of the parties. Considering how competent reasoners can disagree about the answer to a given practical question requires an excursion into meta-ethics.

Meta-ethics investigates the metaphysics, epistemology, and semantics of moral judgment. Put another way, it attempts to determine what is

happening when someone makes a moral judgment. In the context of ordinary moral discourse, moral judgments seem to be reports of the existence of facts of a certain sort, moral facts, and thus to be characterizable as true or false on the basis of whether they correspond to these facts. Further, if moral judgments can be true, there may be a place for moral knowledge, for the idea that we can be justified in making these judgments. But moral judgments are also generally understood to be action-guiding. They, so to speak, point people in the direction of the performance of particular actions.

These features of moral judgment can all be accommodated if we suppose that items in the world can possess not only natural properties, but also non-natural properties that have what J. L. Mackie has called "to-be-pursuedness" built into them.[17] These properties mark actions of certain types as "to be pursued," possibly because the actions will produce states of affairs that are to be pursued. In perceiving that an action which he could perform possesses such a property, an agent becomes aware that he has a reason for action, which in the normal case involves becoming motivated to perform the action. But this picture is usually regarded as unacceptably extravagant, both metaphysically and epistemologically. It is unclear how such properties could combine with natural facts to form a single, inter-connected world, and it is unclear how animals with our particular epistemic capacities could register the existence of such properties.

In the next chapter, I propose that reasonable disagreement about political morality is best accommodated by a meta-ethics that dispenses with moral properties, and thus does not admit moral facts "out there" waiting to be discovered. I call this view *moral nominalism*. But before turning to that, it will be useful to consider whether we can make a place for reasonable disagreement if we opt for a realist meta-ethics that posits the independent existence of moral facts. This will be my general approach to meta-ethical questions. I do not propose to defend moral nominalism by showing that it provides a more satisfactory treatment than other meta-ethical views of the full range of meta-ethical issues. My goal is to save (what I take to be) the phenomenon of reasonable moral disagreement, so my interest in other meta-ethical views is restricted to whether they can do this.

It should be noted at the outset that I mean to distinguish moral realism from constructivism about morality. Both views are cognitivist. They regard moral judgments as expressing beliefs. In a recent book on moral realism, Russ Shafer-Landau proposes that we understand the distinction between

---

[17] J. L. Mackie, *Ethics: Inventing Right and Wrong* (Harmondsworth: Penguin, 1977), ch. 1.

realism and constructivism in terms of what he calls "stance-independence." "Realists believe that there are moral truths that obtain independently of any preferred perspective, in the sense that the moral standards that fix the facts are not made true by virtue of their ratification from within any given actual or hypothetical perspective."[18] For constructivists, by contrast, moral truths are the products of perspectives. The moral nominalism that I am going to propose can be seen as a kind of constructivist view. I say more about this in the final section of the next chapter.

I have suggested that questions of empirical fact admit of reasonable disagreement when the evidence is inconclusive and the personal histories of judgment of competent investigators have given them somewhat different "senses" of how things work in the domain being investigated. Presumably something similar must be the case if questions of moral fact, realistically construed, are to admit of reasonable disagreement. I shall argue, however, that realist views either cannot provide for inconclusive evidence at all, or if they can, it is not inconclusive evidence of the right sort, the sort that sets the stage for competently reasoned judgments articulating conflicting views of the structure of moral normativity.

Moral realism comes in two main versions. One regards moral properties and facts as non-natural, where a natural property or fact is a property or fact that could find a place in one of the special sciences. Let us begin with this. The theory Mackie describes posits non-natural moral properties of a certain sort and a quasi-perceptual way of registering their presence. As has been noted, it is open to objections in both these respects. But even if these objections can be met, it does not appear that a theory of this sort can accommodate reasonable moral disagreement. Moral properties supervene on natural properties. So presumably, the perception of moral properties posited by the view supervenes on the perception, or cognizing in some other way, of the natural properties of an action or outcome. But then there can be no such thing as inconclusive evidence for the presence of the supervening moral properties. If the perceptual apparatus is functioning properly, when an individual is aware of certain natural properties, a perception of the presence of a particular moral property will supervene. The detection of additional natural properties might change the moral properties taken to be present, but this does not mean that the earlier registering of moral properties was based on inconclusive evidence. It was fully warranted in the context in which it occurred.

---

[18] Russ Shafer-Landau, *Moral Realism: A Defence* (Oxford: Clarendon Press, 2003), p. 15, emphasis removed.

There may be another way of formulating a version of moral realism that regards moral properties as non-natural, in the sense that they have no place in the special sciences. It might be suggested that we can establish basic moral principles, at least, by tracing conceptual connections. The acquisition of moral concepts brings with it the understanding that certain naturalistically characterized actions or outcomes possess moral properties as well. An example would be a principle holding that, other things being equal, the intentional infliction of pain is morally wrong. It may be that such a theory – basically, an approach to moral realism via moral rationalism – avoids the metaphysical and philosophical extravagance of the theory Mackie describes. The theory may be committed to the existence of normative facts only in the way that any theory which makes a place for a distinction between what we actually believe and what we are justified in believing is committed to the existence of such facts. One possible complication is that the moral judgments that are produced will presumably establish the actions or outcomes to which they refer as "to be pursued," to use Mackie's words. This means that the theory must provide for moral concepts the content of which makes possible such judgments, and must explain how such concepts are acquired. The moral nominalism that I am going to propose in the next chapter does this, but in a way that has constructivist implications.

Again, however, we can leave these issues unresolved because this rationalist form of realism also seems incapable of making a place for the kind of inconclusive evidence that is a precondition of reasonable disagreement about any matter of fact. Someone who truly possesses the relevant moral concepts will already have all the "evidence" that could be available. If disagreement arises, it must be attributed to the fact that some people are not processing this conceptual material correctly. But then we cannot say that the different conclusions reached are all competently reasoned. Rather, disagreement means that mistakes are being made.[19]

---

[19] A view of this general sort, developed with much greater sophistication than my brief description would suggest, can be found in Christopher Peacocke's *The Realm of Reason* (Oxford: Clarendon Press, 2004), chs. 7 and 8. Peacocke, however, does not understand the view as a version of moral non-naturalism. He suggests (pp. 233–234) that on such a theory, the answers to some moral questions can be indeterminate. The conceptual nexus may not force a particular answer. Indeterminacy of this sort would give us a way in which different, incompatible answers to a moral question could be competently reasoned. But the answers would be competently reasoned only in the sense that the existing conceptual evidence did not rule out any of them. They would have no further support. In a case of genuine reasonable disagreement, by contrast, each of the different conclusions is supported (or forced) by competent reasoning which, since the conclusions are different, has a somewhat different character in each instance.

There may be other versions of moral realism that regard moral properties as non-natural. But it seems likely that any such view will have the same difficulty providing for competently reasoned judgments that nevertheless disagree. Disagreement will mean that at most one person can be reasoning correctly. This conclusion depends, however, on an assumption that might be questioned, the assumption that any competently reasoning human is capable of making full epistemic contact with any moral facts there may be. An alternative possibility is that the cognitive capacities of human beings are, so to speak, crude, at least in the moral case. The normal condition of humans, considered as cognizers of moral reality, is a kind of myopia. Everything is a bit out of focus.

The myopia hypothesis figures in the realist theory that Shafer-Landau has offered.[20] In response to the familiar argument that the existence of widespread moral disagreement is evidence against moral realism, he argues that moral realism is compatible with the possibility that humans do not have full epistemic access to the moral truth. Applied to our present concerns, this means that even people whose reasoning about moral matters is as competent as any human's can be may still fall into disagreement. Thus we can legitimately speak of reasonable disagreement even though some people are making mistakes. But if moral disagreement is to be attributed to moral myopia, one would also expect the parties to such disagreements to be tentative in their judgments. An aspect of epistemic competence, when epistemic access is doubtful, is a retreat from certainty. Yet as I have noted, reasonable disagreements about questions of political morality often do not display this feature. The parties are adamant that their views are correct. A theory of reasonable disagreement must accommodate this fact.

The other main approach to moral realism regards moral facts as natural facts of a certain kind, and thus as empirically accessible. At one time, proposals of this sort took the form of suggestions that terms like "good," in the moral sense, could be regarded as synonymous with particular naturalistic phrases, for example, "conducive to the survival of the species." Such proposals are usually regarded as falling to G. E. Moore's open-question argument. The question "This is conducive to the survival of the species, but is it good?" seems to be perfectly in order, yet if "good" is synonymous with "conducive to the survival of the species," it should be as puzzling as the question, "This is conducive to the survival of the species, but is it conducive to the survival of the species?"[21]

---

[20] Shafer-Landau, *Moral Realism*. See especially ch. 9.

[21] There is a good account of the history of meta-ethics in Mark Timmons, *Morality Without Foundations: A Defense of Ethical Contextualism* (New York: Oxford University Press, 2004), ch. 1.

Contemporary naturalistic proposals dispense with the synonymy criterion. Thus moral properties might be held to be identical with non-moral properties in the way that water is identical with H_2O. The term "water" is not synonymous with "H_2O," but the property of being water is identical with the property of being H_2O. It is possible, however, to do without property identities of any sort. One recent approach focuses on moral theories and understands the concepts provided by such theories, for example, the concept of depravity, as picking out certain features of the natural order that supervene on features picked out by other naturalistic theories, but that cannot be reduced to features of the latter sort.[22] The confirmation of such a moral theory can be understood in the same way as the confirmation of a scientific theory. It can be confirmed by its ability to explain what happens in the world.

Since competent investigators can disagree about which explanatory theory of a particular domain is correct, it might appear that a realist view of the naturalistic sort just described can accommodate reasonable moral disagreement. But it is not clear that this is so. The questions such theories seek to answer concern the causal structure of a certain part of the natural world. Understanding a situation as presenting a moral problem, however, involves understanding it as posing a normative question, in particular, a question about what morally ought to be done. Reasonable moral disagreement is disagreement about what constitutes the correct answer to such a question. But it is not clear that realist views of the naturalistic sort can provide for reasonable normative disagreement. These theories typically attempt to make a place for normativity by incorporating a motivational assumption. Thus it might be assumed that psychologically normal humans will possess motivational dispositions that result in their promoting moral goodness and avoiding moral badness, as these are understood by the best naturalistic moral theory.[23]

The basic view of normative reasons invoked here is Humean. One is justified in performing a particular action if and only if one's beliefs about the way the world is give one good reason to suppose that the action will satisfy one's desires. Hume provides for the rational criticism of desires if

---

[22] The main texts are Nicholas Sturgeon, "Moral Explanations" and Richard Boyd, "How to Be a Moral Realist," in G. Sayre-McCord, ed., *Essays on Moral Realism* (Ithaca: Cornell University Press, 1989), pp. 229–255 and pp. 181–228 respectively.

[23] See Boyd, "How to Be a Moral Realist," pp. 214–216. Boyd also proposes that moral goodness can be understood as what he calls a homeostatic cluster property. This makes it readily intelligible that competent researchers will disagree about what actually possesses the naturalistic property of moral goodness.

they are based on false beliefs. The desire to see a unicorn can be criticized on the ground that there is no such animal. The Humean view can, then, allow for reasonable practical disagreement of a sort. When the members of a group reasonably disagree about a factual question germane to the satisfaction of a common desire, each will be able reasonably to reject the practical judgments made by some of the others.

But an adequate normative theory of practical reasons must allow for the rational criticism of desires in a further respect, one that goes beyond criticism of the beliefs on which they depend. It must provide a way of distinguishing desires whose objects an agent genuinely has reason to pursue from desires the agent merely happens to experience. Since the desires posited by realist moral theories of the naturalistic sort are simply desires that, as a matter of natural fact, are often found in humans, it does not appear that these theories possess the resources necessary to do full justice to moral normativity.

If the observations in this section are correct, accommodating the phenomenon of reasonable disagreement in the moral domain, reasonable disagreement about what there is sufficient moral reason to do, will require the acceptance of a non-realist meta-ethical theory. But this cannot simply be a theory according to which moral judgments give expression to, or are otherwise grounded in, the attitudes that a particular agent happens to have. Such a theory can account for practical conflict, but not for disagreement. Providing for reasonable moral disagreement requires making a place for judgments that are, as I shall put it, *target setting*, judgments that establish certain states of the world as targets to be aimed at in action. I use the word "target," in contrast to "end" or "goal," because the latter terms suggest a distinction between what one is aiming at and the means employed to achieve it. I want to leave room for the possibility that one's aim in performing an action can just be the performance of that action.[24] Attitudes that an agent simply happens to have may also establish states of

---

[24] The following passage from S. L. Hurley may provide some support for this usage: "Choosing how to act in response to reasons is closely related to the idea of control. Reason-responsiveness is a kind of control, which operates through choice. Not all control involves choice and reasons: consider a thermostat. But when someone chooses how to act in response to reasons, her choices and the reasons to which they respond form a control system. Her reasons provide a target, which may involve characteristics of her own behavior as well as external states of affairs. Her choices combined with exogenous events in the environment and acts by others produce joint results, in which the target is either achieved or missed to some degree. Her choices are adjusted in light of information about the exogenous events and the joint results of them and her earlier choices in order to reduce error, or the gap between the target and the joint result" (S. L. Hurley, *Justice, Luck, and Knowledge* [Cambridge, MA: Harvard University Press, 2004], pp. 42–43).

the world as targets, but in this case, the targets have been brought into existence by the mere unfolding of various causal processes.[25] By contrast, when target setting is effected by a judgment, it can be regarded as well or poorly grounded. And if conflicting target-setting judgments made in answer to a given practical question can be well grounded, the result will be reasonable disagreement.

The judgments that are the focus of this study are judgments of political morality, judgments that concern how political cooperation morally ought to be organized. A judgment of political morality sets as a target a particular way of structuring some aspect of political cooperation. Disagreements within a group of potential cooperators concerning how to organize a particular cooperative endeavor have a distinctive character. They demand resolution in a way that disagreements of other sorts do not. I say more about this in chapter 3. For present purposes, the important point is that if we are to accommodate reasonable disagreement about questions of political morality, it appears that we need a view that, while dispensing with independently existing moral facts, nevertheless enables us to understand how judgments that set ultimate targets to be aimed at in action can be well grounded or poorly grounded. I propose such a view in the next chapter.

---

[25] One can want something that one regards oneself as completely unable to bring about. One cannot, one thinks, even increase its likelihood. Here, the want does not establish a target, although it might be more appropriate in such a case to speak of a wish.

CHAPTER 2

Moral nominalism

At the end of the previous chapter, I argued that standard versions of moral realism cannot provide an adequate account of reasonable moral disagreement. I also noted that standard non-realist views, according to which moral judgments describe or express wants or desires that people simply happen to have, display this defect as well. To accommodate the practicality of moral judgment, however, we need to retain the idea that moral judgments set targets. The task, I concluded, is to explain how target-setting judgments can be understood as well or poorly grounded, and thus as competently or incompetently made, without introducing some kind of perception of objectively existing targets.

Jürgen Habermas has suggested that this goal can be achieved by employing a single notion of well groundedness: validity.[1] An empirical judgment is well grounded when it is supported by adequate evidence. Well-grounded empirical judgments can be regarded as true, where truth is understood as correspondence with independently existing facts. A moral judgment, by contrast, is well grounded when there is sufficient moral reason to perform the action it directs. In this case, Habermas says, validity is to be understood as rightness rather than truth. There are, to be sure, normative facts associated with validity in the moral domain, but these are logical facts, facts to the effect that a certain conclusion is supported by certain reasons. A moral ought-judgment, a judgment that some action morally ought to be performed, can be understood as recording the existence of such a fact. But Habermas does not regard the supporting reasons as evidence that the action possesses a distinctive moral property, rightness. The rightness of the action is rather constituted by the fact that reasons of a certain kind justify its performance.

---

[1] See Jürgen Habermas, "Discourse Ethics: Notes on a Program of Philosophical Justification," in his *Moral Consciousness and Communicative Action*, trans. C. Lenhardt and S. W. Nicholsen (Cambridge, MA: MIT Press, 1990), pp. 43–115.

Habermas's view is a step in the right direction, but it does not appear to be adequate as it stands. We still face the problem of the status of the reasons for action the force of which is recorded by a moral ought-judgment. Such a reason consists in the possession by an action, or of something that will be produced by an action, of features that, other things being equal, warrant the performance or non-performance of the action. Thus the fact that an action will benefit someone in distress constitutes a moral reason for performing it, and the fact that an action involves making a false assertion with the intention to deceive constitutes a reason against performing it. In the case of political morality, where what is at issue is the appropriate way of organizing political cooperation, the relevant reasons are often attributes that enable members to make claims against other members or against the polity as a whole. Examples might include needing medical care or having worked harder or more effectively than others. What I shall call morally important social values can also provide a basis for judgments concerning the appropriate organization of political cooperation. Thus the fact that a particular social arrangement would enhance the health of the population, or that it would instantiate a "patterned" principle of justice calling for social equality in some respect, might be regarded as a reason for organizing political cooperation a certain way.

In admitting reasons for action of these sorts, we appear to be countenancing, in a different form, the very kinds of moral facts that Habermas seeks to avoid. The fact that benefiting someone in distress is something we have a moral reason to do seems to be a moral fact. Habermas's notion of validity does not help us here. These facts cannot, like rightness, be construed as logical. Instead of dispensing with objective targethood, then, Habermas seems simply to have shifted its location.[2]

In the present chapter, I attempt to explain, without making use of the idea of objective targethood, how judgments that establish the existence of moral reasons for action can be understood as well or poorly grounded. My proposal focuses on moral concepts, concepts such as beneficence and justice. I call the view I propose *moral nominalism.* I have chosen this label because the possession of a moral concept is understood to consist in

---

[2] Habermas's moral theory makes use of a principle of universalization, which he calls (U), to justify moral norms. (U) requires that all be able to "accept" that the consequences of the general adoption of a norm would be in everyone's interest. But if accepting that the general adoption of a norm would be in everyone's interest is judging that it would be, (U) appears to presuppose the existence of reasons relevant to this conclusion, for example, reasons relevant to the fairness of the resulting arrangement. I discuss Habermasian universalization in "Why There is No Issue Between Habermas and Rawls" (*The Journal of Philosophy* 99 [2002], pp. 111–129).

the mastery of the use of a moral term, which in turn is explained without invoking moral properties. As was mentioned in the introduction, the view is also nominalistic in the sense that moral judgment involves what Nelson Goodman calls worldmaking. In making moral judgments, we construct and alter, make and remake, the moral worlds in which we live. I do not, however, claim that my moral nominalism possesses all the features of serious nominalistic programs in metaphysics. After explaining how moral nominalism works, I discuss more directly its meta-ethical features. My case for moral nominalism is not limited to this chapter. I regard the argument for moral nominalism as resting in part on the use to which it can be put in providing an account of reasonable disagreement. This is explored in the subsequent chapters.

WILLIAMS'S SUBJECTIVISM

It may be helpful, by way of introduction, to say a little more about views that regard practical targets as set, ultimately, by wants or desires that people simply happen to have. A sophisticated view of this sort has been developed by Bernard Williams. According to Williams, all practical reasoning pre-supposes a particular "subjective motivational set," the possession of which by a given agent is a matter of contingent fact and not amenable to rational evaluation. Practical reasoning elaborates and refines the motivational forces exerted by this set. The operations performed in practical reasoning include: determining that some action would be the most convenient, economical, or pleasant way of satisfying some element of one's subjective motivational set; thinking how different elements of one's subjective motivational set can all be satisfied by time ordering; deciding, when there is irresolvable conflict among elements of one's subjective motivational set, which element one attaches the most weight to; and finding what Williams calls constitutive solutions, ways of specifying a more general want or desire. Williams notes that the employment of these deliberative processes can result in the addition of elements to a subjective motivational set or the subtraction of elements from such a set.[3]

Considered as providing a basis for an account of reasonable political disagreement, Williams's view encounters the problem mentioned in the previous chapter. In reasoning about how political cooperation ought to be organized, each party is seeking to determine the mode of organization that

[3] Here I am following Bernard Williams, "Internal and External Reasons," in his *Moral Luck* (Cambridge: Cambridge University Press, 1981), pp. 101–113.

is most appropriate in light of his or her subjective motivational set. To the extent that different ways of organizing cooperation are judged best in light of the different subjective motivational sets, political life will be marked by practical conflict, by attempts to achieve incompatible ends. But this need not involve any disagreement. The parties may agree about what would be best in light of their respective subjective motivational sets.[4]

If we are to make a place for reasonable political disagreement, then, we must suppose that practical reason can do more than elaborate and refine subjective motivational sets. We must suppose that it can set ultimate targets. The following sections develop a way of understanding this idea. Before turning to that, however, we should take advantage of the opportunity provided by Williams's view to say something about the difference between reasonable disagreement and "unreasonable" disagreement. It is plausible, as a matter of general sociological observation, that much of the difference of opinion we find concerning how political cooperation ought to be organized is merely advocacy of policies justifiable by reference to different subjective motivational sets. People proceeding from different sets may argue with one another, but these arguments can produce agreement only by showing that some course of action is suitable in light of all the sets in play.

This puts reasonable political disagreement in perspective. Even if we suppose that a particular political issue admits of reasonable disagreement, or is one about which reasonable people can disagree, much of the actual difference of opinion surrounding it will not usually constitute reasonable disagreement. The political reasoning of many people, maybe most, will be concerned with how to achieve the particular organization of political cooperation that would be most satisfactory in light of their subjective motivational sets. Although many political issues may admit of reasonable disagreement, then, we must be careful to distinguish what I shall call the "zone" of reasonable disagreement from the positions actually taken when a polity addresses a given issue. The zone is the range of opinion we would

---

[4] The account of moral reasoning proposed by Michael Smith in his book *The Moral Problem* (Oxford: Blackwell, 1994) can be regarded as a further development of Williams's view. Smith defines the morally right action in a particular situation as the action one would desire to perform if one's desires had the appropriate content (advancing the welfare of others, for example) and one were fully rational. The difference between the two views is that Smith adds to Williams's characterization of rationality a further condition. One's desires must be, as Smith puts it, systematically justified. Systematic justification brings into play a kind of rational interconnection among desires that goes beyond those mentioned by Williams. For our purposes here, the important point about Smith's view is that it appears unable to accommodate reasonable disagreement. He regards considerations of systematic justifiability as working in such a way that what one would desire when fully rational is the same for everyone. Competent (fully rational) reasoners cannot reach different conclusions. So where there is disagreement about what is morally right, someone is making a mistake.

find if the parties were competently making genuine target-setting judgments. Similarly, the depth of reasonable disagreement may be less than one would suppose from the positions actually taken. The positions that count as reasonable, while disagreeing, may not be as far apart as the positions actually voiced in connection with a given issue.

DESCRIPTIVE JUDGMENT

The members of a polity can be understood as having available to them a shared set of moral concepts, if (1), concepts are acquired in learning how to use words, and (2), the members of a polity typically share a language and a vocabulary.[5] Under these conditions, the problem of accounting for reasonable moral disagreement in politics can be formulated as follows. First, we must explain how people can acquire and correctly employ concepts that have target-setting content in a world where there are no objectively existing targets. And second, we must explain how, consistent with the correct employment of these concepts, people can make target-setting judgments that disagree. It will be useful, however, to begin by considering the case of descriptive judgments. I do not intend to propose a descriptive nominalism. I am happy to countenance descriptive – non-normative – properties. But starting with the descriptive case will allow us to set out some of the main features of the moral nominalism that I am proposing.

According to a more or less Wittgensteinian picture of the acquisition of descriptive concepts, we acquire such concepts by being presented with examples of the correct use of a term. Employing the term correctly is then a matter of "going on" appropriately from the examples. For example, by being presented with examples of the correct use of the term "bottle," a child becomes able to classify various items in the world as bottles. In going on appropriately, we seem to be following a rule for the correct use of the term, and the question of how rule following of this sort is to be understood has received much discussion. But we can sidestep this debate if we borrow an idea from Alvin Plantinga and invoke the normative notion of proper

---

[5] I intend to state only a sufficient condition. Connecting the possession of a concept with mastery of the use of a word makes possible, I believe, a plausible explanation of the existence of reasonable moral disagreement. There is some similarity between the account of the acquisition and possession of descriptive concepts that I present in this section and the account offered by Jerry Fodor in *Concepts: Where Cognitive Science Went Wrong* (Oxford: Clarendon Press, 1998), ch. 6. He does not focus on learning the use of words, however, and I have not adopted his conceptual atomism. His chapter 6 is intended as a way of meeting an objection to his atomistic view, but it seems to me that the general picture he presents there does not require the acceptance of atomism. I say more about Fodor in note 15 below.

functioning. The distinction between the correct and incorrect use of a term is the distinction between proceeding from examples of correct use in a way that manifests the proper functioning of the relevant capacities and proceeding in a way that does not. The normative dimension of the employment of concepts, noted by Saul Kripke and others, is thus an aspect of the normativity of proper functioning.[6] For present purposes, however, the important point is that a human whose cognitive capacities are functioning properly can acquire a mastery of the use of a term by being presented with examples of its correct use. We should be clear about what this means. The claim is not that an aspect of the proper functioning of human cognitive capacities is grasping an independently existing rule for the correct use of a term. Rather correct use is constituted by the way of proceeding that manifests the proper functioning of the relevant capacities. I expand on these points in the next section.

Someone who has mastered the use of a descriptive term will possess a particular descriptive concept. In employing the term in a way that manifests this mastery, he will be making descriptive judgments the content of which is partly specified by that concept. The mastery of the use of a term has a holistic aspect. The correct use of some descriptive terms is closely tied to sensory inputs, while the correct use of others is determined by patterns of inference within a framework of concepts anchored to sensory inputs at the periphery.[7] The inferences that would be made by a properly functioning human exposed to examples of the correct use of terms in observational and inferential contexts are constitutive of the relations of implication and exclusion among the associated concepts.[8]

---

[6] Kripke discusses the normative dimension of the employment of concepts in *Wittgenstein on Rules and Private Language* (Cambridge, MA: Harvard University Press, 1982). Plantinga responds to Kripke's puzzle about "plus" and "quus" in the following way. "[W]hat makes the concepts she acquires the *right* ones, what makes the others wrong, is that a properly functioning human being will acquire the first kind; acquiring the second, in these circumstances will be pathological, out of accord with our design plan. So the normativity involved is the normativity that goes with proper function." *Warrant and Proper Function* (Oxford: Oxford University Press, 1993), p. 136.

[7] This familiar picture is due to Willard Van Orman Quine, "Two Dogmas of Empiricism," *The Philosophical Review* 60 (1951), pp. 20–43.

[8] In *Articulating Reasons: An Introduction to Inferentialism* (Cambridge, MA: Harvard University Press, 2000), p. 28, Robert B. Brandom distinguishes between weak and strong inferentialism. Weak inferentialism is the view that inferential articulation is a necessary element in the demarcation of the conceptual. Strong inferentialism is the view that inferential articulation, construed in a certain way, is sufficient to account for conceptual content. The role of inferential articulation in the nominalist view I am proposing is of the weak sort. In a properly functioning human, the extrapolative dispositions acquired by exposure to examples of the correct use of terms in observational contexts, and inferential dispositions to move from the employment of some terms to the employment of others, are interrelated.

These points can again be illustrated with the concept "bottle." Acquisition of this concept is a matter of becoming able to employ the word "bottle" correctly after having been exposed to examples of its correct employment. Of course, a learner is in no position to identify particular uses as correct or incorrect. She takes the uses she observes as correct and proceeds on that basis. But examples of use will be provided by a variety of people. So by attending to the different examples she encounters, a learner will become able to employ the term "bottle" in a way that is recognized as correct in her speech community. In doing this, she will acquire a concept shared by others in that community.

The process of mastering the use of the word "bottle" will involve learning to distinguish bottles from jars and glasses. An item is correctly identified as a bottle if it is relevantly similar to the items identified as bottles by those who have already mastered the use of the term, but relevant similarity is not a feature that a newly encountered item possesses independently of the extrapolative dispositions of those who have mastered the use of the term. Rather, relevant similarity is constituted by these extrapolative dispositions. Someone who has mastered the use of the term "bottle" may be able to identify a newly encountered item as a bottle even if it has a shape or other features different from the examples she is familiar with. And since someone who has mastered the use of the word "bottle" will be able to distinguish bottles from jars and glasses, she will be able to infer from an item's being correctly described as a bottle that it cannot be correctly described as a jar or a glass.

Two features of this way of thinking about descriptive concepts deserve special mention. First, proper functioning is understood as a real normative attribute of persons, the detection of which involves a form of self-awareness. I am thus committed, to this modest extent, to normative realism. What we are aware of, in the first instance, may be malfunction. We may in the first instance experience the result of an exercise of our cognitive capacities as not "making sense." We can then take awareness of the proper functioning of our cognitive capacities to consist in an awareness that we are not having such experiences. Since the proper functioning of our cognitive capacities underlies the correct employment of concepts, the content of the experiences that register the proper or improper functioning of these capacities should probably be understood as non-conceptual. Of course, the self-awareness of proper cognitive functioning, or of cognitive malfunction, is not infallible. We may fail to have the experience of malfunction when we are actually falling into malfunction, and we may have the experience of malfunction when our capacities are functioning

properly. The account I am proposing does not, then, bring with it the unwelcome consequence that what seems right is going to be right. What is right is determined by the normativity of proper functioning. Our cognitive functioning is completely proper only if the experience of proper functioning tracks actual proper functioning.[9]

The fallibility of our awareness of proper functioning is relevant to the phenomenon of reasonable disagreement. Because the parties to a political disagreement can fail to detect the malfunction of their own cognitive capacities, they may all be confident that they are manifesting reasonableness (in the dual sense explained in chapter 1) when none are. Thus in a disagreement about whether fairness requires that tax revenues be used to finance day care that is free to parents, all parties may be confident that they are employing the relevant concepts correctly when none are. Genuine reasonable disagreement must be distinguished from this phenomenon. Reasoning about fairness is discussed in the fourth section below.

Plantinga regards human cognitive capacities as having been designed by God to yield true beliefs when employed in the normal circumstances of human life. The resulting epistemology is externalist. One is warranted in forming a belief if the belief is the product of cognitive capacities that are functioning properly, regardless of whether one is aware that they are functioning properly (that is, functioning as they have been designed to). On the view I am proposing, the proper functioning of human mental capacities does not presuppose their intelligent design. Proper functioning is a real normative attribute of the exercise of these capacities. It corresponds to a certain sense of "normal," not the statistical sense, but the normative sense that is roughly equivalent to "healthy." It might be suggested that proper functioning, as a real normative attribute of persons and their capacities, could be given a naturalistic construal. I am doubtful, however, that normativity can be understood naturalistically. Consequently, I shall suppose that the proper functioning of human mental capacities is a non-natural attribute that can be possessed by the exercise of these capacities.[10] The proper functioning of human mental capacities, understood as a

[9] The normativity of proper functioning is resistant to what Christine Korsgaard calls the normative question – in this case: "Why should I function properly?" See *The Sources of Normativity* (Cambridge: Cambridge University Press, 1996). In asking any question, we take the capacities we exercise in asking it to be functioning properly. Thus one cannot question the appropriateness of proper functioning without presupposing it. The moral nominalism that I am going to propose is different from Korsgaard's own view, but there are points of similarity.

[10] For a naturalistic account of the normativity of proper functioning, grounded in evolutionary considerations, see Ruth Garrett Millikan, "Truth Rules, Hoverflies, and the Kripke–Wittgenstein Paradox," *The Philosophical Review* 99 (1990), pp. 323–353.

normative attribute of which we can be aware, can be termed rationality, broadly construed. In his book *The Last Word*, Thomas Nagel suggests that the universe may be so ordered that rationality is a possibility that becomes available at a certain level of biological complexity.[11]

Like certain forms of moral realism, the view I am proposing posits a domain of objective targets and something like an intuitive apprehension of them. But only one kind of target is at issue, and apprehending it is apprehending a state of oneself. Apprehension of the proper or improper functioning of the mental capacities of other people, or of oneself at an earlier time, involves reenactment, and is in that sense filtered though self-awareness.[12] The epistemology associated with this view is internalist since whether we are warranted in making the relevant judgments is something of which we can be aware.

The second point that requires mention concerns the social dimension of proper functioning. Proper functioning, understood in the way I have proposed, is in the first instance an attribute of individuals, so the distinction between proceeding appropriately from examples of correct use and proceeding inappropriately is not socially constituted. But if we suppose that an aspect of proper cognitive functioning is taking the disagreement of others as a reason to reconsider one's own judgments, there is a sense in which correct use of a term is a social achievement. Thinking with concepts does not, on the view I am proposing, presuppose membership in a group, but thinking *well* does.[13] This point is relevant to the awareness of proper functioning. The mutual reconsideration that will characterize the cognitive lives of the members of a group of properly functioning humans is the best defense we have against the failure to perceive our own cognitive malfunction. Ultimately, each must go by whether he has the experiences characteristic of proper or improper cognitive functioning when he reconsiders positions with which others disagree. But the readiness to reconsider, especially when this involves confronting arguments made by others,

---

[11] Thomas Nagel, *The Last Word* (Oxford: Oxford University Press, 1997), ch. 7.
[12] I take the notion of reenactment from R. G. Collingwood. In *The Idea of History* (Oxford: Clarendon Press, 1946), esp. part V, Collingwood proposes that historical knowledge is acquired by a method of reenactment. For a discussion of Collingwood's theory, see Rex Martin, *Historical Explanation* (Ithaca: Cornell University Press, 1977). Martin notes that Collingwood regarded his method as appropriate for the human sciences generally, and Martin interprets this method as involving an effort to make sense of actions in light of thoughts.
[13] I thus depart from the view of Philip Pettit in *The Common Mind: An Essay on Psychology, Society, and Politics* (Oxford: Oxford University Press, 1993). Pettit holds that the capacity for thought depends constitutively on certain social relations.

makes malfunction less likely.[14] Of course, reasonable disagreement will survive mutual reconsideration by properly functioning reasoners, so we cannot suppose that proper cognitive functioning in the context of a group will always bring with it agreement.

I said earlier that I do not mean to extend to descriptive judgments the nominalist picture I am going to propose for moral judgments. But it may be helpful, as a way of setting the stage for the moral case, to consider how we might provide for the correct employment of descriptive terms without positing the existence of descriptive properties. Responding appropriately to a set of examples of correct use will not be responding to a set of items that are, independently, items of a particular kind. Membership in that kind will be constituted by classificatory judgments employing the relevant concept.[15] Of course, we must suppose that an encounter with an example of the correct use of a term, and the subsequent employment of the term in new situations, involves the receipt of distinctive sensory information. But we do not have to suppose that the items about which all these judgments are made possess, independently of those judgments, descriptive properties. Given this, the employment of descriptive terms in classificatory judgments involves the making of a world. Further this world is continually remade as we encounter novel situations that nevertheless "catch," or can be made to catch, the extrapolative dispositions underlying the correct use of the terms at our disposal.[16] The evolution of our conceptual scheme and the remaking of the world in which we live go hand in hand.

---

[14] The readiness to reconsider figured in the argument of the third section of chapter 1.

[15] Compare Fodor: "Maybe what it is to be a doorknob isn't *evidenced* by the kind of experience that leads to acquiring the concept DOORKNOB; maybe what it is to be a doorknob is *constituted* by the kind of experience that leads to acquiring the concept DOORKNOB" (*Concepts*, p. 134). Later he characterizes this "leading" as follows. "My story is that what doorknobs have in common qua doorknobs is being the kind of thing that our kind of minds (do or would) look to from experience with instances of the doorknob stereotype" (*Concepts*, p. 137, emphasis removed). Fodor also speaks of minds like ours coming to "resonate" to a certain property in consequence of experience with stereotypes. This involves going beyond the stereotypes in the way characteristic of learning to use a term like "bottle" (to take my example). Officially, the moral nominalism that I am proposing dispenses with moral properties, but it may be that no harm would be done by countenancing Fodor's mind-constituted properties. The distinction between moral nominalism and moral realism could then be formulated with the help of the account of natural kinds that Fodor presents in chapter 7. According to moral nominalism, no moral kind is a natural kind in Fodor's sense. The "moral twin-earth" argument of Terry Horgan and Mark Timmons also points in this direction. For an exposition, see Timmons's *Morality Without Foundations: A Defense of Ethical Contextualism* (New York: Oxford University Press, 2004), pp. 59–67. Moral nominalism is, however, an alternative to the expressivist view they propose.

[16] This talk of the catching of extrapolative dispositions by items encountered in experience is, of course, metaphorical, but I think the basic idea is clear enough for our purposes here.

This brings us to a feature of the present picture of concepts and their acquisition that will be important in the later discussion. Proceeding from examples of the correct use of a term is not always automatic. Whether a given term can be correctly employed in a new situation may not initially be clear, and the making of a judgment employing that term will require the exercise of a certain mental power, the power of judgment (as it is usually called). Again, the word "bottle" can provide an example. It may not be initially clear whether what we have encountered is a bottle, and we may have to use our judgment to resolve the ambiguities in the situation. But each time we employ a term, we augment the set of examples of correct use from which we subsequently proceed. So if employing the term "bottle" in a particular situation requires the exercise of what I have called the power of judgment, this can have the effect of subtly altering the content of the associated concept. One proceeds differently in the future than one would have proceeded had that situation not been encountered. And a number of such subtle alterations of content can produce a profound alteration.

The exercise of judgment in the employment of a term can also affect the content of concepts in other ways. We may resolve the ambiguities of a situation by making a distinction, by dividing what was previously a single concept into a number of related concepts. The converse operation of assimilation is also a possibility. The exercise of judgment may result in the introduction of a concept that unites previously distinct kinds into a single kind, for example, a genus of which the distinct kinds are now regarded as species.

EVALUATIVE JUDGMENT

How can this general picture be extended to target-setting judgments, judgments that orient us toward the creation or maintenance of some state of the world? We are primarily concerned with judgments of political morality. But we can prepare the ground for a discussion of these judgments by considering the case of non-moral evaluative judgments. A possible view of such judgments is that they merely express favorable or unfavorable attitudes toward the items being judged. Can they be seen as employing normative or evaluative concepts that possess target-setting content?

The principal term of evaluative appraisal is "good." In labeling some-thing – an item, action, or state of affairs – as good, we indicate that we regard it as worthy of some kind of response. In the simplest case, this response is choice. Like ought-judgments, good-judgments can be

understood as asserting the existence of reasons.[17] A judgment of either kind is liable to be met with the question, "Why?" which is a demand to be given the reasons. If the reasons for choosing an item of a particular kind are judged to be weightier than the reasons for refraining from choosing it, it can be said to be a good item of that kind. Thus a bottle might be judged good because, although it is inconveniently heavy, it resists breaking and is reclosable. This does not entail that it ought, in the end, to be chosen. That depends on how it compares with any other bottles that might be chosen instead. A decision about what in the end to choose will be expressed by an all-things-considered ought-judgment that takes into account the known positive and negative features of all the options being considered. Thus one might conclude that although bottles A and B are both good, A is the one that ought to be chosen.

If we understand good-judgments in this way, the principal problem we face is explaining what makes a feature of something a reason for choosing it, or for responding to it in some other way. As an example we can take the judgment that an item is beautiful. It should be emphasized that the judgment is to be understood as practical, as presumptively target setting. "Beautiful" is a term of aesthetic appraisal, and it might be argued that there can be aesthetic judgments that are not target setting. I leave this possibility aside. In what follows, a correctly made judgment that something is beautiful will be regarded as establishing the existence of a reason for action, a reason, for example, to display it, or to contemplate it, or to seek better vantage points from which to view it or listen to it.

In accordance with the general program of this book, I understand possession of an evaluative concept to consist in the mastery of the use of a term. We acquire mastery of the use of an evaluative term by being presented with examples of its correct use from which we "go on." Going on involves recognizing new situations as relevantly similar to the learning situations. Again, relevant similarity is not an independently existing fact. It is constituted by the judgments that a properly function human would make. But evaluative terms are used in judgments that set targets. So targethood must somehow enter into the learning situations and into the situations in which the term is subsequently employed. We begin acquiring

---

[17] In *What We Owe to Each Other* (Cambridge, MA: Harvard University Press, 1998), pp. 95–100, Scanlon presents a "buck-passing" account of value according to which to judge that something is good or valuable is to judge that there are reasons for responding to it in a particular way. Scanlon emphasizes that the responses may be different in different cases. One difference between Scanlon's view and the one I am going to propose is that on my view, to judge that there is a reason to choose something, or to adopt some other posture toward it, is already to make a value judgment.

concepts, including evaluative concepts, in childhood. I propose that initially the "sensing" of targethood associated with acquisition and employment of evaluative concepts consists simply in the experiencing of desires or aversions, inclinations or disinclinations. As was noted at the end of the previous chapter, experiencing a desire or want involves finding oneself oriented toward a target.

On the view I am going to present, the concept of proper functioning has application in connection with human motivation. An aspect of proper functioning is the disposition to experience certain kinds of motivation in certain situations. This fact will play an important role in the account of political morality developed in the next section. Applied to the particular case we are now considering, it gives us the result that properly functioning children will experience certain specific inclinations when presented with examples of the beautiful. Thus a child might experience an inclination to display or contemplate such an item. Alternatively, properly functioning children will be amenable to the induction of such inclinations by a process of conditioning administered by adults who have mastered the concept.

The important point, however, is that for a child to acquire the concept "beautiful" in a context where an adult employs the evaluative term "beautiful" to establish the existence of a reason for action, some desire or inclination must be elicited in the child. Mill says that the sole evidence that something is desirable is that people actually desire it.[18] Initially, on the view I am now proposing, the target-setting content of an evaluative concept consists in its being a mark of desirability in this sense. The employment of the term "beautiful," understood as setting a target, is taken as marking the experience of a certain kind of motivation, which is to say, a mental state that already involves orientation toward a target.

The child's proceeding correctly is a matter of her employing the term "beautiful," or being prepared to employ it, in new situations that are relevantly similar to the learning situations. When full competence is achieved, this similarity has two aspects. First, the descriptive features of the item judged beautiful are taken to be relevantly similar to the features of the item or items labeled beautiful by the teacher. Second, the child is experiencing motivation that registers as similar in kind to the motivations experienced in the learning situations. In both of these respects, relevant similarity to the learning situation is not an independently existing fact. It is constituted by the extrapolative dispositions possessed by those who have mastered the use of a term. Typically, there will be some reciprocal

---

[18] John Stuart Mill, *Utilitarianism*, ed. G. Sher (Indianapolis: Hackett, 2002), chap. 4.

influence between these two aspects of relevant similarity. Whether a motivational state registers as relevantly similar to the states experienced in the learning situations is determined in part by whether the descriptive features of the item eliciting the motivation are taken to be relevantly similar to the descriptive features of the items involved in the learning situations. Likewise, whether the descriptive features register as relevantly similar is determined in part by whether the motivation elicited is taken to be relevantly similar.[19]

It may be useful to say a bit more about the notion of a kind of motivation. In the case of the term "beautiful," the relevant similarity of a new situation to the learning situation will consist in part of the similarity of the descriptive features of the new item to the descriptive features of the items labeled beautiful in the learning situation. In this sense, the desires can be said to have relevantly similar objects. But this is not the only sort of similarity that is relevant. As was mentioned earlier, an aspect of the proper functioning of human motivational capacities is the disposition to experience certain kinds of motivation in certain situations. Thus in a properly functioning child, motivation of a certain kind will be elicited in a situation where the use of the term "beautiful" is being learned, for example, a desire to display, or contemplate, the item labeled beautiful. It may be the case, however, that some subsequent desires elicited by items descriptively similar to those that figured in the learning situations are of a different motivational kind. Thus a child might experience a desire to eat something possessing features of the sort labeled beautiful by the teacher, or to throw it. Such a desire would not provide, in a child whose linguistic capacities were functioning properly, an occasion for the employment of the term "beautiful." This point will become clearer when we consider moral motivation in the next section.

It must be emphasized that we are talking about evaluative judgment. The "proceeding correctly" that we are now considering is not a matter of correct description. In particular, it is not a matter of the correct description of motivation. It is target setting. One proceeds from examples of correct target setting to the setting of analogous targets in new situations taken to be relevantly similar, in the senses specified, to the examples. Thus the making of judgments that various items are beautiful involves the construction of an evaluative world, a world of targets. We can imagine a child whose

---

[19] Compare John McDowell, "Non-Cognitivism and Rule-Following," in his *Mind, Value, and Reality* (Cambridge, MA: Harvard University Press, 1998), pp. 198–218, esp. p. 201. The whole essay is relevant to my project in this book.

encounters with the learning situations initially lead him to label as beautiful anything he wants in the requisite way, anything he wants to display, for example. But even in this case, we can speak of a world of targets distinct from those provided by desires that merely happen to assert themselves because the target setting involves judgment. It involves the proper functioning of human linguistic capacities.

The introduction of this linguistic species of proper functioning enables us to accommodate the idea that when we are dealing with value, the items that elicit our responses must merit those responses.[20] When a motivational response to an item possessing certain features catches the extrapolative dispositions associated with the mastery of a positive evaluative term, the item can be regarded as meriting the response. Although the judgments are not descriptive but target setting, they are still judgments. This provides some basis for regarding an agent who makes such a judgment as believing that a reason for action of a certain sort obtains, as believing that an item is beautiful, for example. I say more about this last point in the final section.

Once the distinction between a target set by an ordinary desire and a target set by an evaluative judgment has been established in childhood, it can be expanded. Thus some motivational states that are found to be similar in kind to those elicited in the learning situation may be rejected as occasions for the employment of the associated evaluative term because their objects lack the requisite descriptive similarity to the objects of the motivational states involved in the learning situation. The association of judgments employing terms of aesthetic appraisal like "beautiful" with increasingly precise specifications of the descriptive features of the items about which the judgments are being made is central to the cultivation of taste. By the same token, some motivational states, even of the relevant kind, that are elicited in a given situation may be rejected as occasions for

---

[20] For the idea that an item of value must not merely elicit a response but merit it, see John McDowell, "Values and Secondary Qualities," in *Mind, Value, and Reality*, pp. 131–150. Since McDowell accepts the reality of secondary qualities, it seems he would reject my evaluative nominalism. He says that the explanations of our responses that serve to establish the reality of secondary qualities are constructed from the relevant evaluative point of view (p. 145), so there are some similarities. But a view according to which values are secondary qualities is one that regards "values as genuine features of the world, which we are able to detect by virtue of our special affective and attitudinative propensities" ("Non-Cognitivism and Rule-Following," p. 200). Presumably the features of the world the detection of which is marked by our use of value terms, unlike the properties of objects the detection of which is marked by our use of color terms, must be normative, not merely physical. Otherwise, we get the non-cognitivist picture McDowell wants to reject. My moral nominalism provides, I think, a way of accommodating McDowell's insights while avoiding this particular commitment. The only normative property it invokes is the proper functioning of our mental apparatus, which we detect by a kind of self-awareness. Fodor's approach (see note 15) may also have application here.

the employment of an evaluative term because the motivational dispositions differ in subtle ways from those experienced in the situation where use of the term was learned.

As these points make clear, the learning of the correct use of evaluative terms – the acquisition of a critical vocabulary – can extend well into adulthood, and can involve discovery as well as instruction. For present purposes, however, the key point is that through processes of this sort, a distinction begins to emerge between motivation that we merely find ourselves with and motivation that, in a certain sense, we give ourselves. Following an established tradition in philosophy, we can label motivation of the latter sort rational motivation.

On the view I am proposing, rational motivation is not motivation that has its source in reason. It has the same ultimate source as non-rational motivation, the general capacity, which we possess as animals of the kind we are, to experience motivational dispositions. It is distinguished from non-rational motivation by the fact that the targets involved are set by judgments employing concepts that have target-setting content, which is to say, judg-ments employing terms whose mastery has the two aspects I have described. Judgments employing a term such as "beautiful" set targets when the associated extrapolative dispositions are caught by complexes of motivation and sensory information (or cognition). In this way, a set of targets is established that differs from those set by desires that simply assert them-selves. Desires fall into the latter class by virtue of the fact that they do not catch the extrapolative dispositions underlying the mastery of the use of normative or evaluative terms. As in the descriptive case, evaluative judg-ment has a holistic aspect. Relations of implication and exclusion with other evaluative judgments condition the possibility of making a particular eval-uative judgment.

As well as separating rational from non-rational motivation, evaluative judgment can give novel forms to rational motivation. This involves the exercise of what I called, in the previous section, the power of judgment. It may not be initially clear whether a given item is appropriately labeled beautiful, and an exercise of judgment may be required to resolve the ambiguities in the situation. As a history of judgment involving an evaluative term like "beautiful" is assembled, later judgments taken to be correctly made are added to the stock of examples of correct use from which a given individual proceeds. As a result, the concept of the beautiful, as it is employed by a given individual, can alter its content. New complexes of sensation or cognition, and motivation, framed as they are by other concepts in one's possession, may be perceived as relevantly

similar to the existing examples in novel ways. And when the resulting judgments are added to one's examples of correct use, the content of the associated concept will be altered. Items – pieces of music, for example – previously deemed beautiful may no longer be judged to possess this attribute, and items previously deemed to lack beauty may be judged to possess it.

An aspect of this process is that targets can undergo fission or fusion. What was previously a single target may be divided into several different, but related, targets. Different kinds of beauty, understood as aesthetic choiceworthiness, may be distinguished, or the term "beautiful" may be reserved for only one kind of aesthetic choiceworthiness. And what were previously different targets may be amalgamated into a single target. Earlier distinctions may no longer be regarded as making sense. Occasion may also be found for the introduction of new evaluative concepts to fill perceived gaps in the framework of concepts one initially possesses. Evaluative judgment thus has the effect of reshaping – giving new structure and articulation to – the human capacity to generate motivational dispositions. It makes and remakes evaluative worlds.

The reason for choosing something provided by the fact that it is beautiful may have to be weighed against reasons of another sort for declining to choose it or for choosing something else. An item that is not deemed beautiful might, for example, be judged to have "sentimental value" because it is associated by the agent with a cherished person, location, or time of life. We must, then, consider how all-things-considered normative and evaluative judgments are to be understood within the framework of the nominalist theory I am proposing. In particular, we must consider how the assignment of relative weights to conflicting reasons can be understood as manifesting proper functioning. My answer to this question is presented in the next section.

It should be noted that as in the case of descriptive judgments, properly functioning agents will have a reason to reconsider evaluative judgments with which others disagree. By this process, a change in an individual's employment of an evaluative term like "beautiful" can spread to other members of the community, and be given further refinement by them. The evaluative worlds we make are thus, in an important sense, social products. This fact contributes to the normative dimension of concept acquisition. Adults can be taken to be using evaluative terms correctly in the learning situations because they are part of a linguistic community in which use is socially refined. And of course, the same was true of the adults who taught them. As Goodman points out, we come to the process of

worldmaking *in medias res*, receiving a world from our teachers and elaborating it before handing it on.[21]

MORAL JUDGMENT

The account of judgments employing the term "beautiful" presented in the previous section envisages the possession by all properly functioning humans of motivational dispositions that can be shaped into a particular, conceptually articulated aesthetic sensibility. Parallel points apply to the moral case. Moral nominalism envisages the possession by all properly functioning humans of a form of motivation that can be shaped into a particular, conceptually articulated moral sensibility. Motivations such as sympathy or a benevolent concern for the welfare of others might be mentioned in this connection. It might be argued that all humans whose mental capacities are functioning properly will experience such motivations.

For an account of political morality, however, motivation of another sort is the most suitable candidate. This is the motivation associated with the human capacity for cooperation. A properly functioning human will, I shall assume, be cooperatively disposed. Certain aspects of morality need not have any special connection with cooperation, for example, the imperative to come to the aid of someone who has been injured (although people can cooperate to establish a practice of mutual aid). But political society is a cooperative venture among the residents of a particular territory, and political morality is most plausibly regarded as concerned with the appropriate structuring of this kind of cooperative enterprise. In the case of political morality, then, the motivational "matter" that is given form by judgments employing socially available concepts can be understood as cooperative motivation. It may be possible to extend the resulting picture to the whole domain of right – the domain of what we owe to each other, to use T. M. Scanlon's phrase – but here I propose to focus on political morality. Reasonable disagreement looms largest in this region of the domain of right.

I have suggested that a properly functioning human will be cooperatively disposed. This means two things. First, she will be disposed to contribute to a cooperative venture that produces an outcome she judges, on balance, to be good – to have value of some kind. This judgment should be understood as taking into account the cost to her of contributing. Second, she will be disposed to make concessions from her most preferred cooperative scheme

[21] Nelson Goodman, *Ways of Worldmaking* (Indianapolis: Hackett, 1978), p. 6.

so that the other potential cooperators can find participation worthwhile.[22] A full discussion of the proper functioning of human cooperative capacities would have to say more about the first aspect of cooperative motivation. It would, for example, have to explain how the disposition to contribute manifests itself when an agent must choose among different cooperative ventures all of which satisfy the stated condition. I say a little more about this in chapter 4. For present purposes, however, it is cooperative motivation of the second kind, the disposition to make concessions, that is most important. This is the motivation that is elaborated into moral worlds.

Cooperation proceeds on the basis of an explicitly or implicitly formulated cooperative scheme that assigns contributions and distributes benefits. Cooperation presupposes that each cooperator values something other than cooperation itself, something that cooperation brings into existence, for example, a concert series. We might call this the cooperative benefit (for a given cooperator). The term is not entirely apt since the value an individual attaches to what is produced by a particular cooperative enterprise may be impersonal. Thus she may value the enterprise as enhancing the health of the population. Still, it is the value of the scheme as judged by a given cooperator that is relevant.

An individual whose cooperative dispositions are functioning properly will not participate in a cooperative venture unless she judges the benefit produced, in the sense just specified, sufficient to justify incurring the cost of her contribution. Thus being disposed to make concessions from one's most preferred cooperative scheme will consist, in part, in being disposed to concede what is necessary to secure the cooperation of everyone whose participation one seeks. In the case of a concert series, one might have to accept the inclusion of some performers one has no desire to hear. In the political case, the people whose cooperation is sought, and thus to whom one must be prepared to make concessions, are the residents of a particular territory.

There is, however, more to be said about the disposition to make concessions. Each member of the cooperating group will benefit most if the cooperative scheme that is implemented gives the others only the minimum necessary to secure their participation, with the result that the cooperative surplus goes entirely to him. Considered simply as an instrumental reasoner, each member of a group of potential cooperators will have

---

[22] These two aspects of a cooperative disposition have analogues in the moral philosophy of Kant. The Formula of Universal Law works best as a prohibition on free riding. And being prepared to make concessions to other cooperators when one has the de facto ability to secure their participation on terms more favorable to oneself is one thing that can be meant by treating people not merely as means to one's ends but also as ends in themselves.

a reason to seek the implementation of a scheme that benefits him in this way. Insisting on this, however, will prevent cooperation from going forward, so an instrumental reasoner will typically be prepared to engage in bargaining that produces a particular pattern of concessions.

But as was noted in the previous chapter, I shall assume that a properly functioning human will be cooperatively disposed in a further sense. He will be prepared to make concessions to people whose bargaining power is not sufficient to force the concessions, provided everyone involved is similarly motivated. When all the members of a group that could benefit from cooperation are cooperatively disposed in this sense, they will normally participate in a collective effort to identify, through a process of reciprocal concession, a cooperative scheme that is mutually satisfactory to them as people so disposed.[23]

In accordance with the usage of chapter 1, we can call the disposition to participate in such a process of reciprocal concession "reasonableness." In displaying this disposition, the participants manifest reasonableness. By extension, a cooperative scheme that is acceptable to a reasonable cooperator can be said to be reasonable. Reasonableness has a moral dimension because a reasonable scheme will embody concessions that go beyond those required by self-interested bargaining. As was noted in chapter 1, "fairness" is another term often employed to characterize the sort of concession now under discussion. I suggested employing the term "reasonableness-as-fairness" to mark the contrast with reasonableness-as-competence. A fair scheme is one that would be acceptable to a reasonable-as-fair person.

People who are cooperatively disposed in the respect just described can be understood as possessing a sense of fairness. But for moral nominalism, fairness is not an independently existing normative property, so the sense of fairness is not a perceptual capacity of a certain kind. It is a form of self-awareness, an awareness of the proper functioning of certain human capacities in the case at hand. Awareness of this sort of proper functioning has two aspects. It is partly an awareness that the motivational disposition to make and seek concessions in cooperative contexts, the disposition to be reasonable, is functioning properly. And it is partly an awareness that the linguistic

---

[23] The proviso that others must be similarly motivated also plays a role in Scanlon's theory. He speaks of "principles that could not be reasonably rejected, by people who were moved to find principles for the general regulation of behavior that others, similarly motivated, could not reasonably reject" (*What We Owe to Each Other*, p. 4). In chapter 1, I suggested that one mark of reasonable disagreement in politics is each of the contending positions can be reasonably rejected by someone. But we can still understand the disposition to make and seek concessions in cooperative contexts, which underlies reasonable rejection, as contingent on the perception that the others involved possess this disposition as well.

capacities exercised in judgments employing the terms "fair" and "unfair" are functioning properly. A scheme is appropriately describable as fair when the distribution of benefits and burdens that it specifies, and the motivation it elicits in properly functioning humans, are together capable of catching the linguistic dispositions of someone who has mastered the use of the term "fair." But more needs to be said about what this mastery involves.

Agreement on the fairness of a cooperative scheme can be understood as a kind of equilibrium of motivational inputs of a certain kind. No member of the group is motivated to make or seek further concessions given the concessions specified by the scheme. The process of mutual concession involves reacting to the concessions of others, and may achieve equilibrium in a variety of ways. There is, then, no such thing as *the* fair pattern of concessions in a particular case. A process of reciprocal concession will be initiated within a group of properly functioning humans that is considering how to structure a cooperative venture, but proper functioning does not determine a specific pattern of concessions with which it must terminate. A judgment that a cooperative scheme is fair marks the fact that the person making the judgment is motivated, as a cooperatively disposed person, to accept the specified pattern of concessions. When all the actual or potential participants in a cooperative venture find themselves able, as cooperatively disposed people, to judge a scheme for that venture fair, there will be agreement on its fairness. That is, the different judgments of fairness will be in agreement. Disagreement about the fairness of a cooperative scheme is explored in the next chapter.[24]

---

[24] The points in this paragraph are relevant to the possibility of obtaining a principle of fairness valid for all human beings simply by reflecting on the disposition to make and seek concessions that will be possessed by properly functioning humans. People exercising this disposition will participate in a process of mutual concession with others similarly disposed. But there is no way to extract from the concept of such a process a single form that the product should take. One reason for this is the path dependence described in the main text. But in addition, to anticipate a bit, proper functioning in the manifestation of the disposition involves making judgments employing socially available normative and evaluative concepts that identify various features of social situations as justifying concession. The acquisition of such concepts gives each individual's disposition to make and seek concessions an initial shape. And the concessions that each individual is subsequently prepared to make or seek will depend on this initial shape. We cannot bypass this problem by imagining how the process of mutual concession would unfold if the disposition were unconceptualized. In the absence of conceptualization, the unfolding would be indeterminate.

It may be helpful to put these points another way. It is natural to suppose that an egalitarian standard is implicit in any process of genuinely mutual concession. But what counts as equal concession will be determined by the claims each party can make, and this will depend on the concepts available for articulating claims. These serve to pick out, from the set of things the parties might want to acquire or retain, those they can call upon the other members of the polity, acting collectively, to secure for them. As I explain further in the later chapters, for moral nominalism, the concepts that do this picking out are the product of a historical process that has generated, at different times and places, different concepts, and thus different understandings of what can justifiably be claimed.

Our initial encounters with the concepts of fairness and unfairness as children typically involve simple problems of distribution, for example, the distribution of benefits and burdens within a family, or a group of students in a classroom. The issue might be how chores in a household, or opportunities to use a computer in a classroom, are to be distributed. It is plausible that children learn the correct use of "fair" and "unfair" in contexts where a cooperative scheme is being negotiated. The child observes adults employing these terms to accept or reject proposals made by others and in this way acquires an understanding of their correct use. The learning situation has both descriptive and motivational aspects. A specification of the distribution of benefits and burdens to be realized within the relevant group constitutes the descriptive component of the examples of correct use. The motivational component is provided by the disposition to make or seek concessions that will be experienced by properly functioning humans. The process of reenactment described in the second section above enables the learner to experience motivation in connection with situations in which others are using the terms "fair" and "unfair" in the course of making or seeking concessions. The terms "fair" and "unfair" will be correctly employed in the future when the descriptive features of a cooperative scheme, and the motivation it elicits in a properly functioning individual, together catch the extrapolative dispositions created by the initial encounters with examples of correct use.

When the term being used is "unfair," the motivation that catches the extrapolative dispositions is motivation to make, or seek, concessions different from those specified by the scheme. To make a judgment of unfairness, one need not have some alternative scheme in mind. Just as our awareness of the proper functioning of our cognitive capacities may consist in the absence of an awareness of malfunction, so our awareness of fairness may consist in the absence of an awareness of unfairness. That is, we may judge a scheme fair when we find ourselves disposed neither to make nor to seek further concessions. In the case of both "fair" and "unfair," a crucial role is played by the examples of correct use provided by a particular individual's teachers, whether in contexts of negotiation or not. These give her sense of fairness its initial shape. In addition to enabling us to experience motivation in connection with learning situations in which others are using the terms "fair" and "unfair," the process of reenactment enables us to apply the terms "fair" and "unfair" to schemes in which we do not expect to participate.

The term "fair," like the term "good," can be regarded as marking a kind of choiceworthiness. In this case, however, the choice is understood to be collective. A cooperative scheme that is correctly judged to be fair has this

status by virtue of its possession of features that a cooperatively motivated individual, armed with a socially provided set of normative and evaluative concepts, could regard as supporting its collective choice. Parallel points can be made about unfairness. A cooperative scheme is correctly judged unfair by virtue of its possession of features that a cooperatively motivated individual, operating with the available normative and evaluative concepts, could regard as supporting its collective rejection. We must now consider how these supporting reasons are to be understood.

Although the motivation associated with the correct employment of the terms "fair" and "unfair" is experienced by an individual, it is conditioned by that individual's expectation regarding the concessions that the other participants, as reasonable, will be prepared to make. What one is willing, as reasonable, to give up is a function of what one thinks the other members of the group, as reasonable, should be willing to give up. Thus the correct employment of the terms "fair" and "unfair" involves the registering of a pattern of *claims* that the members of the group can legitimately make against other members or against the group as a whole.

In the most fundamental case, the features of a scheme that constitute reasons for collectively choosing it are features that ground such claims. Terms marking different ways that someone can be deserving of a particular package of benefits and burdens, such as by virtue of having worked hard, provide examples. Thus the socially available concepts might enable a member of a cooperating group to claim a particular package as a suitable reward for the effort she has expended, or will expend, in contributing to the cooperative venture. Alternatively the socially available concepts might enable a member to claim a particular package on the basis of a specific need, such as a medical need. Such claims are evaluated by determining whether granting them is, other things being equal, required by fairness to the person making the claim, or on whose behalf the claim is made. Structural features of a cooperative scheme, such as some sort of equality of benefit or burden, can also provide a basis for claims. A child may learn that he can judge his exclusion from a trip to the zoo unfair on the ground that all the other children in the class are being allowed to go. Claims of both sorts are discussed in more detail in the next chapter.

The correct use of the terms with which claims are expressed is, again, learned from examples of correct use. Thus a child might see an adult claiming a larger distributive share on the ground that she has worked harder than the others, or has contributed more to the cooperative product. As before, the learning situation will be one in which motivation is experienced, in particular, the disposition to make or seek concessions as a part

of a process of mutual concession. The feature of the situation that is identified as grounding a claim will elicit motivation of the requisite kind, either motivation to make a concession or motivation to seek a concession, in the learner. In the example just given, the child's mental reenactment of the adult's claim will involve his experiencing the same kind of motivation the adult is experiencing. Claims, so understood, can support judgments of unfairness as well as judgments of fairness.

In the discussion of evaluative judgment in the previous section, I suggested that in making target-setting judgments, we separate rational from non-rational motivation. This distinction receives further elaboration in the case of political morality. The motivation to which judgments of political morality give form is a manifestation of a particular disposition that all properly functioning humans will experience. It can thus be regarded as possessing a normative dimension prior to having a specific structure imposed on it by target-setting judgments employing socially available normative and evaluative concepts. We may suppose that in a properly functioning human, this cooperative motivation displaces motivation of other sorts that might compete with it, for example, a desire to secure acceptance of a scheme maximally beneficial to oneself through the exercise of bargaining power.

In the case of the judgments of fairness characteristic of political morality, then, two kinds of proper functioning are involved. There is the proper functioning of human cooperative dispositions, which results in the presence of a certain sort of motivation. And there is the proper functioning of human linguistic capacities, which is manifested in judgments that employ socially available concepts to give form to this motivational matter – for example, in a claim of a particular sort, or in a judgment of fairness. These two kinds of proper functioning can be understood as corresponding to the two kinds of reasonableness I have distinguished. The competent operation with relevant reasons that is marked by the term "reasonableness-as-competence" is basically a matter of mastery of the use of terms. Especially important for our purposes are target-setting terms, normative and evaluative terms. But in the case of the reasons that are germane to the fairness or unfairness of a particular scheme of political cooperation, this proper linguistic functioning presupposes the presence of the disposition to make or seek concessions that I have labeled reasonableness-as-fairness.

The points made earlier about the elaboration of rational motivation have application here as well. In the cooperative case, the motivation that engages the extrapolative dispositions associated with the correct use of the relevant terms is the willingness to make or seek concessions when others are

similarly disposed. And this general disposition acquires a particular, conceptually articulated structure as terms suitable for expressing claims, or marking other features of cooperative schemes relevant to their fairness, are acquired. Similarly, features of cooperative situations may be perceived as relevantly similar in novel ways to the accumulated examples of correct use. As a result, the target-setting content of the judgments establishing a specific reason for organizing political cooperation in a certain way may undergo alteration. New distinctions may be created or old distinctions superseded. Through these processes, we make and remake moral worlds, in particular, worlds of right. It should be borne in mind that the available concepts, and thus the process of moral worldmaking, will differ somewhat from polity to polity. I say more about this in the later chapters.

In the discussion of evaluative judgment in the previous section, it was noted that evaluative judgments include not only judgments identifying a particular option as good, or articulating particular reasons for choosing an option, but also all-things-considered ought-judgments capturing the collective force of all the reasons germane to a particular decision. Such judgments have a place in connection with the choice of cooperative schemes as well. We can make these points using the notion of target setting. A judgment establishing the existence of a moral reason for action can be regarded as a particular kind of target-setting judgment, one that sets a presumptive target. An all-things-considered ought-judgment then becomes a judgment that extracts from the various presumptive targets operative in a situation a single target capable of guiding action. How are such judgments to be understood?

To answer this question, we need an account of the relative strength of conflicting reasons. On the view I am proposing, the relative strength of a reason for adopting a particular cooperative scheme must be understood as the strength of the motivation that is given form by the judgment establishing the existence of that reason. For example, the strength that a given individual assigns to the reason for giving a larger distributive share to someone who has expended more effort will be determined by the strength of the motivation to make or seek a concession that is elicited by the claim. But it does not follow that the relative strength of reasons has no rational basis. It will have such a basis if the strength of the motivation to which the judgment gives form can be regarded as a manifestation of the proper functioning of the appropriate motivational apparatus. In general, relative strength will have a rational basis if we can attribute the experience of relatively strong or relatively weak motivation to the proper functioning of the appropriate motivational apparatus, as it has been configured by the available concepts.

In the present case, the appropriate motivational apparatus is that associated with the disposition to make or seek concessions in a cooperative context when others are similarly disposed. The greater strength of the motivation experienced in connection with the entertaining of a given consideration translates into stronger rational support for a particular pattern of concessions only if it is a manifestation of the proper functioning of that apparatus. So we can say that the relative strength, for a specific individual, of the reasons germane to the fairness of a cooperative scheme is determined by the strength of the motivation that she, as someone who has mastered a particular moral vocabulary and whose disposition to make or seek concessions is functioning properly, would experience.

The correctness of an all-things-considered judgment reconciling the competing claims relevant to the fairness of a cooperative scheme can be approached in a similar way. Such a judgment might, for example, have to reconcile claims made on the basis of effort with claims made on the basis of need. An all-things-considered judgment will reflect the combined force of the different claims that have been acknowledged, and will be correct if the way the forces are combined is appropriately responsive to the force each exerts individually. Appropriate responsiveness will be responsiveness that manifests the proper functioning of the disposition to make and seek concessions.[25] It should be borne in mind, however, that claims can also attract what I have called non-rational motivation, for example, a selfish desire for more, and this can distort judgment. When non-rational motivation has this effect, the result is a failure of proper functioning.

---

[25] In her paper "All Things Considered" (*Philosophical Perspectives* 18 [2004], pp. 1–22), Ruth Chang argues that to make sense of all-things-considered judgments, we must posit the existence of a comprehensive value, of which the different considerations that need to be taken into account can be regarded as parts. This value determines the weight to be given to the different considerations in a particular context. The account I have proposed is similar in that a form of motivation that will be experienced by properly functioning humans provides the basis for the different weights that different considerations are appropriately given. But if a comprehensive value is understood as a conceptualized goal, such values do not play a role. The different sources of motivation have no conceptualized structure prior to the making of the reason-judgments that give form to them. The relative weight of a given reason is, then, sensed more than judged. Similar points can be made about evaluative judgments. I mentioned that it is plausible that properly functioning humans will experience certain motivations when presented with items correctly labeled beautiful. They will be correctly so labeled in part because they elicit this motivation. There may, however, be cases in which the motivation given form by two different reason-judgments has its source in the proper functioning of different components of the human motivational apparatus. A conflict between beauty and sentimental value may be of this sort. In such cases, we may have only motivations that, as a matter of fact, differ in strength, with no possibility of attributing these differences to the proper functioning of a single human capacity. There may thus be no rational basis for assigning different relative weights to the reasons.

As we saw in the previous section, the construction of an evaluative world has a collective aspect, at least where the same terms are being employed. Encounters with conflicting judgments give a properly functioning human a reason to reconsider, and this makes the construction of evaluative worlds a collective endeavor. Earlier it was noted that in the case of the construction of a world of right, the process is collective in a further sense. The reasons identified by judgments making or accepting claims are reasons that are to be acted on collectively. They are reasons for the members of the group to adjust the overall scheme of cooperation in particular ways. When views about the required adjustments conflict, properly functioning cooperators will reconsider the judgments they have made. Where the disagreement is reasonable the judgments will not converge, but the pattern of disagreement may change.

In other respects, however, the process of constructing a world of right is the same as the process of constructing an evaluative world. In learning the correct employment of the terms "fair" and "unfair," and the terms used in making the claims that constitute reasons for regarding a particular cooperative scheme as fair or unfair, we are inducted into a moral world. In the course of our lives as practical reasoners, we remake this world. As Goodman says, worlds are made out of worlds. The highly articulated world of right that we now occupy is thus the latest stage in a long history of moral worldmaking stretching back to what were presumably the relatively simple worlds of right occupied by the earliest humans capable of constructing such worlds, the earliest of our forebears capable of living a life with a conscious normative dimension.

META-ETHICAL DETAILS

According to the nominalist theory that I have proposed, possession of a target-setting concept consists in the mastery of the use of a target-setting term. This mastery is displayed in judgments employing the term. Such judgments give structure and form to motivational matter of a particular kind. In the case of judgments of political morality, this matter is provided by the disposition, which will be possessed by all properly functioning humans, to participate in a process of mutual concession when others are similarly disposed. Judgments of political morality are correctly made if making them constitutes "going on" appropriately from previously encountered examples of the correct use of the terms employed. The import of this way of understanding moral judgment will become clearer in the subsequent chapters, where it is put to use in providing an account of reasonable disagreement

concerning questions of political morality. But a few further observations about the meta-ethics of moral nominalism may be useful here.

First, in chapter 1 I distinguished moral realism from constructivism, and suggested that moral nominalism can be regarded as a kind of constructivist view. According to Russ Shafer-Landau, "[w]hat is common to all constructivists is the idea that moral reality is constituted by the attitudes, actions, responses, or outlooks of persons, possibly under idealized conditions."[26] Shafer-Landau calls constructivist theories that incorporate some sort of idealization "objectivist," and he says that, like moral realism, constructivist theories of this kind can provide for the impartiality of morality, for the categorical nature of moral demands, and for moral error.[27]

Moral nominalism can be understood as a constructivist theory of this objectivist sort. The idealization is provided by the stipulation that human motivational and conceptual capacities are functioning properly. Shafer-Landau argues that constructivist theories can be expected to give intuitively plausible results only if the conditions imposed by the idealization are already implicitly moral. The process of construction can yield an intuitively acceptable output only if the input is, in some respects, already moral. He takes this to be a point in favor of moral realism. The idealization associated with moral nominalism is implicitly moral by virtue of the assumption that properly functioning humans will be disposed to make and seek concessions when others are similarly disposed. Further, moral nominalism construes proper functioning realistically. But this disposition yields no determinate moral requirements prior to its being given conceptualized form by judgments employing the available normative and evaluative concepts, and the moral worlds constructed by such judgments are not construed realistically. Further, where the concepts available within two polities differ, the constructive process will generate different ways of understanding the appropriate organization of political cooperation.

Constructivist views can provide for moral truth. A judgment can be regarded as stating a moral truth if it accurately records the output of the specified constructive process, when that process is appropriately carried out. But the word "true" is often taken to mark correspondence with facts that have, to borrow Shafer-Landau's term, stance-independent existence. So I prefer to speak of moral judgments, on the nominalist construal I have proposed, simply as correct or incorrect. They are correct when they are made in a way that manifests the proper functioning of the capacities

---

[26] Russ Shafer-Landau, *Moral Realism: A Defence* (Oxford: Clarendon Press, 2003), p. 14.
[27] Ibid., p. 40.

engaged. It is not, however, essential to the moral nominalism I am proposing that talk of truth be excluded, provided it is understood that no correspondence with independently existing moral facts is involved. I say more about this below.[28]

We can now turn to some more specific points. The rational motivation that moral nominalism regards as created by practical judgment can be understood as autonomous because it involves the setting of targets that may differ from those set, directly or indirectly (through the mediation of beliefs about effective means) by ordinary desires. But rational motivation in the moral case is not the completely independent target-setting capacity that Kant seems to have envisaged. It is created by judgments that give conceptualized form to motivational dispositions that will be experienced by properly functioning humans. As the process of conceptual refinement proceeds, rational motivation undergoes articulation. Since the motivation that receives structure is human motivation, biological facts may constrain the moral worlds we can construct. Nevertheless, these worlds can achieve a subtlety and refinement far exceeding anything produced by desires that merely assert themselves.

On the view I have developed, practical judgment cannot create motivation. Motivation must present itself, to be accepted, rejected, and ultimately shaped by judgments whose content is provided by target-setting concepts. But the account does not require any specific phenomenology of motivation. Being motivated in a particular way can be understood as possessing a set of dispositions to move from the cognizing of particular states of the world to the manifestation of particular behaviors.[29] Being motivated to acquire a conch shell can be understood as possessing a disposition to move from the perception of one to the grasping of it, or from the belief that there is one at a particular location, to going there and getting it. An aspect of the proper functioning of human mental capacities is that the activation of such motivational dispositions can provide the occasion for a judgment employing a normative or evaluative term. As we have seen, whether these terms are correctly employed depends in part on whether certain kinds of motivation are present. In this way, the proper

---

[28] As we saw in the last section of chapter 1, Shafer-Landau says: "Realists believe that there are moral truths that obtain independently of any preferred perspective, in the sense that the moral standards that fix the facts are not made true by virtue of their ratification from within any given actual or hypothetical perspective" (*Moral Realism*, p. 15). He thus seems to be making room for a non-realist way that moral standards can be true, that provided by constructivism.

[29] The phenomenology of desire, and the possibility of a dispositional account of desire, are discussed by Michael Smith in *The Moral Problem*, ch. 4.

functioning of our linguistic capacities enters into the proper functioning of our motivational capacities, yielding target-setting judgments – judgments setting ultimate targets – that possess motivational content. Thus if the attributes whose perception activates the disposition to examine a conch shell, and the disposition itself, are of the right sort, as determined by the agent's history with the relevant terms, the shell can be judged beautiful. That is, a judgment establishing a particular reason for action will be possible.

In the case of judgments of fairness, the motivation is provided by the general disposition to make and seek concessions in cooperative contexts when others are similarly disposed. As we acquire more normative and evaluative concepts identifying particular ways social arrangements can be fair or unfair, and refine them in practical judgment, we effect a reconfiguration of the disposition to make and seek concessions in cooperative contexts. In its subsequent appearances, this motivation possesses a new shape, which may itself be reshaped by further judgments. On the view I am proposing, the fact that our linguistic and motivational capacities interact in this way is simply an aspect of the proper functioning of the human mental apparatus. It is of a piece with the interaction of our linguistic and sensory capacities, and is no more (or less) mysterious. As I have said, the reshaping of our motivational dispositions has a historical dimension. Through moral judgment, we remake the normative worlds we receive from our teachers, just as they remade the worlds they received from their teachers. Our moral worldmaking is the latest stage of a process that began when the human race did and will last as long as it does.

The interaction between our linguistic capacities, on the one hand, and our motivational or sensory capacities on the other may enable us to explain why reasonable disagreement plays a greater role in connection with moral judgments than with observational judgments. It is plausible that the proper functioning of our motivational apparatus displays more interpersonal variability than the proper functioning of our sensory apparatus. Moreover, on the account I have presented, interpersonal variability of the proper functioning of the motivational apparatus is especially to be expected in the case of political morality because proper functioning itself has an interpersonal aspect. The relevant disposition is a disposition to make or seek concessions when others are similarly disposed. So the motivational idiosyncrasies of the people with whom a given individual is interacting can affect the pattern of concessions he finds acceptable.

If motivation of a certain kind, a disposition to make and seek concessions, for example, would be experienced by a properly functioning human

in situations of a particular sort, we can criticize the lack of it. And we can say that people who are capable of experiencing such motivation have a reason to do what they can to create the capacity in anyone who lacks it. Can we say in addition that an individual who lacks the requisite motivational capacity has reason to do what he would judge himself to have reason to if this capacity were active and functioning properly in all respects? For moral nominalism, the possession of moral reasons for action presupposes the possession of both of the required capacities, linguistic and motivational. So anyone who completely lacks either of these capacities cannot be said to have the corresponding moral reasons for action. For example, if a sociopath is an individual who completely lacks the motivational dispositions presupposed by judgments of fairness, he cannot be said to have a reason to treat people fairly. Similarly, although some species of animals possess cooperative dispositions, they cannot be said to have moral reasons for action since they lack the requisite linguistic capacities.

The more common case, however, is that where the capacity is present, but is sometimes dormant or disabled. Here the problem is the occasional non-activation of the motivational dispositions underlying the sense of fairness in situations where proper functioning calls for their activation. In such cases, moral nominalism allows us to say that the individual in question has a reason to act in the requisite way even though she is not on that occasion able to make a fully formed moral judgment. The fact that she has the capacity for such a judgment, even though it is dormant or disabled on that occasion, enables us to describe her as possessing a reason for action despite its being motivationally inert. Of course, she may still do what she has moral reason to do for another reason, such as that provided by coercive sanctions.[30]

---

[30] Can we add to that an individual of the sort described not only has a reason for action but knows this? We can regard someone who has the requisite motivational dispositions but finds them dormant or disabled in a particular situation as knowing that she has a moral reason for action if she can recall judgments that she made in similar situations where these dispositions were active. But it may be that such a person can rely on the judgments of others as well. One issue in meta-ethics concerns the possibility of an "amoralist," someone who knows what morality requires but is always unmoved. In "Knowing Enough to Disagree: A New Response to the Moral Twin Earth Argument" (in Russ Shafer-Landau, ed., *Oxford Studies in Metaethics* [New York: Oxford University Press, 2006], pp. 161–193), Mark Van Roojen argues, in response to the problem of the amoralist, that the correct use of moral terms has a social dimension. Thus even if their correct use requires appropriate motivation, someone who completely lacks moral motivation can use moral terms correctly provided that the community generally satisfies the conditions for correct use, and her usage follows that of the community. I am doubtful that the usage of someone, such as a sociopath, who completely lacks moral motivation could actually follow that of the community. Still, the possibility Van Roojen describes may serve, within the framework of moral nominalism, to ground the usage of someone

It should be noted that moral nominalism allows for the evaluation of possibilities. Generally, I have been speaking as if we judge an existing cooperative enterprise to be fair or unfair. But practical judgment often involves the assessment of objects or outcomes that do not exist at the time the judgment is made but could, we think, be produced by actions available to us. We make judgments about the moral acceptability of a proposed modification of an existing institution, for example. In this case, there can be no question of the perception of the factual features of the item being judged. The place of perception is taken by the imagination, or by reasoned beliefs about what would follow the performance of certain actions. But the human capacity to experience motivation, understood as a kind of disposition, is capable of activation in connection with states of affairs that are imagined, or entertained in some other way, and the complex of motivation and cognized descriptive features that results may catch the extrapolative dispositions associated with a particular moral concept.

The moral nominalism that I have proposed is not an expressivist view. According to expressivist meta-ethical theories, normative terms are linguistic tools for expressing attitudes toward actions of particular kinds, or for expressing the endorsement of particular norms. For expressivists, the grammatical fact that normative judgments employ normative terms as predicates is misleading as to the actual semantic status of these judgments. They are not attempts to describe something. With the exception of judgments about proper functioning, the nominalist view that I am proposing agrees that normative judgments are not, ultimately, descriptive. A moral judgment uses a socially available set of moral terms to give form to a kind of motivation that will be experienced by all properly functioning humans. But the judgment is formulated in a declarative sentence, and it expresses the associated motivational state in the way an ordinary factual judgment expresses a belief. The judgment expresses a motivational state in that the existence of the state can normally be inferred from the judgment.

Expressivist meta-ethical views are typically contrasted with cognitivist views, according to which moral judgments are to be understood as giving voice to beliefs of a certain kind. As I suggested earlier, it may be possible to regard the moral judgments envisaged by moral nominalism as expressing beliefs. It may thus be possible to classify moral nominalism as a cognitivist

---

whose moral motivation occasionally lapses, thus allowing us to attribute to her knowledge that she has, in a particular situation, a moral reason for action. It should be noted, however, that when moral judgments admit of reasonable disagreement, there will no such thing as the community's usage. In this case, we must hope it will suffice if usage follows that of at least one reasonable member of the community.

view.[31] But even if one wishes to reserve the term "belief" for states whose entire content is descriptive, moral nominalism envisages practical judgments that can be regarded as correctly or incorrectly made. This gives it some of the character of a cognitivist view.

Expressivist meta-ethical theories encounter the so-called Frege–Geach problem. Simple inferences employing moral terms, such as "Murder is wrong; if murder is wrong, then inciting murder is wrong; so inciting murder is wrong" seem valid. But although the wrongness of murder is asserted in the first premise, it is not in the antecedent of the conditional, and for expressivist views, attitudes are expressed only where assertions are made. So expressivist views are apparently forced to regard the inference as trading on an equivocation, and consequently as invalid. The "quasi-realist" theories of Simon Blackburn and Allan Gibbard constitute, in part, attempts to address this problem. These theories seek to explain how the expression of a moral attitude can take on the logical trappings of ordinary, fact-reporting speech, in which our statements have truth values and inferences of the kind at issue go through.[32]

The moral nominalism that I have proposed does not encounter the Frege–Geach problem. With the exception of facts about the proper functioning of human mental capacities, the only normative facts are those created by our normative judgments. So judgments of political morality cannot be understood as true by virtue of their correspondence with independently existing normative facts. But as I have indicated, such judgments can still be understood as correctly or incorrectly made. They are correctly made when they are made in the way I have described, a way that manifests the proper functioning human conceptual and cooperative capacities. And to place a judgment employing a moral term in the antecedent of a conditional is to hypothesize its correctness in this sense. Thus there is no equivocation and the inference goes through.[33]

---

[31] Terry Horgan and Mark Timmons have defended a position that they call cognitivist expressivism. They argue that even on an expressivist construal, moral judgments can be regarded as beliefs because a state can count as a belief without having overall descriptive content. See their "Cognitivist Expressivism," in T. Horgan and M. Timmons, eds., *Metaethics After Moore* (Oxford: Clarendon Press, 2006), pp. 255–298.

[32] See, for example, Simon Blackburn, *Ruling Passions* (Oxford: Clarendon Press, 1998), esp. pp. 68–77, and Allan Gibbard, *Thinking How to Live* (Cambridge, MA: Harvard University Press, 2003), esp. pp. 41–59.

[33] As I said at the beginning of this section, although I prefer to speak of correctness, I do not think anything vital turns on excluding talk of truth, provided it is not understood to require the positing of an independently existing domain of moral properties and facts. See also note 28.

When normative or evaluative properties are admitted, they are usually understood as supervening on non-normative properties, where this means that they are determined by non-normative properties. Thus the beauty of a piece of music supervenes on its auditory properties. Realists about normative or evaluative properties who resist the naturalistic construal of such properties have traditionally had difficulty explaining how normative facts could stand in this relation to non-normative facts. The proper functioning of human mental capacities, viewed as a non-natural normative attribute, must similarly be understood as supervening on non-normative properties, in particular, non-normative properties of the brain and nervous system. Thus the account I have presented faces the difficulty just mentioned, although it can be argued that in the case of the proper functioning of our mental capacities, the supervenience of the normative on the non-normative is an aspect of the supervenience of the mental on the physical. Moral nominalism does not, however, admit the existence of any normative or evaluative properties beyond proper functioning. It understands fairness, for example, as supervening on non-normative properties, but this just means that when a judgment employing the term "fair" is correctly made, the associated extrapolative dispositions are caught, in part, by the perception, or the cognizing in some other way, of non-normative features of a cooperative scheme. The catching is the determining.

Similar points apply to multiple realizability, which is associated with supervenience. The supervenience of bottlehood on shape shows how multiple realizability can be accommodated within the framework of the nominalist theory I have proposed. Vessels with a variety of different shapes can all be judged to be bottles because the extrapolative dispositions of a user of the term "bottle" whose conceptual and sensory capacities are functioning properly will be caught by vessels possessing different shapes. Similarly, cooperative schemes with a variety of non-normative features can all be judged to be fair because the extrapolative dispositions of a user of the term "fair" whose conceptual and cooperative capacities are functioning properly will be caught by schemes possessing different non-normative features.

CHAPTER 3

Agreement and disagreement

In the previous chapter, I developed a theory of moral judgment, and moral worlds, that I called moral nominalism. Moral nominalism is a meta-ethical theory, and I believe that it has some appeal as an intermediate position between realist theories that countenance independently existing moral properties and facts, and anti-realist theories that view moral judgments as expressing attitudes that particular people simply happen to have. I suggested that it can be regarded as a constructivist view. As I have indicated, however, my principal argument for moral nominalism is that it enables us to "save the phenomenon" of reasonable moral disagreement in politics. It does not require disagreement. A certain amount of agreement concerning how political cooperation ought to be organized is to be expected under moral nominalism. But moral nominalism explains how disagreement among competent reasoners can be a persistent fact of political life. Showing this is the main task of the present chapter.

Disagreement concerning questions of fact plays a significant role in political contexts. I explained in chapter 1 how such disagreements can be reasonable. But factual judgments purporting to identify effective ways of achieving given ends presuppose evaluative and normative judgments that set the ends. In accordance with the program outlined in chapter 1, our principal focus will be judgments of the latter sort, in particular, judgments of political morality.[1]

I have characterized reasonable disagreement as disagreement that survives, or would survive, shared deliberation conducted in good faith over an extended period of time. After briefly considering why political communities will seek agreement, I explore the circumstances under which shared

---

[1] Disagreements that concern neither empirical questions nor questions of political morality may sometimes be politically relevant, and such cases may have been more common in the past. Especially important here are religious disagreements. I believe, however, that when disagreements of this sort are politically relevant, they can be modeled on disagreements concerning questions of political morality. I say more about religion in chapter 5.

deliberation can produce moral agreement and the reasons why it is often unable to secure that result. Disagreements about the fairness of political cooperation will be the focus. I make a distinction between narrow and broad fairness. I also address a possible objection to the idea that moral nominalism can provide for genuine disagreement concerning questions of political morality, and I introduce the notion of the zone of reasonable disagreement.

With the possible exception of a revolutionary situation, people deciding how to organize political cooperation will not be selecting a total cooperative scheme. Rather they will be considering how a particular aspect of political cooperation, for example, the provision of unemployment benefits, ought to be organized. This may mean adding some new components to the overall scheme of political cooperation, or it may mean revising some components already in place. Either way, however, agreement will be necessary. Why is this?

Let us assume that the members of a polity share a vocabulary of normative and evaluative terms. On the view I have proposed, mastery of the use of such terms is a matter of proceeding appropriately from examples of their correct use. In introducing this idea in the previous chapter, I noted that properly functioning humans will take the fact that others disagree as a reason to reconsider the judgments they have made. Reconsideration can result in agreement, and since reconsideration is dictated by proper functioning, we can speak here of a form of rational pressure that is capable of producing agreement.

This cannot be the whole story in the political case, however. The reason to reconsider in the face of disagreement is also operative in connection with non-moral judgments such as the judgment that a piece of music is beautiful. The process of mutual reconsideration, in a case of that sort, may involve the exchange of reasons germane to the beauty of the piece, such as the presence or absence of dissonance, and agreement may result. But if it does not, the parties can just "agree to disagree," that is, they can reconcile themselves to continuing disagreement. Continuing disagreement will constitute a kind of irritant, since it gives each party a reason to suppose he may be making a mistake and also threatens his standing with outsiders as a competent judge of musical matters. But the parties will have no reason beyond eliminating this irritant to try to resolve their disagreement.

The political case is different. Political cooperation requires the coordination of interaction among the members of a polity. Agreement is thus

necessary if the benefits of political cooperation are to be achieved. This means that disagreement is not merely an annoyance. It is an obstacle that must be overcome. To be sure, one possible mode of political organization involves licensing people to act on their own convictions about certain normative and evaluative questions. But the appropriateness of this mode of organization may itself be something about which the members of a polity can disagree. Some may feel that particular answers to certain normative or evaluative questions should be woven into the fabric of political cooperation. Disagreement at this higher level must be resolved if political cooperation is to proceed.

This point is independent of the issue of moral realism. Correct representations of an independently existing state of affairs will agree. The rational pressure that observers are under to make correct representational judgments may thus bring about agreement. But here again, rational pressure that can result in agreement must be distinguished from rational pressure specifically to agree – to eliminate any disagreement that may remain after reconsideration, or after more careful adjustment by each party of his representational apparatus.

On any view that provides for the correctness or incorrectness of moral judgments, including the moral nominalism that I have proposed, disagreement can be expected to be accompanied by argument. We respond to what we regard as mistakes by trying to correct them. The presentation of arguments for one's view, and the criticism of arguments for opposing views, plays a central role in the mutual reconsideration that, in competent reasoners, is prompted by disagreement. But the fact that the members of a group are being subjected to the pressure of argument must be distinguished from their collectively facing a rational requirement to agree.

DELIBERATION AND DISAGREEMENT

Disagreement exists where people answer a given question differently. In the political case, the question concerns how political cooperation ought to be organized. I have distinguished rational pressures that can result in agreement, in particular the pressure to reconsider when confronted with disagreement, from the rational pressure to specifically to agree – to reach agreement – that will be experienced by properly functioning cooperators. But the two kinds of pressure are not completely unrelated. As was noted in the previous section, the reconsideration that, in properly functioning humans, is prompted by disagreement will typically involve examining arguments. People may have a variety of reasons for arguing with those

who disagree with them, but in all cases, the result is the bringing to bear of argumentative pressure. This pressure can play a role in the achievement of the agreement that is required for cooperation. That is, one way that the members of a group of cooperatively disposed humans can respond to the requirement they confront, as cooperatively disposed, to agree on a cooperative scheme is by presenting each other with arguments that cooperation ought to be organized in a particular way. When this happens, in a context where all are prepared to respond in good faith to opposing arguments, we can speak of a process of *shared deliberation*. In the case of political cooperation, shared deliberation will typically focus on the organization of some part of the overall endeavor. How, within the framework of moral nominalism, is such shared deliberation to be understood? And to what extent can it be expected to produce agreement?

In the usual case, the members of the polity, or the subset with an interest in the aspect of political cooperation at issue, will already have made provisional judgments concerning how cooperation ought to be organized, and these judgments will disagree. The judgments will normally be expressed with terms taken from a shared vocabulary, but they will articulate conflicting – mutually incompatible – conclusions. The judgments will be all-things-considered judgments that attempt to capture the combined force of all the considerations that those making the judgments regard as relevant to the organization of political cooperation in the case at hand.

Claims that different members of the polity can make against other members, or against the polity as a whole, constitute an important class of such considerations. Claims are reasons purporting to establish that political cooperation must be organized in a certain way if it is to be fair to one or more individuals. Such claims are made by members of a polity on their own behalf, or on behalf of other members, and they compete with claims that can be made by or on behalf of different members. There is thus a sense in which to make a claim is to put oneself in an adversarial position with respect to the other members of the polity. A cooperative scheme that appropriately reconciles all the claims that can be made by or on behalf of the members of a polity can be said to be fair in the narrow sense. I explain the distinction between narrow and broad fairness in the fourth section.

A judgment of narrow fairness is ultimately an all-things-considered judgment encompassing the full set of claims that can be made in a given case. It is a judgment that the reconciliation of these claims requires a particular pattern of concessions. But it will be useful to focus initially on a single claim presented as a reason to suppose that narrow fairness requires organizing political cooperation in a certain way. Let us take a claim of need.

The claim, which we can understand as being made in the United States, is that fairness requires the polity to provide care in an assisted living facility for those elderly members who need it. To put it another way, the claim is that if it were to fail to provide such care for those who need it, the polity would be countenancing unfairness.

According to an online encyclopedia, "Assisted living as it exists today emerged in the 1990s as an alternative on the continuum of care for people who cannot live independently in a private residence, but who do not need the 24 hour medical care provided by a nursing home."[2] An assisted living facility typically provides a more congenial residential environment than a nursing home, but at the present time, the federal Medicare program does not cover the cost of residence in an assisted living facility, so this option is available only to those who are able to tap private financial resources. After private resources have been exhausted, the federal Medicaid program for low-income individuals will usually pay for care in a nursing home. I shall speak here of the claim that fairness requires the public provision of assisted living. The claim is presumptive, a claim that, other things being equal, fairness requires this.

We can refine the issue by making two further assumptions. First, there is no disagreement about whether the individuals in question have a genuine need. We are speaking of people who are no longer capable of accomplishing on their own all the tasks of day-to-day living. The question that gives rise to disagreement rather concerns fairness. Given the need, does fairness require the polity to meet it by providing assisted living?[3] Second, the claim is that fairness requires the public provision of assisted living regardless of the ability of the recipients to pay for this service out of their own resources. Later, this assumption will be lifted.

There will, we are supposing, initially be disagreement about whether the public provision of assisted living is required by fairness. How should shared deliberation undertaken to resolve this disagreement be understood? One possibility involves employing philosophical theories of justice, but most members of a polity will not be prepared to deliberate in these terms. I say more in the final section about the role of philosophy in the deliberation undertaken to resolve political disagreements. Most people confronted with a question like the one we are considering will reason by analogy. Those

---

[2] http://en.wikipedia.org/wiki/Assisted_living

[3] The concept of a need can be understood biologically, as something that is required for survival in a given environment. When it is understood more broadly, as something that is required for a normal life in a given social setting, the question whether a particular item or service constitutes a genuine need cannot be clearly separated from the question whether fairness requires providing it.

favoring the public provision of assisted living will present cases where, they hope, all will agree that fairness requires meeting a need by public provision. They might, for example, expect all to agree that fairness requires the public provision of hospital services to the elderly, to agree that it would be unfair to deny such services to elderly citizens. They will then attempt to establish that the case of assisted living is relevantly similar. Those opposed will present cases where, they hope, all will agree that fairness does not require meeting a need by public provision, and then attempt to establish that the case of assisted living is relevantly similar to those cases. They might offer for this purpose the need for household maintenance or companionship, which they take to form a large part of what the residents of assisted living facilities receive.

For moral nominalism, relevant similarity is not a property that two cases possess independently of the judgments that properly functioning humans would make. Relevant similarity is implied by the fact that a properly functioning human, proceeding from a given set of examples of the correct use of certain terms, would find her extrapolative dispositions caught in the same way by the situations associated with both cases. For present purposes, it will be useful to work with a slight modification of this picture. The relevant similarity of two cases is constituted by the fact that someone proceeding from a set of examples of the correct use of a given term would find her extrapolative dispositions caught first by one of the cases and then, after that case was added to her examples of correct use, by the other.

Shared deliberation about whether fairness requires the public provision of assisted living will involve the collective assembling of a set of cases held to be analogous in different ways to this case, where the claimed analogies may either support the policy or fail to. The process could produce agreement in the following manner. Competent reasoning is a matter of proceeding appropriately, that is, in a way that manifests proper functioning, from examples of the correct use of a given term. Each judgment taken to be correctly made is added to the examples of correct use from which a given individual proceeds. In the instance we are considering, there will be some people who, extrapolating from what they take to be examples of the correct use of the relevant terms, will conclude that (presumptively, pending the establishment of conflicting claims) fairness requires the public provision of assisted living. When a person of this sort finds that others disagree, she will offer to them the cases from which she is extrapolating, for example, the public provision of hospital services, hoping that they will agree that fairness requires public provision in those cases. The expectation is that if they do,

they will experience increased pressure, as competent reasoners, to conclude that the public provision of assisted living is, after all, required by fairness. Those whose examples of the correct use of the relevant terms lead them to the conclusion that fairness does not require the public provision of assisted living will similarly offer to the group the cases from which they are extrapolating, such as the need for household maintenance or companionship. In their view, while these are genuine human needs, the meeting of them is not a public responsibility. The cases presented may be actual cases of which the participants are aware or hypothetical cases that engage the relevant extrapolative dispositions.

It is possible that after all the parties have presented to the group the cases they take to be relevant to the question whether fairness requires public provision of assisted living, all will find that the same conclusion is warranted. That is, all will find their extrapolative dispositions, as these have been modified by the new material now available, engaged in the same way by the public provision of assisted living, either for or against. The probability of this can be increased by the collective examination of the extrapolative moves that each individual is making. Thus it may be possible to change the mind of someone who does not find the provision of assisted living relevantly similar to the provision of hospital services by calling on him to explain exactly how they differ.

Suppose, for example, that some party to the debate concedes that fairness requires the public provision of hospital services to the elderly but does not agree that it requires the public provision of assisted living. When challenged to explain how the two cases differ, he may present a particular sort of hospital service, for example, emergency care for heart attack victims, that he regards as disanalogous. To this, those in favor of the public provision of assisted living might respond by offering a different sort of hospital service that they think everyone will have to concede is analogous to the provision of assisted living, care in a mental hospital, perhaps. Since the skeptic has accepted that fairness requires the public provision of all hospital services to the elderly, if he concedes the analogy in the case described, he will face increased rational pressure to accept the public provision of assisted living.

Of course, the increased rational pressure may not be decisive. The skeptic may still find the public provision of assisted living relevantly similar in other respects to cases where, in his view, public provision is not required or appropriate. And he may challenge those who do not see these similarities to explain their view that assisted living is different. But the collective examination of the extrapolative moves being made or resisted by the

participants in a process of shared deliberation that employs reasoning by analogy will typically have the effect of refining everyone's thinking and modifying the initial disagreement. This in turn may be sufficient to produce a convergence of judgment among the people participating in, or witnessing, the deliberative process.

It should be borne in mind that according to moral nominalism, the extrapolative dispositions associated with judgments of political morality are caught, in part, by a certain motivational disposition, the disposition to make concessions to, or seek concessions from, the other participants in a cooperative venture when they are similarly disposed. This disposition will be experienced, in some form or other, by all properly functioning humans. How it is experienced in the case of judgments concerning the fairness or unfairness of the public provision of assisted living will be influenced by the shape it has been given by the previous judgments that a particular individual has made about the fairness of different aspects of political cooperation. Shared deliberation taking the form of collective reasoning by analogy thus reshapes – gives a new conceptualized shape to – the particular sense of fairness that each of the participants initially brings to the deliberative process. The ultimate result of this reshaping may be agreement on the fairness of a particular way of organizing some aspect of political cooperation, for example, the fairness of the public provision of assisted living.

In theory, then, shared deliberation of the sort described is capable of producing agreement about the presumptive fairness of a particular way of organizing a cooperative venture. It will accomplish this by creating a partial overlap in the personal histories of judgment of the parties. As engaged by the case at hand, they follow the same path. Nevertheless, this result is unlikely when what is at issue is the organization of political cooperation. In the first place, it will not be possible bring critical attention to bear on the thinking of each member of a polity. But even where critical attention can be brought to bear, there are reasons why shared deliberation taking the form of collective reasoning by analogy may not produce agreement. The sense of fairness of a given member will be determined by her entire history of judgment. Where the members have had extensive prior experience employing the concepts associated with a particular claim – extensive experience employing the concept of need to support judgments of the fairness or unfairness of different aspects of political cooperation, for example – it will not usually be feasible for each individual to present all the examples of correct employment that influence her thinking. She may not even recall all the prior judgments that influence her thinking. She may simply find herself, after participating in good faith in a process of shared

deliberation, failing to see the analogies others see, or intuiting the unfairness of policies that others regard as paradigmatically fair. Intuitive judgments of these sorts could reflect, in a way that manifests the proper functioning of the capacities engaged, a given individual's history of judgment with the relevant terms, despite her not being able to bring the details of that history to mind.

The difficulties just described are partly practical. There will not be enough time to do what is required to produce agreement among all the members of a polity, or all those with an interest in a particular issue. But the difficulties are not solely practical. Even if the members of a polity were able to present to each other all the cases that influenced their thinking, and to subject everybody's judgments to critical attention, human cognitive limitations would probably prevent the full assimilation of the assembled information. Since competent moral reasoning is reasoning that displays the proper functioning of *human* cognitive and motivational capacities, these limitations do not impugn the competence of the people involved. We thus get the result that in political contexts, a process of shared deliberation that displays human competence to the highest degree may still fail to produce agreement.

The inability of competent reasoning to produce political agreement has other aspects as well. The collective effort to create a common pool of relevantly similar cases will involve the presentation of cases in speech. This will produce states of mind whose content is provided by the concepts associated with the terms employed, for example, the term "hospital services." But for two reasons, it is inevitable that the process will leave out some of what influences the members of a polity. First, the ability to capture experience in speech requires what might be called literary skill, and the members of a polity will differ in the degree to which they possess this skill. They will thus differ in their ability to share with the group the import of their personal experiences. Those who have had extensive experience in hospitals, either as providers or patients, may be unable, because of a lack of literary skill, to make others see what they take to be relevant similarities, or dissimilarities, between the public provision of hospital services and the public provision of assisted living.[4] Second, each individual's experience will typically have some non-conceptual content which can bear on the question of relevant similarity. But non-conceptual content cannot be fully captured in speech, regardless of literary skill. These two features of the human

---

[4] In *Contingency, Irony, and Solidarity* (Cambridge: Cambridge University Press, 1989), Richard Rorty emphasizes the role of literary skill in changing moral minds.

situation provide further reason to doubt that collective reasoning by analogy will produce a convergence of judgment among the members of a polity.

These points can be put in terms of the Habermasian idea that shared deliberation involves mutual perspective taking.[5] Each person's perspective on the relevant reasons is made available to the rest. One's perspective on the relevant reasons is, however, determined by one's personal history of judgment, and this will consist partly of the judgments one has made in situations one has actually experienced. So because of the limitations we face in translating experience into speech, it cannot be expected that the presentation of cases in speech will result in the full comprehension of the different perspectives of the members of the group. Mutual perspective taking through shared deliberation will inevitably be incomplete.

The upshot is that shared deliberation taking the form of collective reasoning by analogy will usually not be able to produce agreement among all the members of a polity. If the relevant capacities, cognitive and motivational, of all the members are functioning properly, there is, however, reason to expect collective reasoning by analogy to eliminate, or at least reduce, incompetent reasoning. There is reason to expect it to winnow out the unreasonable views. The disagreement that remains will thus have the character of reasonable disagreement of the kind described in chapter 1. It will be disagreement among competently reasoned judgments about what would be reasonable-as-fair. As I have said, my main argument for moral nominalism, as a meta-ethical theory, is that it saves the phenomenon of reasonable disagreement. It should now be clear why this is so. The extrapolative dispositions, that, according to moral nominalism, underlie the correct use of normative and evaluative terms will differ to a certain extent from person to person, even if the cognitive and motivational capacities of the people involved are functioning properly and they are employing a common set of terms. The dispositions may converge in a particular case, but there is no rational requirement that they do so. It is thus possible for judgments of fairness that are competently reasoned nevertheless to disagree.

Three further points should be made about this argument. First, the disagreement that remains after shared deliberation is reasonable only if everyone is reasoning competently. This has implications for the identification of actual political disagreements as reasonable. The positions that are

[5] As I mentioned in note 16 to chapter 1, I discuss Habermasian perspective taking in "Why There is No Issue between Habermas and Rawls," *The Journal of Philosophy* 99 (2002), pp. 111–129.

actually taken may not be the product of competent reasoning in the context of a good faith effort to respond to the arguments of others. This was mentioned in the first section of the previous chapter. Further, as was noted in chapter 1, a claim that an actual political dispute constitutes an instance of reasonable disagreement typically has a counterfactual aspect. The claim is that if the parties were reasoning competently with the available conceptual materials, they would still disagree. But the disagreement that would remain will usually differ somewhat from that actually found. The positions that the members of the polity would take if they were reasoning competently will differ from those actually voiced in political exchanges. What we usually find, then, is an actual dispute that contains a core of reasonable disagreement, the outlines of which may not be immediately evident.

Second, it should be noted that the existence of reasonable disagreement is not the only feature of contested cases that is relevant for political purposes. Also important is the distribution of judgments within the polity. The example we have been considering involves a yes–no question: whether (other things being equal) fairness requires the public provision of assisted living. But where there is reasonable disagreement, opinion could be evenly split or there could be a large majority on one side. Most people might think that fairness requires the public provision of assisted living, or that it does not. Facts of this sort will be important when we consider the resolution of reasonable disagreement in the next chapter.

Third, the obstacle to agreement created by the fact that the parties have different personal histories of judgment has an important, and quite intuitive, implication for the possibility of securing agreement by shared deliberation. The more similar the personal experience, and thus the histories of judgment, of the members of the group, the more likely shared deliberation will be to produce agreement. Conversely, the more their personal experience differs, the more likely they are to remain in disagreement even after a process of shared deliberation. Because of their different experiences, they are likely, even when reasoning competently, to respond in different ways to the cases in the common set constructed by shared deliberation. It is partly because large modern polities contain people who have diverse personal experiences that reasonable disagreement has a prominent place in the life of such polities.

The example we have been considering might be thought too simple. In reality, those dissenting – those judging that fairness does not require the public provision of assisted living – would be likely to be especially resistant to public provision to people who can afford to pay for the care they receive. But

deliberation would still proceed in the same way, and disagreement might still result. Some might feel that all needs for care in the elderly population create a claim on the polity as a whole, and that the fairness of political cooperation thus requires the public provision of whatever is required to meet these needs. Indeed, some might feel that in a fair society, no elderly person will be personally responsible for meeting any genuine need.

These observations bring us to a further issue. I have suggested that shared deliberation about the requirements of narrow fairness will involve reasoning by analogy from cases held to be relevantly similar or dissimilar. It could be objected that some will also, or instead, come to these questions armed with general principles. One group might hold a principle like the one just mentioned, asserting that in a fair society, one displaying an appropriate pattern of concessions, no elderly person will be personally responsible for meeting any need for care, or, perhaps, any genuine need at all. Another group might hold the principle that in a fair society, no one will be expected to help pay for items needed by people who are financially able to provide those items themselves. But when a principle of this sort is advanced in shared deliberation, other people will have to decide whether it has any validity in the case at hand, and this will require considering what it implies about cases regarded as relevantly similar to that case. So even when general principles are invoked, reasoning by analogy from cases held to be relevantly similar or dissimilar to the case being considered will play a large role.

It might be suggested that reasoning by analogy actually involves the employment of relatively fine-grained principles, but this is not my view of the matter. A general principle of political morality is a conditional stating that if circumstances of a particular kind obtain, political cooperation morally ought to possess certain features, other things being equal. An example would be, "If the elderly members of a polity have a need for care, it morally ought, other things being equal, to be met at public expense." On the view of moral judgment that I have proposed, however, proceeding from examples of the correct employment of moral terms is not a process of inference employing conditionals. It is rather a matter of the "catching" of extrapolative dispositions by situations possessing both cognitive and motivational aspects.

Reasonable disagreement of the kind we have been considering can be understood as disagreement concerning how to interpret the concepts expressed by a shared vocabulary of normative and evaluative terms. On this construal, all the properly functioning members of the polity will find it appropriate to employ these terms. When they reasonably disagree, they show that they interpret the associated concepts differently. If disagreement

is understood in this way, shared deliberation can be regarded as an attempt to arrive at a common interpretation in a particular case.

It should be mentioned that political disagreement can also be grounded in the fact that some members of a polity do not employ all the normative or evaluative terms employed by others. Thus Oscar Wilde is said to have remarked that "blasphemous" was not one of his words. In cases of this sort, the parties to a political disagreement are employing somewhat different sets of concepts. To the extent that the rejection of a concept is compatible with proper functioning, such disagreements can be reasonable. The rejection of a concept will not always be compatible with proper functioning, however. I have suggested that all properly functioning humans will be disposed to make or seek concessions in the context of a cooperative endeavor, and I have labeled this disposition the sense of fairness. So no one can legitimately say that "fairness" or "justice" is not one of his words.

The points made above apply as well to disagreement concerning all-things-considered judgments of political morality. Someone who judges that fairness presumptively requires the public provision of assisted living may nevertheless conclude that it should not be provided because funds are limited and the money would be better spent in some other way, for example, meeting the need of working families for day care for their children. This would be, in effect, a judgment that allowing the former need to go unmet would be less unfair than allowing the latter need to go unmet. Others may reach the opposite conclusion. Of course, some may reject the assertion that funds are limited and judge that both needs should be met. But this will itself be a judgment concerning what fairness requires all things considered, since it presupposes that the requisite level of taxation would not be unfair.

Shared deliberation concerning all-things-considered judgments of political morality can be understood in the way described earlier. What is at issue is the relative weight of different reasons. This was discussed in the previous chapter. All properly functioning humans will experience a disposition to make or seek concessions in cooperative contexts. When the question is one of narrow fairness, the relative weight that a particular individual gives to two competing claims, for example, the claim that fairness requires the public provision of assisted living and the claim that fairness requires the public provision of day care, will be determined by the strength of this disposition as it is experienced in connection with those claims. That is, it will be determined by the strength that the individual finds this motivational disposition to possess when it is structured by the concepts articulating these two different claims of need. Shared deliberation takes the form of

the presentation of arguments intended to produce a change of mind about the relative strength of the two claims. For example, cases requiring the balancing of analogous claims might be offered in the expectation that this would make it possible to see the appropriateness or inappropriateness of a particular way of striking the balance in the case at hand. Here again, obstacles of the sort presented earlier can be expected to result in reasonable disagreement in a large political society. Indeed, there is likely to be more disagreement about the relative weights to be assigned to different claims, or other reasons for organizing political cooperation in a particular way, than about the judgments establishing that those reasons obtain – judgments establishing that other things being equal, fairness requires the honoring of a particular claim, for example.

The observations in this section comport with Rawls's account of reasonable disagreement, as described in chapter 1. Rawls attributes reasonable disagreement to what he calls the burdens of judgment. It will be useful to quote Rawls more fully on the most important of these burdens. He says:

> To some extent (how great we cannot tell) the way we assess evidence and weigh moral and political values is shaped by our total experience, our whole course of life up to now, and our total experiences must always differ. Thus in a modern society with its numerous offices and positions, its various divisions of labor, its many social groups and their ethnic variety, citizens' total experiences are disparate enough for their judgments to diverge, at least to some degree, on many if not most cases of any significant complexity.[6]

The moral nominalism that I have proposed enables us to explain how differences in total experience can influence the interpretation of socially acknowledged values, and the weights assigned to them in particular contexts. Differences in total experience mean differences in judgmental history. Further, the explanation provided by moral nominalism makes it clear that the resulting disagreements can be reasonable, in the sense of being compatible with the proper functioning of the relevant capacities. Political disagreement need not be attributed to factors that bias or otherwise corrupt judgment.

CONCEPTUAL IDENTITY

I have said that I understand possession of a concept to consist in the mastery of the use of a term. Disagreement arises because the parties proceed from different examples of the correct use of a term, or proceed

---

[6] John Rawls, *Political Liberalism* (New York: Columbia University Press, 1993), p. 57.

differently from the same examples. Such disagreements can be reasonable if the parties, although coming to different conclusions, are manifesting the proper functioning of the relevant mental capacities. But if the mastery of the use of a term can take different forms in different people, don't we have to say that they are using the term to express different concepts? This possibility might call into question the idea that we are dealing with genuine disagreement. If the parties to a dispute are using a particular term to express different concepts, their judgments do not actually disagree.

One way of addressing this problem is to follow a suggestion that S. L. Hurley makes concerning how to provide for reasonable disagreement within a Wittgensteinian framework. She proposes that some concepts are responsible to structured sets of potentially conflicting criteria and that when this is so, agreement about certain exemplary cases, as well as agreement in practices of theorizing about relations among conflicting criteria, enables us to regard the members of a group as employing the same concept even though their judgments often disagree.[7] The concepts of fairness and justice can be fitted to this model. A number of different considerations, for example, different claims that might be made, are relevant to whether a given arrangement is fair or just. Hurley's proposal may not completely solve our problem, however. We are concerned not only with concepts such as justice or fairness but also with concepts, like need and desert, that are used to articulate particular claims. I have said that disagreement in judgments that articulate particular claims may be attributable to the fact that the parties interpret the associated reasons differently, which again suggests that they are employing different concepts.

It might be proposed that we should simply accept the conclusion. Difference in judgment means difference in concepts, so we cannot understand reasonable disagreement as disagreement among people employing the same concepts. This is acceptable because the key point about reasonable disagreement is that it is not resolvable by shared deliberation, no matter how openly it is conducted or for how long. If the parties are employing different concepts, the fact that deliberation does not produce agreement is readily

---

[7] S. L. Hurley, *Natural Reasons: Personality and Polity* (Oxford: Oxford University Press, 1989), p. 51. She also says that "Wittgenstein's views about what it is to follow a rule apply ... both to the understanding of reasons and to the understanding of the relationships among reasons" (p. 49). Similar points might be made about "ought," understood as reporting the existence of good or sufficient reason to do something. The members of a polity can reasonably disagree about how political cooperation ought to be organized without using the word to express different concepts. For related discussion, see Ralph Wedgwood, "Conceptual Role Semantics for Moral Terms," *The Philosophical Review* 110 (2001), p. 29. Wedgwood discusses "ought" explicitly in "The Meaning of 'Ought'," in Russ Shafer-Landau, ed., *Oxford Studies in Metaethics* (New York: Oxford University Press, 2006).

explained. But this proposal still leaves us with a problem. If the parties are using a given term to express different concepts, what is the point of deliberation? Why would they try to convince one another by argument?

Although the members of a group are using a given term to express different concepts, they may not recognize that they are doing this. On the view I have proposed, possessing a concept is a matter of having mastery of the use of a term, which in turn is a matter of proceeding, in a way that manifests proper functioning, from (what are taken to be) examples of the correct use of the term. In light of this, two people can be said to be employing the same concept, tokening the same type, if and only if their histories of judgment with a given term are the same. But when, by this criterion, two concepts differ, they may nevertheless be similar to a high degree. There may be considerable overlap between the histories of judgment of the people employing the term. Further, in considering whether two people possess the same or different concepts, we cannot simply consult their actual histories of judgment with a given term. We must consider, counterfactually, what judgments they would make about different situations they might encounter. When we expand in this way the range of opportunities for judgment, we may find that the judgments the two people would make diverge in only a small subset of cases.[8]

If this is the correct account of the matter – that the concepts expressed by different people using the same moral term will rarely be exactly the same, but may be similar to a high degree – it is easy to understand why the parties to a political dispute would attempt to resolve it by shared deliberation. They may take themselves to be employing the same concept. Further, shared deliberation may not disabuse them of this conviction. The construction of a set of cases taken to be analogous or disanalogous to the case that is the focus of dispute might be sufficient to produce agreement about that particular case, even if there are some situations where the parties would employ the term in question differently. In addition, the presentation of cases taken to be analogous or disanalogous to the

---

[8] Adopting this suggestion requires a way of interpreting sameness of judgment that does not depend on the idea that what makes the judgments the same is that they employ the same concepts. Perhaps it will suffice to understand judgments as the same when the same sentence is used in the same way (in assertion or denial). In *Concepts: Where Cognitive Science Went Wrong* (Oxford: Clarendon Press, 1998), p. 29, Jerry Fodor ties the possibility that different people can share the same concept to the success of intentional explanations in psychology. But it is a feature of reasonable disagreement that we do not really understand those with whom we disagree. We understand what they are saying, but we do not understand how, as competent reasoners, they can say it. (We construe in accordance with our own linguistic practice the words being used, but so construed the words seem, in that particular instance, to be misused.)

case at issue may alter to a certain extent how the parties understand the correct employment of the relevant term. If shared deliberation has this effect, it could again produce agreement about the case at issue even if the concepts employed are merely similar to a high degree. Of course, where disagreement is reasonable, the expectation that agreement can be achieved through argument will be disappointed. But if the concepts being employed are similar to a high degree, the expectation is readily intelligible.

The resolution of reasonable disagreement by engineering conceptual change will be discussed in more detail in the next chapter. Here, it is enough to note that these issues concerning the identity of concepts also arise in connection with the general phenomenon of conceptual change. Should conceptual change be understood as the replacement of one concept, or set of concepts, by another? Or should we rather speak of one and the same concept undergoing a change in its content? If concepts are individuated by their possession conditions, possession is understood as mastery of the use of a term, and mastery is constituted by a history of judgment in which earlier correct uses of a term ground later correct uses, we will have some basis for speaking of identity through change. The employment of a term in new circumstances adds to the examples of correct use from which further judgments proceed. And when a new circumstance has novel features, assimilating it to one's history of judgment may involve, so to speak, a bending of the concept. Subsequent cases will be handled differently than they would have been had the novel case not been encountered. Since properly functioning humans will reconsider judgments with which others disagree, a change of this sort in the content of a concept can spread to an entire community. After enough such bending, however, it would probably be more natural to say that the terms employed have come to express different concepts.

BROAD FAIRNESS

I have proposed that the experiences that catch the extrapolative dispositions associated with the concept of fairness are, in part, experiences of a certain kind of motivation, the disposition to make concessions from one's most preferred cooperative scheme when actual or potential cooperators are similarly disposed. This motivational disposition, together with the reciprocal disposition to seek concessions when others are similarly disposed, will be possessed by all properly functioning humans, although the form it takes in a particular case will be determined by the socially provided normative and evaluative concepts that are employed to give structure to it, and by a given individual's history of judgment with those concepts. As has been

noted, the concepts will include some that the members of a polity can use to articulate claims against other members or against the polity as a whole. Such claims constitute reasons for thinking that a particular way of organizing political cooperation is, presumptively, required by fairness.

I said earlier that I would call fairness of this sort, fairness that consists in the appropriate reconciliation of claims that can be made by or on behalf of the individual members of a polity, narrow fairness. The claims are typically claims of desert or need. That is, they identify particular kinds of accomplishment or experience, or particular kinds of need, as creating claims against other members or the polity as a whole. Narrow fairness is thus concerned with the distribution of benefits and burdens to individuals. Whether a polity is fair in this sense admits of reasonable disagreement because people may disagree about the interpretation of the claims that can be made with the available normative and evaluative terms, or about the relative weight to be accorded to different claims when they conflict.

If the fairness of a polity is understood as a matter of appropriate concession, however, it is not exhausted by narrow fairness. In considering how political cooperation is to be organized, the members of a modern polity typically take into account considerations that only indirectly concern the distribution of benefits and burdens to individuals. I call these considerations *morally important social values*. A partial list includes: the defense of national territory; the maintenance of the rule of law or, more generally, social peace; the promotion of social prosperity; the fostering of community; the preservation of the health of the population; the advancement of knowledge (understood broadly as encompassing the creation of an educated and informed populace); and the development of culture.

The members of a modern polity will think it important that political cooperation be organized so as to promote these values and others of their kind, as well as narrow fairness. Indeed, narrow fairness can itself be viewed as a morally important social value, albeit one that differs from those just mentioned by virtue of its connection with claims of the sort described above. Like the claims with which narrow fairness is concerned, the concepts articulating morally important social values are amenable to different interpretations, and the values can be accorded different weights when they conflict. Thus their introduction brings with it a new dimension of reasonable political disagreement. This disagreement will sometimes have factual as well as evaluative aspects, since questions about the means to be employed to promote a given value, interpreted in a given way, will also have to be addressed. A view of what is required by the full set of morally important social values, appropriately reconciled, can be understood as a conception of the public good.

If judgments invoking morally important social values other than narrow fairness are to be understood on the model I have proposed, the relevant linguistic dispositions must be caught, in part, by motivation that will be experienced by all properly functioning humans. The morally important social values identify social states of affairs that contribute to, or partly constitute, the flourishing of human beings in social contexts. I shall not speculate about the precise motivational dispositions involved in the acknowledgment of such values, but I think it is plausible that properly functioning humans will experience forms of motivation that can be shaped in the specified ways. And this motivation can be understood as implicitly cooperative, since it is primarily through collective action that the morally important social values are realized.

Narrow fairness, viewed as a morally important social value, will form a component of the public good. But the concept of fairness can be understood as playing another role in connection with the public good. We can speak of fairness wherever concessions are held to be justified, and a particular pattern of concessions by the members of the polity will be required to realize a given conception of the public good, a given conception of what all the morally important social values, taken together, require. I call fairness in this larger sense *broad fairness.*

This is not the place for a discussion of the public good in all its aspects. The principal point to be made about the public good, and about broad fairness, is that questions concerning how these notions are to be understood, and what they require, present issues of interpretation and weighing that admit of reasonable disagreement. Especially important is the fact that the requirements of narrow and broad fairness can conflict. Narrow fairness, understood as a morally important social value, might be regarded as outweighed, in certain respects, by other morally important social values. That is, the public good might be held to require some sacrifice of narrow fairness, some disregarding of the requirements of narrow fairness, as they emerge from judgments employing the relevant concepts to establish claims. It will be useful to consider a few examples that illustrate this point. It should be emphasized that these examples are not meant to establish any specific conclusions about how the public good ought to be understood. Their purpose is simply to illustrate the distinction between broad and narrow fairness.

A simple example is provided by the value of national defense. If a polity is fighting a just war, this value enjoins the structuring of political cooperation so as to ensure that the war effort is effective. The promotion of national defense, in time of war, will require that some people fight, and perhaps die, in battle. But it will also require that people who have skills that

are important for the war effort, but that involve, say, doing scientific research, or producing vital materiel, be exempted from military service, or at least the kind of service that involves combat. The structuring of political cooperation that results will bring with it a particular pattern of concessions on the part of the members of the polity, and if the associated moral reasoning is sound, this pattern of concessions can be regarded as fair in the broad sense. But some people will be living better than others, and not because of claims of desert or need that they can make, or that can be made for them. Thus a well-organized war effort, though fair in the broad sense, will typically involve some sacrifice of narrow fairness.

Affirmative action provides a further example. In modern Western societies, non-discrimination is generally acknowledged as an important social value. It can be understood as a component of narrow fairness. Each member of a polity has a claim not be discriminated against, which can plausibly be regarded as a claim of desert. On one common interpretation, the avoidance of discrimination in employment requires that employment be based solely on ability to do the job in question. But in some cases, there may be a number of equally qualified candidates for a given job, and it may be thought appropriate to give some weight in the employment decision to membership in a group that has, historically, suffered from discrimination. There are two ways of understanding this appropriateness. The policy might be understood as required by narrow fairness. That is, it might be thought that an individual's membership in a group that has historically suffered discrimination establishes that he or she deserves preferential consideration in employment, and thus that preferential consideration is required independently of any contribution it might make to the promotion of various morally important social values. Alternatively, it might be thought that narrow fairness requires that all qualified candidates, regardless of group membership, have an equal chance of getting a particular job. But this requirement is regarded as outweighed by other components of the public good that will be advanced by the preferential hiring or promotion of members of groups that have in the past suffered discrimination. Thus the policy might be thought to advance the value of community. The overall pattern of concessions within the polity could be the same in both cases. But since, in the second case, the concessions are not justified by claims that can be made by or on behalf of the particular individuals who happen to be hired or promoted, the fairness of affirmative action will be broad fairness.

For a final set of issues that illustrate the distinction between narrow and broad fairness, we can turn to the promotion of social prosperity. By this I mean the general enjoyment of things that satisfy non-moral wants. The

value of social prosperity, like all moral values on the view I am proposing, requires interpretation, and these issues of interpretation admit of reasonable disagreement. Social prosperity might be understood narrowly as the general enjoyment of (individually or collectively) purchasable goods and services, in which case the promotion of prosperity is a matter of increasing productivity and income. Alternatively, it might be suggested that the want satisfaction associated with the promotion of prosperity should be understood as happiness, with the result that there is more to prosperity than the enjoyment of purchasable goods and services. For purposes of discussion, however, let us take the first view, which seems to play a role in much modern thinking about the public good. To adopt this interpretation is to suppose that the general enjoyment of purchasable goods and services has moral value even if the items enjoyed themselves lack moral value.

How might the promotion of social prosperity, so understood, conflict with narrow fairness? Some writers have proposed that justice be interpreted as luck neutralization. Justice, here, is what I have called narrow fairness. Luck neutralization is a way of understanding the claims that members of a polity can legitimately make on their own behalf or on behalf of others. In the present context, these will be claims to a share of the social product. Justice as luck neutralization has two main elements. First, some differences in actual distributive shares are due to luck, to factors for which the people receiving a particular share cannot claim responsibility. For example, it is partly a matter of luck that people have talents that enable them to secure a high income in a market system. Justice as luck neutralization calls for the elimination of differences in distributive shares that can be explained in this way. Some other differences in distributive shares, however, are not due to luck in this sense. What people get in a market system is also influenced by how diligently they work to develop their talents and to apply these talents to productive tasks, and from a commonsense perspective, people can claim responsibility for the diligence they display. Justice as luck neutralization thus accepts differences in distribution that can be explained in this way.

The best known statement of the luck-neutralization view is by G. A. Cohen. He characterizes it as calling for equal access to advantage.[9] The view is a contribution to the debate, initiated by Rawls's theory of justice, concerning what, exactly, an egalitarian polity will distribute

---

[9] G. A. Cohen, "On the Currency of Egalitarian Justice," *Ethics* 99 (1989), pp. 906–944. Cohen suggests that the purpose of egalitarian arrangements is to eliminate involuntary disadvantage, "disadvantage for which the sufferer cannot be held responsible, since it does not appropriately reflect choices he has made or is making or would make" (p. 916).

equally. The value of equality, in this context, can be understood as another social value which, like narrow fairness when it is interpreted as a social value, is capable of grounding claims that can be made by or on behalf of individual members of a polity. The proposal that resources are to be distributed equally may be thought inadequately responsive to the claims of need that some members of a polity may have. Some may need more than an equal share of resources would give them. Proposals advocating the equal distribution of welfare – that is, advocating the maintenance of equal levels of want satisfaction – can address this problem, on the assumption that people's wants reflect their needs. But equalizing welfare seems to create the possibility that a member could exploit the polity by deliberately cultivating expensive tastes, which the polity would have to satisfy to prevent his welfare falling below that of others. Justice as luck neutralization is designed to avoid these problems. Genuine needs are usually a result of factors for which the people experiencing the needs are not responsible. So justice as luck neutralization will meet these needs. But people who cultivate expensive tastes are responsible for any frustration they experience as a result of not being able to satisfy those tastes. So the frustration creates no claim against the polity as a whole.

The luck neutralization view of justice is more subtle than this description suggests, and it has generated some well-argued critical responses.[10] For our purposes here, however, the important point is that luck neutralization can conflict with the value of social prosperity if this requires the full exploitation of all the productive resources of a polity. Among the productive resources will be the talents of the members, understood as their de facto ability to contribute in various ways to overall social production. From the standpoint of the promotion of social prosperity, and also of many other morally important social values, it does not matter whether an individual's possession of a talent in this sense is something for which she can claim responsibility. The effective promotion of the values requires the exploitation of the talents, regardless of their provenance. But exploiting the talents of highly talented people will usually make their lives better in a number of different ways. For example, it can result in their occupying upper-level positions in hierarchies. Since the possession of the talents is partly a matter of luck, so is the receipt of these benefits. If narrow fairness is understood as luck neutralization, then, exploiting the talents of the talented will involve

---

[10] Important criticisms can be found in Elizabeth Anderson, "What is the Point of Equality?" *Ethics* 109 (1999), pp. 287–337, and S. L. Hurley, *Justice, Luck, and Knowledge* (Cambridge, MA: Harvard University Press, 2004).

sacrificing narrow fairness, to a certain extent at any rate. But if the exploitation of these talents is nevertheless justified by the values thus promoted, the associated pattern of concessions in the society as a whole will also be justified, which means that the way political cooperation is organized will be fair in the broad sense.

One reason that exploiting the talents of highly talented people can make their lives better is that they may be unwilling to contribute their talents in the socially most useful way unless they are paid more. Cohen has discussed whether accommodating such a fact about the dispositions of the talented is compatible with justice.[11] He plausibly argues that how much the talented have to be paid to induce them to deploy their talents in the socially most useful way is influenced by the general ethos of a society. The ethos of one society may encourage the talented to get as much as they can for themselves. The ethos of another may emphasize service to the society as a whole, with the result that the talented do not have to be paid a lot more than other people to get them to deploy their talents in the socially most useful way. Given this fact, Cohen argues, the ethos of a society should itself be subject to assessment from the standpoint of justice, rather than serving as a background fact that a theory of justice must accommodate.

Again, for present purposes we do not need to resolve this issue. Cohen is concerned with whether a society in which the talented demand a relatively larger distributive share as the price for putting their talents to productive use can be said to be a just society. Justice here is what I have called narrow fairness. But even if accommodating a demand by the talented for extra pay gives rise to narrow unfairness, the pattern of concessions that results may be judged by some people to be justified by the consequences for the promotion of social prosperity and other morally important social values. For those who hold this view, the society will be fair in the broad sense. The overall pattern of concessions will be appropriate. Cohen takes himself, in making his argument, to be identifying a problematic feature of Rawls's understanding of his difference principle, an understanding according to which it governs the design of institutions, in particular, legally defined institutions, not the choices that individuals make. Let us suppose that as employed by Rawls, the difference principle does not provide an adequate interpretation of the requirements of narrow fairness. It might nevertheless be possible to regard Rawls as offering a particular theory of broad fairness in

---

[11] See, for example, G. A. Cohen, "Where the Action Is: On the Site of Distributive Justice," *Philosophy and Public Affairs* 26 (1997), pp. 3–30.

which part of the justificatory work is done by what is in fact necessary, in a given social setting, to enhance the prosperity of the less fortunate.[12]

We should be clear about the significance of the concept of broad fairness for the present study. According to moral nominalism, what catches the extrapolative dispositions associated with the employment of normative and evaluative terms in political contexts is, in part, experienced motivation. I have spoken in this connection of a general disposition to make and seek concessions in cooperative contexts when others are similarly disposed. This motivational disposition grounds the sense of fairness. In the course of moral maturation, a human being will acquire more specific normative and evaluative concepts that identify particular reasons for regarding the organization of political cooperation as fair or unfair. These concepts will be socially provided, which means that there will be some social variation in the reasons supporting particular ways of structuring political cooperation. I say more about this in the later chapters.

The reasons may take the form of specific claims of desert or need that can be made by or on behalf of a member of the polity, and the appropriate reconciliation of these claims gives us one form of fairness, which I have called narrow fairness. It is arguable that the sense of fairness is especially responsive to considerations of this sort. The general disposition to participate in a process of mutual concession finds direct expression in judgments of narrow fairness. But once morally important social values are acknowledged, they, too, can provide reasons to make or seek concessions in

---

[12] For the difference principle, see John Rawls, *A Theory of Justice* (Cambridge, MA: Harvard University Press, 1971), pp. 75–83. The difference principle licenses departures from an equal distribution of income and wealth within a polity if the shares of those who get the least in the resulting unequal distribution are larger than they would be in an equal distribution, and cannot be made larger still by further redistribution. The basic idea is that it can be acceptable to give more to those whose talents enable them to make an important contribution to the social product if this is necessary to secure the deployment of those talents. The surplus that remains after these payments have been made goes to the less well off members of the polity. If the shares of the less well off members are to be as large as they can be, the talented must receive only the minimum required to induce them to contribute in the most productive way. Cohen's point is that this minimum can be influenced by the social ethos. Thus the ethos should itself fall within the scope of a theory of justice.

The possible interpretation of Rawls mentioned in the text is that if, given the prevailing ethos, a certain set of payments would in fact maximize the prosperity of the less well off members of a particular polity, it may be possible to regard the resulting pattern of concessions within the polity as a whole as fair in the broad sense even if it is not fair in the narrow sense. It is worth bearing in mind that even if we take this view of the matter, the requirement that the prosperity of the less fortunate be maximized would constrain the distributive shares of the talented. It would be appropriate, for example, to test, with tax policy, the limits of what could be accomplished for the less fortunate given the prevailing ethos. Cohen's distinction between a just society, in which everyone's choices are informed by (what are taken to be) the correct principles of justice, and a just government that applies the correct principles to a society some members of which do not accept them, is relevant here.

cooperative contexts. So if fairness is understood as appropriate concession, we must expand our view of it. The result is what I have called broad fairness. Someone who judges social arrangements that effectively promote various morally important social values to be fair will often be employing the notion of fairness in the broad sense.

The examples above are meant to illustrate the fact that judgments of narrow and broad fairness can diverge. In particular, what is fair in the broad sense may be unfair in the narrow sense. We are interested in the implications of this for the possibility of reasonable political disagreement. I have suggested that there can be disagreement concerning the interpretation of the reasons and values germane to the structuring of political cooperation, and concerning their relative weights when, interpreted in particular ways, they conflict. Such disagreement will be reasonable when it is possible for competent reasoners to reach different conclusions. The fact that shared deliberation conducted in good faith for an extended period of time does not resolve disagreements of a particular kind is an important sign that such disagreements are reasonable. The moral questions raised by the distinction between narrow and broad fairness – questions concerning whether various ways of organizing political cooperation involve a sacrifice of narrow fairness and whether, if they do, the sacrifice is nevertheless appropriate – are the focus of continuing, energetic debate. So it is likely that they admit of reasonable disagreement. It bears repeating, however, that the zone of reasonable disagreement about these issues cannot be equated with the set of views we actually observe.

THE ZONE OF REASONABLE DISAGREEMENT

I have defined reasonable political disagreement as disagreement among competently reasoned views of what would constitute a fair way of organizing some aspect of political cooperation. Fairness consists in an appropriate pattern of concessions by the cooperators. As we have seen, this idea can be given a narrow and a broad construal. Ultimately, political disagreement concerns what would be fair in the broad sense, what would constitute an appropriate pattern of concessions on the part of the members of a polity given the full range of moral considerations relevant to the organization of political cooperation. I have also suggested that one mark of reasonable political disagreement is that it will survive shared deliberation conducted in good faith over an extended period of time. Shared deliberation conducted in good faith can be expected to eliminate mistakes in reasoning and thus winnow out the unreasonable views. But different reasonable views will remain.

Political disagreement typically concerns the organization of a specific aspect of political cooperation. Let us call the set of reasonable positions, the set of competently reasoned views concerning what fairness requires, that can be taken with respect to a given political issue the *zone of reasonable disagreement* associated with that issue. As I have mentioned several times, the zone of reasonable disagreement cannot be equated with the set of positions actually taken. It consists rather of the positions that would be taken if all the members of the polity were reasoning competently with the available concepts – were proceeding appropriately within the context of their judgmental histories. The zone of reasonable disagreement thus has a counterfactual aspect which can make it difficult to identify. It is possible that some actual political disagreements would be resolved if the parties deliberated long enough. But where there is freedom of political speech, the fact that a particular pattern of disagreement reemerges in a variety of different decision contexts gives us some basis for supposing that we are dealing with reasonable disagreement.

For political cooperation to be achieved, there must be agreement on a cooperative scheme. The mechanisms that can produce such agreement when shared deliberation is not able to produce it will be discussed in the next chapter. In the present section, I want to consider some issues that arise in connection with the idea that a zone of reasonable disagreement is associated with many political questions.

I have been restricting the discussion to a single polity, and assuming that the members of the polity, by and large, share a set of normative and evaluative concepts relevant to the structuring of political cooperation. This might be questioned. Concepts such as freedom and equality, and more specific concepts such as non-discrimination, are shared by all the members of modern Western polities, although they may be interpreted differently in the judgments that are made about particular cases. But the conceptual resources germane to political cooperation that are available in a modern Western polity also include philosophical theories of the good polity. These typically contain a number of specialized, indeed technical, concepts generated by reflection on more familiar concepts such as those just mentioned. Most members of modern Western polities are unacquainted with these theories and thus with these concepts. What are the implications of this for the specification of the zone of reasonable disagreement? In particular, should we say that because only philosophers are working with all the available conceptual resources, the zone of reasonable disagreement can be equated with the set of positions taken by competently reasoning philosophers?

There is some basis for thinking that we should. In the discussion of shared deliberation in the second section, I proposed that for most people, deliberation about what fairness requires in a particular case involves reasoning by analogy. But this constitutes only one part of the reasoning employed to establish and defend philosophical theories of the good polity. Reasoning by analogy generates particular judgments of fairness or unfairness. But in the crafting of a philosophical theory, these judgments have the status of data to be systematized by a coherent structure of general principles, and considerations of various sorts are relevant to this process. Reasoning that generates a theory of the good polity by taking all these considerations into account employs what Rawls calls the method of reflective equilibrium.[13] It can be argued that reasoning about how political cooperation is to be organized is not fully competent unless it moves beyond reasoning by analogy to encompass the method of reflective equilibrium.

This suggestion must be approached with some care, however. In the first place, we need to ask who is to count as a philosopher. If it is among philosophers that we are most likely to find competent reasoning about how political cooperation ought to be organized, this is because they employ the method of reflective equilibrium and are able to devote more time than most members of a polity to thinking about issues of political morality. But this description is satisfied by a number of people who are not members of academic philosophy departments. The set of political philosophers must be understood to include as well specialists in political theory in academic political science departments. And that is not all. Many academics in other areas of the humanities or the social sciences devote much thought, employing some version of the method of reflective equilibrium, to the question of how political cooperation ought to be organized, so these people must also be counted as philosophers for the purposes of the suggestion we are now considering. Similar points apply to some legal academics and to specialists in business ethics working in business schools. Indeed, the set of political philosophers cannot even be restricted to academics. Some fellows of "think tanks" such as (in the United States) the Brookings Institution and the American Enterprise Institute, and some conceptually sophisticated journalists and writers of other kinds, must also be included if we are going to equate the zone of reasonable disagreement with the range of opinion found among people who competently employ some version of the method of

[13] For the method of reflective equilibrium, see Rawls, *A Theory of Justice*, pp. 46–53. A useful discussion is Norman Daniels, "Wide Reflective Equilibrium and Theory Acceptance in Ethics," *The Journal of Philosophy* 76 (1979), pp. 256–282.

reflective equilibrium to reach conclusions about how political cooperation ought to be organized.

Once this is understood, however, the suggestion we are now considering confronts a problem. The zone of reasonable disagreement consists of competently reasoned views concerning how political cooperation ought to be organized, and in general, views can be regarded as competently reasoned only if they are the product of shared deliberation conducted in good faith. We find shared deliberation among people working on political philosophy in philosophy departments, and among people working on political theory in political science departments, but even in the case of these two closely allied fields, the discussions are somewhat disconnected. And the absence of shared deliberation becomes more marked as we add to the mix other academics interested in questions of political philosophy, including legal academics and business ethicists, and members of think tanks and other writers who reflect philosophically on the appropriate way of organizing political cooperation. We cannot, then, simply equate the zone of reasonable disagreement with the range of opinion actually found within all these groups. The zone consists rather of the views that would survive inter-group deliberation conducted in good faith. Since, especially at the extremes – for example, between academic philosophers and members of the American Enterprise Institute – there is little such deliberation, the actual range of opinion among "philosophers" cannot be regarded as a reliable guide to the boundaries of the zone of reasonable disagreement.

The proposal that the zone of reasonable political disagreement be equated with the range of opinion we find among philosophers also confronts another problem. Must we say that because only philosophers, in the expanded sense just proposed, can be regarded as reasoning competently with all the available conceptual resources, no disagreement between a philosopher and a non-philosopher can be reasonable? This is hardly an attractive position in a democratic polity. But if reasonableness is understood as competence, and competence in political reasoning is greater among people who are familiar with all the available conceptual resources and are able to devote their working lives to this reasoning, how is the conclusion to be avoided?

The counterfactual element in the characterization of the zone of reasonable disagreement may help us here. The zone consists of the range of opinion that would be produced by shared deliberation conducted in good faith over an extended period, but the initial reasoning of the parties need not be highly competent. Competent reasoning is rather the outcome of shared deliberation. Thus while philosophers, in the sense in which I am

using the term, may initially be employing the available conceptual resources more competently than non-philosophers, a process of shared deliberation conducted over an extended period of time would reduce these differences. The non-philosophers would become familiar with the specialized concepts employed by philosophers and adept in employing them. They would, in effect, become philosophers. It may be that few non-philosophers have the time to devote to extensive deliberation with philosophers, but what matters for the characterization of the zone of reasonable disagreement is the range of opinion that would exist if the requisite deliberation were to take place.

Given these points, the idea that the zone of reasonable disagreement can be equated with the range of opinion found among competently reasoning philosophers is not as objectionable as it might initially seem. In its final form, the zone may encompass positions taken by people who are not philosophers by occupation. The non-philosophers will have histories of judgment that differ from the histories of the philosophers by occupation, and thus have different perspectives on the relevant reasons. For example, non-philosophers who have had extensive experience managing large, heterogeneous organizations may have a different perspective on certain political values than academics who lack this experience. The same is true for non-philosophers who have had extensive experience in labor or community organizing. Shared deliberation employing the method of reflective equilibrium will refine these perspectives, and reduce some of the initial disagreement, but it is likely that elements of the different perspectives created by different histories of judgment will survive the process. Indeed, the position initially taken by a non-philosopher in a dispute with a philosopher might actually fall within the zone of reasonable disagreement. Shared deliberation employing the method of reflective equilibrium might leave it in place.

We can apply these points to the question whether fairness requires the public provision of assisted living. It seems likely that the introduction of philosophical theories of the good polity will give the zone of reasonable disagreement with respect to this question a configuration different from that produced by analogical reasoning employing commonsense concepts. But as was mentioned earlier, reasoning by analogy plays an important role in the method of reflective equilibrium when that method is employed to generate philosophical theories of the good polity. Analogical reasoning provides data relevant to the construction and confirmation of such theories. The method of reflective equilibrium can thus be regarded as giving a new conceptualized shape to an antecedently existing sense of fairness

created by analogical reasoning. And where these antecedent understandings of fairness differ, because the parties have different personal experiences and histories of judgment, it can be expected that the method of reflective equilibrium will yield different results. It will give the parties different philosophical theories of the good polity, or different interpretations of a single theory. The situation in academic political philosophy appears to confirm that reasonable disagreement among people employing the method of reflective equilibrium is possible, but disagreement is likely to be more pronounced if the set of philosophers is expanded in the ways I have described. When philosophical theories of the good polity generated by the method of reflective equilibrium are brought to bear on an issue like the public provision of assisted living, then, the result will normally be the restructuring, not the resolution, of reasonable disagreement.

CHAPTER 4

The resolution of reasonable disagreement

Cooperation presupposes agreement on a cooperative scheme. In small groups, the process of reaching agreement often involves the offer and acceptance of what I call a coordination proposal. In its canonical form, a coordination proposal is formulated with the words "let us" ("let's"). Thus we might get, "Let's go to the movies," followed by "Okay," said by all the others.[1] If the first proposal is resisted by some group members, different proposals may be made, with the result that the group must decide among proposals. The imperative to decide will typically initiate a process of shared deliberation aimed at securing a consensus on the appropriate way of structuring cooperation in the case at hand.

We are concerned, however, with large groups, in particular, polities. As we have seen, the question of how political cooperation ought to be organized is likely to admit of reasonable disagreement. That is, even if the members engage in shared deliberation conducted in good faith over an extended period of time, a consensus will not be achieved. Decision making in the face of disagreement can be regarded as a defining feature of political association, considered as a general social form. Part of what distinguishes political association from other social forms is the existence of procedures for authoritatively resolving disagreement about how cooperation is to be organized. By this criterion, corporations of all kinds can often be understood as political associations, but polities provide the paradigm.

As has been mentioned, the zone of reasonable disagreement is defined counterfactually, as the set of positions that would be produced by competent reasoning drawing on the available concepts, and we cannot in general be certain whether a particular position lies within the boundaries of the zone. Our most reliable indicator of reasonable disagreement is that a particular pattern of disagreement appears in a variety of decision contexts and persists despite

---

[1] I discuss coordination proposals in *Collective Rationality and Collective Reasoning* (New York: Cambridge University Press, 2001), p. 55.

extended debate. One example is provided by the disagreements surrounding the question of how to exploit the causal powers of the population. Some think that political cooperation should be organized in whatever non-coercive way will, as a matter of fact, achieve the fullest exploitation of these powers. Others are worried that doing this can have undesirable consequences for social equality.

Although the precise boundaries of the zone of reasonable disagreement are unclear, it will be useful, in providing an account of the resolution of reasonable disagreement, to begin by considering a model polity in which all disagreement about how political cooperation is to be structured is reasonable in the dual sense I have described. That is, all the members of the polity are reasoning competently about what would constitute a broadly fair way of organizing political cooperation. In addition, I shall assume that each member knows, perhaps as a result of shared deliberation, what the other positions held within the polity are. To this extent, each knows what the zone of reasonable disagreement in the polity is.

In a polity of this sort, there will be a certain amount of agreement about the form that political cooperation should take. Concerning some issues relating to the organization of political cooperation, there will be judgments that no one can reasonably reject. For example, in a society that possesses the concept of discrimination, there will be disagreement among competent reasoners about how it is to be interpreted, but no reasonable person will regard racial segregation as fair in either the narrow or the broad sense. The question we are concerned with, then, is how the disagreements that remain are to be resolved. As the chapter proceeds, the discussion will be broadened to include cases where some of the positions held within a polity are unreasonable. They represent incompetent reasoning about what would be broadly fair, or do not reflect any reasoning about fairness at all.

AUTHORITY AND DEMOCRACY

A reasonable political view is a view about the pattern of concessions that ought to characterize some aspect of political cooperation, some part of the overall cooperative endeavor. The resolution of reasonable disagreement involves making a particular such view the basis of political cooperation, and this requires further concession at a higher level. The members of the polity must be prepared to make concessions to those holding opposing views about how political cooperation ought to be organized in the case at hand. Thus the question of fairness arises again at this higher level. We confront the question of what would be a reasonable-as-fair way of resolving reasonable first-order disagreement about fairness.

We encountered the idea of higher-order concession in chapter 1. There it was noted that some approaches to political disagreement advocate mutual accommodation among the opposing views, and I suggested that this involves concession at a higher level. I also suggested that the willingness to make such concessions may bring with it a kind of detachment from one's first-order view of the appropriate pattern of concessions. But the procedures of political decision making that are employed to resolve reasonable disagreement – that is, to decide among the reasonable options – need not have this result. The members of the polity will ultimately have to be willing to live with a certain amount of what they regard as moral error, but participation in the decision-making procedure itself need not involve any retreat from what a given individual regards as morally required. Each member can be understood, in participating, as seeking to secure the adoption by the polity of her particular view of the appropriate way of organizing political cooperation.

The resolution of disagreement by a political decision-making procedure requires that the procedure possess de facto authority within the polity. The members of the polity must be prepared to defer to its decisions. Since these decisions are typically given expression in the law, it follows that the members of the polity must be prepared to obey the law. Reasonable members of a polity will insist, in addition, that the authority possessed by the political decision procedure be legitimate. The legitimacy of political authority has two, interrelated, aspects.

In the first place, a source of directives can be regarded as exercising legitimate authority within a polity only if almost all the members of the polity have sufficient reason to comply with the directives produced. Where the issues that require political resolution are moral issues that admit of reasonable disagreement, this means that almost all the members must have sufficient reason to obey some laws that they regard as morally mistaken. I believe that the reason to obey, for a given individual, must ultimately have something to do with the fact that if all the members of a polity were to fail to obey – if there were a breakdown of political cooperation – that individual would find the social condition in which she lived morally worse than that created by political cooperation on the basis of existing law. Conversely, if she can judge that the breakdown of political cooperation would be morally preferable to its continuation, she will be justified in disregarding the law.

There appear to be two basic ways of understanding this idea. The first, the holistic interpretation, envisages the total breakdown of all aspects of political cooperation. That is, the thought experiment involves comparing

the existing form of political cooperation, in its totality, with its complete collapse. It is unlikely, given human cooperative dispositions, that the consequence of collapse would be a "state of nature" of the sort described by the classical contract theorists. Rather a new form of political cooperation would shortly be instituted. Thus conducting the thought experiment will involve making a factual judgment concerning what the new form of political cooperation would look like and also a moral judgment concerning whether it would be preferable to the existing form. The holistic interpretation seems to have the consequence that only those who regard the existing form of political cooperation as a moral disaster will be justified in declining to obey the law. In any other case, there would be too little basis for supposing that the complete collapse of political cooperation would be followed by something better.

Alternatively, the thought experiment can be given a piecemeal interpretation. On this interpretation, the decision whether to obey a given law, or interrelated set of laws, is made by focusing on the particular component of the total system of political cooperation brought into existence by conformity with that law or set. One is justified in obeying that law or set of laws if one judges the total system of political cooperation, understood as containing this component, to be preferable to the system that would exist if the component were to collapse. Again, performing the thought experiment involves making a factual judgment about what the likely consequences of collapse would be, together with a moral judgment concerning the acceptability of these consequences. But it seems that on this interpretation, a member of a polity who judged a particular law or set of laws morally mistaken would often be justified in declining to obey those laws. He could often conclude that the collapse of the corresponding component of political cooperation would be, or lead to, an overall moral improvement.

Neither interpretation is entirely satisfactory. We seem to face a choice between a view that leaves too little scope for disobeying laws one finds morally objectionable and a view that leaves too much.[2] The introduction of the phenomenon of reasonable disagreement enables us to provide a more satisfactory account. On the assumptions we are now making, all the members of the polity are competent reasoners whose views about the appropriate way to organize a given aspect of political cooperation can be regarded as reasonable in the dual sense I have proposed. But as has been mentioned, the fairness of some aspects of the total system of political

---

[2] In *Collective Rationality and Collective Reasoning*, ch. 3, I argue that if a choice must be made, the holistic approach is preferable. But as I explain in the text, I now think there is a third possibility.

cooperation will not be in dispute. It will not admit of reasonable disagreement. Legal specification of the required actions will still be necessary because the shared understanding of the fairness of these aspects must be publicly affirmed. And even if we assume that it is common knowledge within the polity that everyone is cooperatively disposed, legal enforcement will have a role to play in guarding against lapses of judgment. But no one will, on reflection, regard these laws as morally mistaken.

Given this, we can craft an intermediate position on obedience to the particular laws that a given individual judges to be mistaken. A member of a polity who is trying to decide whether to obey a law that she reasonably judges to be morally mistaken need ask only whether the continued existence of those parts of the overall cooperative scheme *that have been put in place to resolve reasonable disagreement* would be preferable to their collapse. This gives us the following result. Someone who objects so strongly to a law resolving a particular reasonable disagreement that she judges the collapse of the total legal effort to resolve reasonable disagreement preferable to its maintenance will be justified in disobeying that law. The collapse of the total legal effort would bring with it many inconveniences. But in any actual polity there is always a certain amount of unresolved reasonable disagreement. So what is at issue is an augmentation of a condition that already obtains to a certain extent.

We are concerned, then, with someone (a competent reasoner, we are supposing) who finds especially galling the concessions imposed on her by a law adopted to resolve reasonable disagreement in a particular case. The possibility we are considering is that she might conclude that living with a substantial increase in the inconveniences that accompany unresolved reasonable disagreement would be an acceptable price to pay for the non-existence of that law. But since a substantial increase in these inconveniences is not a trivial matter, it cannot be supposed that the thought experiment will always have this result. The interpretation of the "compliance test" that we are now considering will, then, leave more latitude for disobeying laws one finds morally mistaken than the holistic interpretation, but less than the piecemeal interpretation.

I said earlier that a source of directives can be regarded as possessing legitimate authority within a polity only if almost all the members have sufficient reason to comply with its directives. This is accurate to a first approximation, but ultimately account must be taken of the percentage of the total set of directives with which a given member can be expected to comply. It is not enough that almost everyone has sufficient reason to comply with some directives. Rather, it must again be the case that

compliance is the norm. So if a substantial subset of the members of a polity judge that they have no reason to obey many of the laws that have been put in place to resolve reasonable disagreement, this will call into question the legitimacy of political authority.[3] A prudent government must therefore approach carefully the decisions it makes resolving reasonable disagreement. As I explain below, an aspect of this carefulness will be the employment of decision procedures that are widely regarded as fair.

It should be borne in mind that if the other members of the polity favor maintaining the forms of political cooperation established to resolve reasonable disagreement, those who competently judge that they have no reason to obey a given law, and act accordingly, may still face punishment of some kind. This may give them a reason of a different sort to obey. And of course in real political life, the way of interpreting the compliance test that we are now considering will be complicated by the fact that the precise shape of the zone of reasonable disagreement, and thus the identity of the particular political decisions that resolve reasonable disagreement, will not be clear. The actual employment of this version of the compliance test thus presupposes the availability of some method, such as reflection on the history of the disputes found within a polity, which makes it possible to discern, in broad outline at least, the zone of reasonable disagreement.

Now let us turn to the second aspect of the legitimacy of political authority in a population of people who reasonably disagree about how political cooperation should be organized. This concerns whether the operative political decision procedure constitutes a fair way of distributing the burden of living with perceived moral error. This burden inevitably accompanies the resolution of reasonable moral disagreement about how political cooperation ought to be organized. If we suppose that competent reasoners will come to different conclusions about what would constitute a fair way of distributing the burden of living with perceived moral error, some way must be found to resolve this disagreement as well. A constitutional convention charged with deciding among broadly fair ways of resolving political disagreement is one possibility, but the form the constitutional convention is to take might itself admit of reasonable disagreement. We thus confront the possibility that the resolution of reasonable disagreement at this level, the process of deciding among competently reasoned views about what would constitute a fair

---

[3] The legal resolution of a reasonable disagreement will sometimes give the force of law to the very view a particular individual holds. In this case, he will have sufficient reason to comply with that law even if, for the reasons described in the text, he has opted out of the overall legal effort to resolve reasonable disagreement.

political decision procedure, must ultimately involve social mechanisms that transcend formal decision-making procedures.

The role of informal social mechanisms in resolving reasonable disagreement is explored below and in the later chapters. For present purposes, we can focus on the formal procedures. What formal procedures for resolving reasonable political disagreement might find favor among competent reasoners seeking a broadly fair way of resolving such disagreements? This issue presents us with a further aspect of the problem of legitimacy. Whether a given individual regards as fair the way the existing decision procedure distributes the burden of living with perceived moral error will be a factor in whether she judges that she has sufficient reason to obey the law. If she regards the existing procedures as fairly distributing this burden, she will be less likely to judge the collapse of the legal effort to resolve reasonable disagreement morally preferable to its maintenance, even when she strongly disagrees with some of the measures put in place by these procedures.

The first question to address in considering this second aspect of legitimacy concerns what would constitute a narrowly fair way of distributing the burden of living with perceived moral error. Narrow fairness, it will be recalled, consists in the appropriate reconciliation of the claims that the members of the polity, considered as individuals, can make against one another or against the polity as a whole. One proposal might be that the decision procedure should give everyone, or each interested party, an equal chance of getting adopted his view of the appropriate way of organizing the aspect of political cooperation at issue. Alternatively, it might be suggested that fairness requires that everyone be given an equal opportunity to affect the way political cooperation is organized.

The difference is illustrated by the choice between a procedure that employs a lottery to determine the view that will be adopted and a procedure that involves voting by the method of majority rule, when everyone has the opportunity to propose measures to be put to a vote. A lottery is probably preferable if the goal is to give everyone an equal chance of getting his view adopted, but it could be argued that the two procedures are equivalent in ensuring that everyone has an equal opportunity to affect the way political cooperation is organized. Voting by the method of majority rule satisfies this condition if its status as a fair procedure is not compromised by the existence of entrenched minorities who are on the losing end of every vote. When the issues decided by voting admit of reasonable disagreement, entrenched minorities may be less likely.

It should be noted that even someone who judges a lottery to be preferable from the standpoint of narrow fairness may find voting by the

method of majority rule preferable from the standpoint of broad fairness. She may judge that any disadvantages possessed by the method of majority rule from the standpoint of narrow fairness are offset by its superior consequences for the promotion of various morally important social values. Here is one argument that might support such a judgment. I have proposed that a member of a polity will be justified in disobeying a law that resolves a reasonable disagreement if she would prefer the collapse of the total legal effort to resolve such disagreements to its maintenance, given that maintaining it involves obeying the law in question. That is, she will be justified in disobeying if she can judge the increase in the inconveniences associated with unresolved reasonable disagreement that would accompany the collapse to be an acceptable price to pay for disregarding the law. But if a lottery is employed to resolve reasonable disagreement in a particular case, the result may be that only a tiny minority agrees with the policy adopted. Thus it is likely that more people employing our compliance test will conclude that disobedience is justified than would be the case if decisions were made by the method of majority rule. And the prospect of more disobedience of the laws that resolve reasonable disagreement when the decision procedure is a lottery may constitute a reason to favor the method of majority rule even though a lottery is fairer in the narrow sense.

Some sort of voting procedure enfranchising all adults is the universal method of making political decisions in modern Western polities, and increasingly in other polities as well, so let us focus on that. When the decision concerning how political cooperation is to be organized in a particular case is made by a voting procedure of any kind, the task of each member of the polity is to try to secure enough agreement from the other members to get her view enacted into law. That is, her task is to assemble a majority, or whatever the voting procedure requires.

The question of how this is to be done when the issue to be decided admits of reasonable disagreement will be discussed further in the next section. But one point can be made here. The resolution of reasonable disagreement about how political cooperation is to be organized must work in such a way that the form of organization selected for implementation is reasonable in the dual sense we have been working with. The form of organization selected must constitute a view of what would be broadly fair that can be supported by competent reasoning. Where disagreement is reasonable, there will be more than one such alternative, but the alternative selected, which may be a new one that emerges after the process of resolution gets started, must possess this character. This has the consequence that bargaining of the usual sort cannot in general be regarded as an

acceptable mechanism for resolving reasonable disagreement. Bargaining involves making concessions from one's most preferred way of organizing political cooperation, but these are motivated by strategic considerations. Each will make only the concessions she judges necessary to secure the participation of people whose involvement would, from her standpoint, add more to the value of the cooperative product than it would cost. Thus there is no guarantee that the final result will correspond to a competently reasoned view of what fairness requires in the organization of political cooperation.

CHANGING MINDS

A member of a polity who reasonably holds a particular position, and whose thinking is in other respects sound, will try to bring it about that political cooperation, or the aspect of it at issue, is organized in the way she judges appropriate. We are supposing that the positions actually taken all fall within the zone of reasonable disagreement and that the decision among them is made by the method of majority rule. We need not consider here the precise procedures that translate majority opinion into legislation. When a polity decides by the method of majority rule, the task of a member seeking to effect the implementation of a particular way of organizing political cooperation is to secure a majority for that way of organizing it. Other democratic decision procedures may not require the assembling of a majority, but success in getting one's view translated into legislation will still depend on convincing a large fraction of the members of the polity that the course one advocates is appropriate. How is a majority, or other sufficiently large group of like-minded others, to be assembled when the issue to be decided admits of reasonable disagreement?

As we have seen, bargaining cannot in general be expected to result in the adoption of a view about what would be fair that can be supported by competent reasoning. Bargaining can change the position a given individual is prepared to vote for, but it will not change a competent reasoner's mind about what would be fair, and can easily result in the adoption of a position that no one judges fair. What, then, are we left with?

Deliberation is the possibility that first suggests itself. This was discussed in the previous chapter. Deliberation cannot in general be expected to eliminate political disagreement, but it can reduce disagreement. In assuming that the positions actually taken are reasonable, we are, in effect, assuming that a certain amount of shared deliberation has already taken place. This might have produced a majority view, although further

deliberation could result in the emergence of a different majority view. But we need to consider in more detail how shared deliberation can create a majority for a particular view.

Some of the members of a polity will have formed, prior to their participation in shared deliberation, a view on the issue being addressed. The changing of minds will consist partly in the revision or abandonment of some of these views as deliberation proceeds. Deliberation can change how the available concepts are interpreted or how the relative weights of the corresponding reasons are understood. It can do this by identifying mistakes in the reasoning underlying the initial positions, or by presenting in speech cases that expand the familiarity of the participants with relevantly similar or dissimilar situations, as was described in the previous chapter. Insofar as the goal is to secure a majority for one's view, attempting to change the thinking of people whose views are already close to one's own will make more sense than attempting to change the thinking of people with sharply opposed views. But argument with people whose views are sharply opposed can be an effective means of changing the thinking of other people if the arguments take place in a public forum. Of course, these options are not restricted to individuals. A group of like-minded people can act collectively in these ways to secure a majority for its view.

As we saw in the discussion of shared deliberation in the previous chapter, the presentation of cases held to be analogous or disanalogous may elicit more than routine, so to speak, linear, extrapolation from examples of the correct use of a normative term. This can happen when it is not initially clear how to assimilate a new case to the examples of correct use from which a given individual is proceeding. In such a situation, the individual must exercise his judgment (as it is usually put), and this can have the effect of altering the content of the concept employed. After the new case has been added to the individual's set of examples of correct use, subsequent cases may be handled differently than they would have been had that case not been encountered.

A change of this sort can also be produced by presenting in a different order cases with which a given individual is familiar. Some people may initially resist the employment of a given term in a particular way because its use in that way seems to be "too much of a stretch," given previous uses taken to be correct. But when this happens, it is sometimes possible, by presenting the familiar cases in a different order, to create a bridge to the new use. In this way, the results produced by shared deliberation can exhibit path dependence. The conclusions reached may depend not only on the set of relevantly similar and dissimilar cases constructed by shared deliberation, but on the route taken through them.

The alteration, through shared deliberation, of the content of the concepts expressed by normative or evaluative terms can, then, play a role in the efforts of an individual or group to assemble a majority for a particular way of organizing political cooperation. It is worth noting that all that is required is agreement about how political cooperation is to be organized. The members of the majority that an individual or group seeks to assemble need not agree on why cooperation is to be organized that way. Of course, if the majority is produced by shared deliberation, it is to be expected that there will be a certain amount of agreement among the members of the majority about why political cooperation ought to be organized as they propose. But it is not necessary that the judgments involved have precisely the same rationale.

Changing minds by a process of deliberation involves inducing people, in a way compatible with the proper functioning of the relevant capacities, to give a particular conceptually articulated structure to the disposition to make and seek concessions that underlies the sense of fairness. It involves getting them to give this disposition, as it is activated by a given situation, a particular conceptualized form. When deliberation produces conceptual change in the way described, the proper functioning of this motivational capacity ensures that any new conceptual materials that may be generated are suitable for expressing reasonable views about how political cooperation should be organized. Whether new conceptual materials are deemed to provide a suitable way of structuring a given individual's disposition to make and seek concessions will also depend on the structure his previous judgments have given it. This is connected with the fact that for moral nominalism, moral worlds are made out of moral worlds.

Some light can be shed on these points by noting an observation made by John Stuart Mill. In the chapter of *Utilitarianism* titled "The Ultimate Sanction of the Principle of Utility," Mill says that the moral faculty can be cultivated in almost any direction, so that almost any view can come to acquire the authority of conscience.[4] He also suggests that the moral views that we construct often yield, over time, to the dissolving force of analysis. But he argues that this fate will not befall utilitarianism because the greatest happiness principle has the support of what he calls the social feelings of mankind.

The view of political morality that I have presented is not utilitarian, but we can avail ourselves of the basic idea that Mill is employing here. A variety of normative or evaluative concepts may be introduced in the course of a

---

[4] John Stuart Mill, *Utilitarianism*, ed. G. Sher (Indianapolis: Hackett, 2002), ch. 3.

polity's collective effort to determine how political cooperation should be organized, but they will not be able to survive the scrutiny of extended deliberation conducted in good faith unless they are capable of giving structure to the disposition, which will be possessed by all properly functioning humans, to make or seek concessions in cooperative contexts when others are similarly disposed. This disposition stands to normative and evaluative concepts as matter to form. It thus constrains the concepts that can appear in competently reasoned judgments specifying particular ways of organizing political cooperation. It should be emphasized that different polities can operate with somewhat different sets of moral concepts. Although the matter constrains form, it can still be given different forms. This point will receive further discussion in the next chapter.

Shared deliberation is not, however, the only way that those seeking to secure a majority for their view can change the minds of people who initially disagree. There is also what might be called a pragmatic procedure. It typically takes a significant amount of time to do its work, but the changes that result can be more extensive and profound than those produced by shared deliberation.

The deliberative approach to assembling a majority envisages a group of people who share a set of normative and evaluative terms, but proceed from different examples of the correct employment of these terms – proceed within different personal histories of judgment. Through shared deliberation, they make the sets of examples from which they proceed more alike by presenting to each other in speech cases they hold to be relevantly similar or dissimilar to the case calling for decision. As we have just seen, linear extrapolation from personal histories may not be able to accommodate all the new material presented. The parties may have to exercise judgment if they are to extend the examples of correct employment that they are working with to certain new cases, and this can have the effect of altering the content of the concepts expressed.

But it is not only through the presentation of cases in speech that the members of a polity may confront situations that require the sort of exercise of judgment that can result in conceptual change. Concrete action may also present such situations. The members of the polity will reasonably hold different views about how political cooperation should be structured. Sometimes they will be able to put their particular views into practice only by securing the adoption by the whole polity, through a political decision-making procedure, of a cooperative scheme embodying those views. But often they will be able to take steps toward the structuring of political cooperation in the way they favor without an explicit political decision.

To take a trivial example from the recent history of Western polities, most people in a polity may think that it is morally unacceptable for a sexually involved man and woman to live together unless they are married. As a result, such couples may not be able, as a matter of social fact, to make various claims that married people can make. For example, landlords may decline to rent them apartments, and hotel managers may decline to give them rooms. Further, this denial of claims may be reasonable. It may be supportable by competent reasoning employing the available concepts. Nevertheless, the conclusion that unmarried couples should have the same housing options as married couples may also be supportable by competent reasoning employing the available concepts. That is, the issue may admit of reasonable disagreement. And men and women who reasonably reject the prevailing view may start putting their convictions into practice by taking advantage of such opportunities to set up a household as are available to them.

By living together without marriage, they present the rest of the society with cases about which judgments will have to be made. But these judgments may involve the sort of non-linear extrapolation that I have described. The assimilation of the cases encountered to a personal history of judgment may have the effect of altering the content of the concepts employed by the person in question. Further, the fact that the cases are not merely described in speech, but experienced in their full particularity, can be expected to facilitate this process. The "stretching" of concepts to fit a new case will be more likely when the case is presented in its full particularity. When couples who see nothing wrong with cohabitation without marriage act on their convictions, then, they may be able to change minds within the larger society.

This way of changing minds is typically supplemented by deliberation involving the exchange of arguments, but it transcends the exchange of arguments. Those who are unconvinced by the arguments, and consequently continue to regard the practice as morally wrong, are nevertheless confronted with the very behavior they reject. And this may produce a change of mind when argument is unable to do so. Since, initially, only a few people will be confronted with actual cases of what they oppose, the changing of minds by a process of this sort will be gradual. But once the process begins, the pace of change can accelerate.

The people seeking to secure acceptance of cohabitation without marriage will want to change the minds of those for whom the issue has no personal significance – because, for example, they are already married – but whose support, or at least acquiescence, would be desirable. But they will

also want to recruit to their cause people for whom the issue does have personal significance, men and women who are contemplating setting up a household. These people, too, may initially think that marriage is required, but come to change their minds when confronted with examples of cohabitation without marriage. To the extent that they act on these convictions, they will add to the concrete instances of cohabitation without marriage encountered by the rest of the society. Eventually, the view that cohabitation without marriage is acceptable may come to be held by a majority, even when deliberation on the basis of cases presented solely in speech could not have achieved this result.

This last point deserves emphasis. Shared deliberation involves bringing to bear what Habermas calls the force of the better argument. This force can produce a change of mind, but it does so in a way that respects the autonomy of the recipients of the arguments. It respects their status as people who are in control of the judgments they make. Argument does not so much change the mind of another person as lead that person to change her own mind. The action-induced changes of mind that we are now considering have a somewhat different character. The changes are again made by the people who undergo them. Presented with concrete instances of cohabitation outside marriage, for example, people change their minds. But although they control the changes they make in response to the cases they confront, they do not control the social environment that presents them with these cases. There is thus a sense in which change is produced by a force which is not the force of the better argument.

It might be suggested that the same could be said of shared deliberation, since an argument may present one with a case that one would rather not think about. But argument trades on the fact that properly functioning reasoners face a requirement, as properly functioning, to consider the arguments of others. Doing this enhances the competence of their reasoning. Changes of mind forced upon one, as an individual whose cognitive and cooperative capacities are functioning properly, by an alteration of the social environment are different. There does not appear to be a rational requirement to confront examples of behavior that one reasonably regards as morally wrong. One may seek to avoid them. Indeed, if one reasonably regards the new way of behaving as morally wrong, it may be permissible to punish those exhibiting it by denying them association. But as the process of social change gains momentum, avoidance becomes increasingly difficult. The result may be a change of mind that is produced, in part, by a force that is not the force of argument.

DOMINANCE

The example just given of the way concrete action can produce a change of mind is trivial. But important changes in moral thinking can be effected in this way, and some of the most consequential historical changes in moral thinking have been effected in this way. When what is at issue is a fundamental moral transformation, shared deliberation is not enough.

This is especially clear in connection with a phenomenon that I shall call dominance. In considering our model polity, we have been supposing that all the positions actually taken are reasonable. In reality, it may not be clear whether a particular political issue admits of reasonable disagreement, or if it does, where the boundaries of the zone of reasonable disagreement lie. Still, I have suggested that when a given disagreement, or form of disagreement, arises in a variety of different decision contexts and survives shared deliberation conducted in good faith over an extended period of time, it can plausibly be regarded as reasonable. The positions taken can plausibly be regarded as grounded in competent reasoning about what would be fair in the broad sense.

An example is provided by the disagreement between those who advocate socialist economic arrangements and those who advocate capitalist economic arrangements. To simplify matters, let us suppose that both sides accept that democracy is the appropriate way of making political decisions. Thus we can regard the disagreement as one between advocates of a basic structure, to use Rawls's term, that is democratic and capitalist, and the advocates of a basic structure that is democratic and socialist.[5] Since each side accepts that political disagreements are to be resolved democratically, each will be prepared to acquiesce in the arrangements preferred by the other if democratic procedures produce that result. The disagreement might take a number of different forms. Individuals with different judgmental histories might regard capitalism as narrowly fair (as justified by claims of desert that individuals can make against other individuals) or as narrowly unfair. And people who regard capitalism as narrowly unfair might, or might not, conclude that it can nevertheless be justified as promoting various morally important social values. Similar differences of opinion could emerge with respect to socialism. It might or might not be regarded as justified by the claims of desert that individuals can make against other individuals. And people who find socialism narrowly unfair might or might

---

[5] Rawls discusses the basic structure in *Political Liberalism* (New York: Columbia University Press, 1993), Lecture VII.

not conclude that it can nevertheless be justified as promoting various morally important social values.

But despite the fact that these issues seem to admit of reasonable disagreement, one view may be dominant. Consider the United States. Advocacy of democratic capitalism is the dominant view in the United States. Too few people advocate democratic socialism for it to have any significant impact on the way political cooperation is organized. This social fact, in effect, resolves the reasonable disagreement between the advocates of capitalism and the advocates of socialism before formal decision-making procedures are brought to bear. The formal procedures are employed to decide how to organize political cooperation that is presupposed to be capitalist in its basic structure.[6] There can be disagreement about the requirements of narrow fairness within a capitalist framework, and about the extent to which other morally important social values are able to justify some sacrifices of narrow fairness. Some disagreements of this sort were discussed in the previous chapter. But the acceptability of capitalism itself is not a live political issue.

Dominance is a status that one reasonable view can possess with respect to the other reasonable views, the marginal views. If a particular view held within a polity is reasonable, it will be a dominant view, in the sense I am proposing, if it is held by most members of the polity. A view is not dominant because it is more reasonable than the marginal views. Dominance is not a logical relation among reasonable views. It concerns the way *people* are distributed within the zone of reasonable disagreement.

How is the dominance of a particular view to be explained? The dominance of democratic capitalism in the United States doubtless has something to do with the fact that the institutions of democratic capitalism are firmly in place. This provides the basis for a possible objection to the phenomenon of dominance. It might be suggested that in a community of competent reasoners, if two views of the appropriate way of organizing political cooperation at the most basic level are both reasonable, each should be embraced by a large subset of the population. If this is not the case, the explanation must be that reasoning has been corrupted in some way.

---

[6] It might seem that where there is dominance, democracy can no longer be regarded as a fair way of distributing the burden of living with perceived moral error. Some central political issues are not put to a vote. But democratic procedures will typically provide for the possibility of a vote. The reason the issues are not put to a vote is that the exercise seems pointless. Given that reasonable disagreement must be resolved if political cooperation is to take place, the only alternative to the method of majority rule, and the attendant acquiescence in dominance, that can be regarded as fair is the employment of a lottery to select a way of organizing political cooperation. As was noted in the first section, however, although the employment of a lottery may be fair in the narrow sense, it can have morally undesirable consequences.

Political theorists discussing democratic decision making sometimes speak of accommodationist preferences, preferences that shape themselves to oppressive institutional arrangements.[7] The existence of such preferences is thought to compromise democratic decision making, understood as a fair way of resolving disputes, since it means that the powerful, who are responsible for the existing arrangements, will have a disproportionate influence on the outcome. Democratic deliberation can be regarded as counteracting this effect, so it might be suggested by those favoring democratic socialism that the dominance of capitalist views in the United States shows that democracy in the United States is not sufficiently deliberative.

Within the framework of moral nominalism, however, the dominance of a particular political view need not be understood as a sign that competent reasoning has been compromised. According to moral nominalism, one acquires a mastery of the use of normative and evaluative terms by being presented with examples of their correct use. One then extrapolates to new cases in a way that manifests the proper functioning of the underlying capacities, including motivational capacities. Over time, each individual amasses a collection of judgments taken to be correct. A given individual's history of judgment will be affected both by her initial instruction in the correct use of normative and evaluative terms, and by the situations she subsequently encounters.

The existing structure of society will permeate both the learning situations and the situations subsequently encountered. If an individual's initial instruction in the correct use of the socially available moral terms takes the form of judgments endorsing the kind of basic structure the polity possesses, her subsequent competent judgments are likely to endorse it as well. Of course, a contrarian judgmental history is also possible. An individual's initial examples of the correct use of the available moral terms may take the form of judgments that the basic structure the polity possesses is in various respects unfair, or perhaps fundamentally unfair. But where the existing structure is democratic and capitalist, most people may be instructed in the correct use of the available terms by exposure to examples of correct use that support democratic capitalism. And if the resulting judgmental histories confirm this training – if obstacles to competent extrapolation are rarely encountered – it will be the case that most people in the polity competently judge democratic capitalism to be morally

---

[7] Accommodationist preferences are discussed by Joshua Cohen in "Deliberation and Democratic Legitimacy," in J. Bohman and W. Rehg, eds., *Deliberative Democracy: Essays on Reason and Politics* (Cambridge, MA: MIT Press, 1997), pp. 67–91.

acceptable. We are assuming that advocacy of democratic capitalism is a reasonable view, so the idea that there will be few obstacles to competent extrapolation is not implausible.

The fact that most receive initial instruction that endorses the existing structure need not be regarded as evidence of some sort of failure of proper functioning. It can be explained as a result of a historical process of the sort described at the end of the previous section. As we saw there, changes in the way some people live their lives can produce conceptual changes that in turn give rise to judgments by others that endorse the new forms of life. What we are dealing with, then, is a process of conceptual change that is conditioned by social change while at the same time conditioning social change. We can speak here of the remaking of moral worlds by a *conceptual-cum-social process*. The process is not merely causal. If, as we are assuming, the capacities engaged are functioning properly, it has a normative dimension.

The dominance of democratic capitalism in a contemporary polity could be a result of the operation of such a conceptual-cum-social process in the past. At an earlier time, when the currently dominant view, endorsement of democratic capitalism, was marginal, the people holding various versions of it acted on their convictions, in much the same way that, more recently, people who regarded cohabitation without marriage as morally acceptable acted on their convictions. This alteration of the social environment led to accommodating conceptual changes elsewhere in the society, which in turn gave rise to further social change. The process can extend over several generations. It is likely that there is a limit to the amount of conceptual change that can take place within a lifetime of a single cohort. But parents will start a child off with the judgments they have come, in the course of their lives up to that point, to regard as correct. So over several generations, the conceptual resources available in a polity, and the percentage of the population employing particular concepts, can undergo a profound transformation. It can, then, be consistent with a history of proper functioning for most of the members of later generations to be presented with learning situations in which the available moral terms are used to endorse the kind of basic structure their polity has come to possess.

If this picture is correct, the charge that judgments supporting the status quo are accommodating in a bad sense can be seen as reflecting skepticism about the proper functioning of the human disposition to make and seek concessions in cooperative contexts, and of the linguistic capacities that give conceptualized form to this motivational disposition. The proper functioning of these mental elements is regarded as easily corrupted by social forces. But confidence in their robustness, their ability to withstand distorting

forces, is an equally tenable position. At the very least, the issue admits of reasonable disagreement. We have been discussing a model polity in which all the positions adopted are reasonable in the dual sense. In actual fact, unreasonableness is common. Usually, however, it takes the form of self- or group-interested bias that is in principle correctable by shared deliberation. So there is a place for confidence in the ability of the mental capacities underlying political judgment to withstand distortion. And for those who possess this confidence, the widespread acceptance of the existing basic structure need not be taken as evidence that these capacities have been corrupted. It can be seen as the result of a conceptual-cum-social process of the sort I have described, a process that, by reciprocally altering both the available concepts and the social environment, has provided the members of the polity with concepts that can be employed in competently reasoned judgments endorsing the kind of basic structure the polity possesses. As was explained at the end of the previous section, there will be an element of force that is not the force of the better argument in the operation of the conceptual-cum-social process. But as we also saw there, this does not mean that the proper functioning of human cognitive and motivational capacities has been compromised.

It is interesting, in light of these observations, to reflect on the endorsement of communist dictatorship. I have suggested that democracy can be seen as a fair way of distributing the burden of living with perceived moral error that is inevitable when political life is marked by reasonable disagreement. But if democratic procedures are to be accepted for this reason, the members of a polity must, at some level, acknowledge the possibility of reasonable political disagreement, and reasonable disagreement itself presents an obstacle to such acknowledgment. It is a feature of reasonable disagreement that opposing positions often seem unreasonable. Confidence in the robustness of the proper functioning of human cognitive and motivational capacities can provide some support for democracy in these circumstances. But people who hold a theory according to which political judgment is routinely distorted by social forces will lack this confidence. They may thus conclude that political power should be given to, or taken by, those who have the correct understanding, their theoretically informed understanding, of the political domain. However, the general skepticism concerning the proper functioning of human cognitive and motivational capacities that is associated with this stance sits awkwardly with the confidence of the people adopting it in the proper functioning of their own capacities.

Dominance, on the view I have presented, will typically be a transitory condition. This can be illustrated by the evolution of the zone of reasonable

disagreement in the West, which has given us the current situation in which democratic capitalism and democratic socialism are both reasonable, although democratic capitalism is dominant, albeit in different forms and to different degrees, in Western polities. According to J. B. Schneewind, in pre-modern Europe, the dominant view, the view held by most competent reasoners operating with the available concepts, was one that regarded human society as a "divine corporation."[8] On this view, social life is under the control of a divine supervisor who can be relied upon to ensure that if everyone plays his or her assigned role, where roles are usually assigned by birth into a particular "office" within the corporation, the result will be morally satisfactory. We can see this as a conception, employing religious concepts to package human cooperative dispositions, of the appropriate pattern of concessions within a population, a conception of narrow or broad fairness. Schneewind regards the transition to modernity as involving, in part, the replacement of this view by one according to which those engaged in political cooperation are understood to be responsible themselves for whether it is morally satisfactory – in our terms, for whether it is broadly fair. Some people in pre-modern Europe may already have held that view, but it was marginal then.

The change in dominant views that Schneewind describes, the emergence to dominance of a formerly marginal view and the concomitant recession to marginal status of the formerly dominant view, was not effected by a process of shared deliberation. The members of pre-modern polities did not debate the issue until most became convinced of the appropriateness of the new view. The change was brought about by a conceptual-cum-social process of the sort I have described. People armed with certain political convictions, marginal at the time, acted on these convictions, altering the social environment in a way that prompted accommodating changes in the concepts and judgments of other people. A new dominant view grew from a conceptual seed provided by a previously marginal view. Argument played an important role in this process, but not a decisive role. It clarified and solidified the conceptual aspect of the overall conceptual-cum-social process.

Similar points can be made about more recent developments in the moral history of the West. The emergence of industrial capitalism and the reaction

---

[8] J. B. Schneewind, "The Divine Corporation and the History of Ethics," in R. Rorty, J. B. Schneewind, and Q. Skinner, eds., *Philosophy in History* (Cambridge: Cambridge University Press, 1984), pp. 173–191. Schneewind does not, of course, employ my categories. I have used my terms to formulate his point.

against its excesses by organized movements of working people changed moral thinking, but deliberation was only part of the story. These historical events are responsible for basic features of the moral world we occupy today.

Some might be tempted to view moral history simply as the unfolding of a sequence of contingencies. "Power," in some form or other, has fashioned conceptual resources in its image. But moral nominalism allows us to understand what has taken place in the West as a transformation of, and within, the zone of reasonable disagreement. Some new concepts were devised, or were rescued from marginality to become widely employed, for example, the political concept of autonomy, autonomy as a right of self-direction. Others, such as the concepts of honor and condescension (understood as a virtue) associated with aristocratic social forms, fell out of regular use. In both cases, moral nominalism attributes the change not to power, but to a conceptual-cum-social process that has a normative dimension because its unfolding involves the proper functioning of human linguistic and cooperative capacities. These points receive further discussion in chapter 6.

In the history of the West, then, we find a progression of moral worlds of the sort Goodman describes. The newer worlds were not created ex nihilo; rather they were fashioned out of older worlds. We may judge the result, our present moral world, an improvement. Indeed, it will generally be the case that the occupants of a moral world, reflecting on the history of that world, will see it as an improvement over its predecessors. But within the framework of moral nominalism, we cannot understand what has taken place as the emergence of the moral truth. The modern moral world, in Western polities, is defined by the present configuration of the zone of reasonable disagreement in these polities. The present configuration can be regarded as right for the current conditions precisely because it is the product of a conceptual-cum-social process that is partly responsible for those conditions. But had the moral history of the West been different, the present zone of reasonable disagreement would have been different too. Analogous points can be made about the currently dominant view. The fact that it is widely accepted now does not entail that it is more competently reasoned than the dominant views of the past.

MILL ON PARTIAL TRUTH

I make some further points about the historical character of moral normativity in the final section. Before turning to that, however, it may be helpful to note that the account of reasonable disagreement we have been exploring

can be employed to provide an interpretation of one of the arguments that John Stuart Mill gives for freedom of political speech.

In *On Liberty*, Mill presents three basic reasons why the freedom to speak one's mind with respect to moral and evaluative issues is important.[9] Perhaps the most familiar is that the received opinion on some matter may be false, and the freedom to contest it makes the discovery of its falsehood more likely. The second point he makes is that even if the received opinion is true, the contesting of it maintains an appreciation of the grounds of its truth and prevents the decay of its "meaning," its ability to influence conduct. But there is a further reason as well. Mill says that the received opinion will seldom or never be the whole truth. Liberty of discussion is important as enabling a society to take possession of the whole truth. He mentions in particular the division of political opinion into a party of order or stability and a party of progress or reform, and he says that both are necessary for a healthy condition of political life.[10]

It is doubtful that Mill regarded truth in moral or political matters as admitting of reasonable disagreement in the sense I have proposed. His third reason seems to be grounded in two observations. First, arriving at a correct answer to a question concerning how political cooperation should be organized requires taking account of a number of different considerations. Second, for psychological and sociological reasons of various kinds, political opinions are normally reflective of only some of these considerations. Liberty of discussion is desirable because it makes possible debate, which in turn makes available to all the members of the polity the full set of considerations relevant to a particular political issue. This puts the members in a position to make true all-things-considered ought-judgments.[11]

Nevertheless, an interpretation in terms of reasonable disagreement is possible. If the disagreements found in a given polity are reasonable, the positions taken by the different parties will be grounded in different, competently reasoned all-things-considered ought-judgments. But there is

---

[9] John Stuart Mill, *On Liberty*, ed. David Bromwich and George Kateb (New Haven: Yale University Press, 2003), pp. 86–120.

[10] Ibid., p. 113.

[11] Mill says, "[O]n every subject on which difference of opinion is possible, the truth depends on a balance to be struck between two sets of conflicting reasons." And in discussing the connection between knowing the truth and knowing how to refute opposing arguments, he characterizes the reasons that can be brought forward in argument as parts of the truth. Someone who has not encountered opposing arguments "will never really possess himself that portion of the truth that meets and removes the difficulty." Ibid., pp. 104–105 (both quotes). It is also relevant that Mill seems to envisage the possibility, in the future, of a party that is equally of order and progress, able to distinguish "what is fit to be preserved from what ought to be swept away."

a sense in which these can be understood as parts of a larger truth. The whole truth about how political cooperation ought to be organized can be equated with the set of ought-judgments that the different members, reasoning competently with the available concepts, would make. The whole truth can be equated with the zone of reasonable disagreement. A number of Mill's observations in this section of *On Liberty* are placed in a new light when the parts of the truth he speaks of are understood as different, competently reasoned, all-things-considered ought-judgments. Three of these observations are particularly noteworthy.

First, Mill says, "[I]n the human mind, one-sidedness has always been the rule and many-sidedness the exception."[12] He evidently associates one-sidedness with possession of part of the truth. But if many-sidedness is, and will continue to be, the exception, he cannot be supposing that a polity's coming into possession of the whole truth is a matter of the elimination of one-sidedness. One-sidedness must remain the norm throughout the process of free political discussion that Mill envisages. If the different parts of the truth are understood as different reasonable all-things-considered ought-judgments, one-sidedness is readily explained. As has been noted, the parties to a reasonable disagreement will not usually recognize the opposing positions as reasonable. In this sense, they will be one-sided.

In saying that many-sidedness is the exception, Mill implies that it is sometimes found. This will be the case, on the interpretation I am now suggesting, if some people are aware that a zone of reasonable disagreement is associated with many political issues. This awareness might be a result of reflection on the fact that certain patterns of disagreement seem to reappear in different contexts and to resist resolution by shared deliberation. Mill clearly regards many-sidedness as desirable. One reason that many-sidedness, as I have interpreted it, is desirable is that a many-sided person will have an understanding of the human condition that a one-sided person lacks. An additional point in favor of many-sidedness is that people who are prepared to acknowledge that most political controversies contain a core of reasonable disagreement will be more receptive to the use of a fair decision-making procedure, such as voting, to determine how political cooperation is to be organized.

The second point Mill makes is that although different parties possess different parts of the truth, there will normally be a generally held view of a given issue, the "received doctrine." He also says that views become

---

[12] Ibid., p. 112.

generally held because they are better adapted to the needs of the time. If a view's being better adapted to the needs of the time is to be taken seriously, we cannot treat the replacement of one generally held view by another as a mere contingent happening, a change prompted by the de facto realignment of social forces. There must be some sense in which the new view is one that ought to be adopted. But if, as Mill says, it remains part of the truth, requiring supplementation with other parts, neither can its being better adapted to the needs of the time be understood as its being uniquely suited to the prevailing conditions.

The phenomenon of dominance described in the previous section provides a plausible interpretation of these observations. As the social environment is transformed, most of the reasonable views held within a polity will adapt their central concepts to the new conditions. Those that do not will lose their status as reasonable and eventually die out. Thus all the views that survive can be said to be better adapted to the needs of the time than the earlier views. But Mill also seems to think that there is a sense in which one view can claim to be more fully adapted to the needs of the time than the others, and to have become the received doctrine as a result. We can explain this if we suppose that the received doctrine has achieved this status through the operation of a conceptual-cum-social process of the sort I have described. The received view is better adapted to the needs of the time because the conceptual-cum-social process that brought it to dominance is partly responsible for the social environment it confronts.

Finally, Mill says, "Truth, in the great practical concerns of life, is so much a matter of the reconciling and combining of opposites, that very few have minds sufficiently capacious and impartial to make the adjustments with an approach to correctness, and it has to be made by the rough process of a struggle between combatants fighting under hostile banners."[13] This observation, too, can be related to the discussion in the previous section. The process by which a particular view emerges as dominant is in part experimental. Those holding the view find that, in the evolving social situation, they are able to get more "traction." They are able to make happen more of what they think ought to happen. Change will thus radiate outward, in the way I have described, from a view that is gaining greater traction. But as I have noted, there will be an element of force, which is not the force of the better argument, in the process by which a view becomes dominant. To the extent that the application of this force meets resistance, we can speak of a struggle.

---

[13] Ibid., p. 114.

The struggle will be morally constrained. The parties, as reasonable, will be acting on competently reasoned judgments employing the available moral concepts. Further, to the extent that there are moral requirements that all properly functioning members of a given polity, or all humans generally, will accept, the struggle, as a struggle among properly functioning humans, will take place within a moral framework that is shared by the parties. Given the existence of reasonable disagreement, the reconciliation that Mill speaks of cannot be understood as the adoption of the same view by all the parties. But a kind of equilibrium can emerge if the forms taken by the newly dominant view and the views dissenting from it are, for the time being, stable. The actions performed by the adherents of each view prompt no further changes in the others.

As I have said, I make no claim that Mill understood the different parts of the truth of which he speaks as different competently reasoned views of the whole truth. But the interpretation I have offered is compatible with the fact that Mill takes himself to be presenting a reason why freedom of political speech is important. The conceptual-cum-social process that I have described will be more likely to unfold in a way that manifests the proper functioning of the capacities engaged if the members of a polity enjoy freedom of political speech.

THE EVOLUTION OF MORAL NORMATIVITY

We have seen how the zone of reasonable disagreement can evolve and how, as it evolves, new dominant views can replace old dominant views. Given moral nominalism, what we have here is not just the evolution of moral thinking. All meta-ethical theories make a place for the evolution of moral thinking, but realist theories, or those that are optimistic, regard the evolution of moral thinking as bringing into better focus a set of timeless and universal moral facts. For moral nominalism, by contrast, the evolutionary process takes the form of the making and remaking of moral worlds. Thus moral normativity itself – moral rightness and wrongness – evolves.

Further, it cannot be supposed that the evolutionary process will produce some final form of moral normativity. The process involves the emergence of new conceptual resources capable of structuring the human disposition to make and seek concessions in cooperative contexts, and as was explained in the second section, the proper functioning of this motivational disposition constrains the judgments of political morality that a properly functioning human can make. But the concepts that provide the structuring change in tandem with changing social circumstances, and it is

always possible for novel forms of behavior that can be regarded as permissible by some competent reasoners to arise and take root. It should also be mentioned that completely fortuitous events like plagues can produce social change that may prompt conceptual change. So there is no reason to suppose that the evolution of moral normativity will ever cease.

It is nevertheless compatible with moral nominalism to posit the existence of a core set of moral judgments that possess universal validity. Some ways of giving form to the human disposition to make and seek concessions in cooperative contexts will be so obviously in accord with the proper functioning of this disposition that all polities, societies, or cultures can be expected to develop conceptual resources suitable for articulating, in some way, the corresponding requirements. Prohibitions on murder provide an example. A society that lacks normative concepts capturing the impermissibility of killing its members will have fallen into collective malfunction.

In general, the evolution of moral normativity proceeds at a faster pace in the political domain than in the personal domain. Political morality is the morality of authority and property. A person's property encompasses all the claims he or she is licensed to make against the other members of the polity or against the polity as a whole.[14] Political morality, so understood, has witnessed great changes in the course of human history. The normative and evaluative concepts that make possible different ways of thinking about the concessions that are appropriate in political contexts have undergone significant alteration. These include concepts that can be used to formulate claims, and also concepts that identify morally important social values relevant to the public good. The significance of the fact that the members of different polities, or the same polity at different times, can in this way live in different moral worlds is explored in the next two chapters. But moral nominalism can still provide for some specifically political judgments that no one can reasonably reject. Indeed, it is plausible to regard some requirements of political morality as a priori, in the sense that they are directly implied by the proper functioning of the capacities engaged, independently of the contingencies of conceptual evolution.

The most obvious example concerns the institution of chattel slavery. This institution deprives certain participants in the overall system of social cooperation of the ability to make any claims at all, either against other

---

[14] For Locke, property, the protection of which is the end of government, is everything a person has a right to. See John Locke, *The Second Treatise of Government*, ed. C. B. MacPherson (Indianapolis: Hackett, 1980), section 87.

members of the polity or against the polity as a whole.[15] Slavery involves cooperation within a segment of the population to deny to other members of the population recognition as sources of claims. It involves cooperation to deny certain members of the population recognition as moral persons.[16] Historically, enslaved peoples have been outsiders, racially, ethnically, or religiously, and held far from home.[17] Making these people the property of established members of a polity is a way of integrating them into the existing cooperative enterprise while denying them recognition as cooperators. Nevertheless, they are clearly participants in the overall system of cooperation that is in effect in that polity. The institution of chattel slavery is thus necessarily unfair in the narrow sense. A system of political cooperation that does not allow certain of the people participating in it to make any claims at all cannot be fair in the narrow sense. Further, no valid morally important social value can support a claim that chattel slavery nevertheless serves the public good, and is thus fair in the broad sense. In the first place, it is hard to imagine that any enhanced realization of other moral values could justify such a radical sacrifice of narrow fairness. But in addition, whatever its components, the public good must be understood as the good of the entire polity, which is to say, the good of all the people participating in the overall system of cooperation in place in the polity. So nothing that involves excluding from the community of moral persons some participants in the overall system of political cooperation can serve the public good.[18]

These points have the consequence that chattel slavery would be morally wrong even in a polity that lacked concepts suitable for articulating this judgment. They also have the consequence that chattel slavery would be morally wrong in a polity that possessed a conceptual apparatus supporting slavery. I earlier described how the operation of the conceptual-cum-social

---

[15] To be more precise, chattel slavery deprives the enslaved people of the ability to make any claims on their own behalf. The property rights of their owners afford some moral protection in dealings with other people.

[16] In *Slavery and Social Death: A Comparative Study* (Cambridge, MA: Harvard University Press, 1982), Orlando Patterson elaborates on the "secular excommunication" of the slave by employing the notion of natal alienation. To be a slave was to be so deprived of socially recognized ties to other persons that one did not even have recognized ties to ancestors and descendants. Patterson explains the inheritability of slave status in these terms (pp. 9–10). He also suggests that the key fact about the connection between slavery and property was not that the slave was property but that the slave could not own property (p. 28). A slave could not possess the claims against others associated with ownership.

[17] For discussion of these points, see David Turley, *Slavery* (Oxford: Blackwell, 2000), ch. 2.

[18] Another requirement of political morality that may be a priori in the sense I have proposed is noted by Bernard Williams in *Truth and Truthfulness* (Princeton: Princeton University Press, 2002), ch. 9. Williams argues that unmediated use of coercion to establish social control – that is, coercion unmediated by a sound justification – is universally an injustice. I say more about this in the following chapters.

process can make acceptance of the existing basic structure the dominant view in a polity. But a view can be dominant, in the sense in which I am employing the term, only if it is reasonable, only if the concepts expressing it are capable, in the existing social environment, of giving form to the disposition to make and seek concessions that will be possessed by all properly functioning humans. Because chattel slavery is morally wrong a priori, its acceptance cannot constitute what I call a dominant view even if it plays a decisive role in the organization of political cooperation. And competent reasoners will make no use of the conceptual apparatus of slavery in their thinking about how political cooperation ought to be organized.[19]

It is interesting in this connection to speculate about the conceptual changes that led to the general acknowledgment of the wrongness of slavery. The religious idea that all people are equal in the sight of God is sometimes mentioned in this connection, but it was familiar long before the wrongness of slavery came to be generally acknowledged. The most that can be said is that more people began to see the incompatibility of this idea with the institution of slavery. It may be that an important role was played by specifically political changes, in particular the emergence of the state, understood as a form of political association involving all the residents of a single, relatively large, territory. This change seems to have made it easier to see political life as a cooperative venture involving everyone living in a given territory, as is shown by the development at approximately the same time of contractarian political theories. Of course, slavery survived into the modern world. But it can take time for the implications of political ideas to be fully appreciated. Another contributing factor may have been the devising of concepts identifying morally important social values. As more such values are acknowledged, people will become increasingly inclined to think in terms of the public good, in contrast to the good of their class or group. Finally, the emergence to dominance of the concept of autonomy in the political sense, the concept of a right to self-direction, may have played a role. I say a little more about this last possibility in chapter 6.

To the extent that consequentialist considerations such as morally important social values influence political decisions, questions of empirical fact will be germane to the organization of political cooperation. This brings us to another way that moral evolution can involve the elimination of

---

[19] The general acceptance of slavery in a polity does not necessarily entail that most of its members are incompetent moral reasoners. Many members of slave societies may have accepted slavery in the sense of regarding it as too firmly entrenched to be dismantled, while still recognizing that it was fundamentally unfair.

unreasonableness. Factual thinking that is not competently responsive to the available evidence can be replaced by thinking that is. It is plausible that the elimination of erroneous factual thinking has contributed to the wide acceptance in modern moral life of the value of non-discrimination, but the trend has broader significance. Thus one historian has suggested that the declining role of prophesy in political decision making contributed importantly to the transition to modernity.[20]

Two further points should be mentioned here. First, the conceptual-cum-social process described earlier is not merely the engine of the evolution of the zone of reasonable disagreement. It can also bring about a reduction of unreasonableness. Reasonable actions that prompt unreasonable responses can play a role in securing the general recognition of the unreasonableness of certain practices or institutions, and the concomitant rejection of the concepts that support these practices or institutions. Second, the growth of media of communication, by creating greater awareness of political debate and of the progress of the conceptual-cum-social process generally, may reduce unreasonableness. It may thus help to ensure that most political opinion falls within the zone of reasonable disagreement, and that the parts that still lie outside the zone do not lie as far outside as would otherwise be the case.

Although reasonable disagreement will always be with us, then, there is some basis for optimism that the straightforwardly unreasonable will, over time, come to play a reduced role in political life. In this way, at least, moral nominalism can make a place for moral progress. Still, it must be acknowledged that the unreasonable can influence the competent construction of moral worlds out of moral worlds. I have described a mechanism of conceptual-cum-social change. Competent reasoners operating with particular normative and evaluative terms confront situations that cannot be handled by routine, linear extrapolation of their judgmental histories. The employment of these terms in the new environment thus requires the exercise of judgment, and this has the effect of altering the available conceptual resources. The content of old concepts undergoes change, and new concepts may be introduced. Actions guided by the practical judgments that result then give rise to further conceptual change. But we need to be clearer about what initiates the process.

In the scenario described earlier, it is initiated by the actions of people whose conceptual and motivational capacities are functioning properly. They hold views about how political cooperation ought to be organized

---

[20] Theodore K. Rabb, *The Last Days of the Renaissance and the March to Modernity* (New York: Basic Books, 2006), ch. 6.

that are marginal, but still reasonable in the existing context. In acting on these views, they alter the social environment that other people confront. I offered as examples the general acceptance of cohabitation without marriage and the emergence to dominance of democratic capitalism. Changes in the social environment can also, however, be created by unreasonable actions, actions taken on the basis of incompetently reasoned judgments concerning how political cooperation ought to be organized, or actions that are not guided by such thinking at all. As was mentioned in the earlier discussion of Mill's observation about the social feelings of mankind, judgments that are not capable of giving form to the disposition to participate in a process of reciprocal concession with others who are similarly disposed will not be able to survive shared deliberation conducted in good faith. But the concepts employed can nevertheless find a place in the thinking of particular groups within a population, and the resulting actions can have significant social effects. These in turn can force competent reasoners to alter the concepts they are working with, and thus the zone of reasonable disagreement. Since moral normativity at a given place and time can be equated with the zone of reasonable disagreement there and then, it follows that unreasonable actions can affect the evolution of moral normativity.

An example may make this point clearer. Actual historical change typically involves change in forms of cooperation, but this has sometimes been brought about by subgroups cooperating to impose particular social arrangements on other subgroups. Thus according to Robert Brenner, the social history of medieval and early modern Europe passed through a number of stages corresponding to forms of cooperation among landowners that were designed to maintain the extraction of a surplus from the serfs.[21] Unlike chattel slavery, serfdom gave the serfs, in theory at least, some claims they could make on their own behalf. On the view I am proposing, then, competent reasoners employing the available moral concepts may have been able to endorse a basic structure that provided for serfdom in some form.[22]

---

[21] Robert Brenner, "The Rises and Declines of Serfdom in Medieval and Early Modern Europe," in M. L. Bush, ed., *Serfdom and Slavery: Studies in Legal Bondage* (London: Longman, 1996), pp. 247–276.

[22] If we consider how serfdom in medieval Europe would have looked to competent contemporary reasoners employing the available moral concepts, one possibility is that the lowest position deemed morally acceptable – deemed compatible with recognition as a cooperating member of society – would have been that of a tenurial serf. A tenurial serf held unfree land (land to which obligations were attached) but was not unfree in his person. For the distinction between tenurial and personal serfdom, see Michael Bush, "Serfdom in Medieval and Modern Europe: A Comparison" (*Serfdom and Slavery*, pp. 199–224). Personal serfdom had many of the characteristics of slavery. In "On Servile Status in the Early Middle Ages" (*Serfdom and Slavery*, pp. 225–246), Wendy Davies discusses various respects in which it is unclear whether serfs in the early medieval period (400–1100) were slaves or not.

But the particular landowner actions described by Brenner could nevertheless have been unreasonable, locally, in the sense I have proposed. If they were, and the resulting social changes provided an occasion for competent reasoners to transform the normative and evaluative concepts they were employing, the evolution of moral normativity in those localities would have passed through a corresponding sequence of stages.

I say more about the history of moral normativity in chapter 6. For present purposes, the important point is that the evolution of moral normativity is embedded in the wider historical process. Much of what has actually happened in political history is unreasonable in our sense. It consists of actions, by individuals or groups, which could not have been endorsed at the time they were performed by reasonable people operating with the available moral concepts. But these actions may nevertheless have led reasonable people to alter the concepts they employed, with the result that moral normativity itself was altered.

According to moral nominalism, the zone of reasonable disagreement is defined counterfactually as the set of judgments that would be made within a particular polity, given the available concepts, if the members were reasoning competently within the framework of their experience about how to organize political cooperation.[23] Because the zone of reasonable disagreement evolves, moral normativity has a history. Views that are straightforwardly wrong now, views that fall outside the zone of reasonable disagreement, may not have been straightforwardly wrong in the past. Competent reasoners operating with the concepts available in the past might have been able to hold those views, or their conceptual ancestors. It does not follow that all the practices and institutions of the past were morally acceptable in the historical context. It may not have been possible for competent reasoners living in the polities of the past, and operating with the available concepts, to endorse certain of the practices and institutions that were actually in place in those polities. But the resulting wrongness consisted in deviation from the requirements of morality as they were then, not as they are now.

---

[23] Characterized in this way, the zone of reasonable disagreement encompasses any moral judgments that all competent reasoners will make, judgments condemning murder or slavery, for example. It thus becomes the zone of the reasonable, which is a zone of disagreement because reasonable judgments can sometimes disagree.

CHAPTER 5

Localism

According to moral nominalism, judgments of political morality employ socially available moral concepts to give a conceptually articulated structure to a motivational disposition that will be possessed by all properly functioning humans, the disposition to make and seek concessions in the context of a cooperative endeavor when others are similarly disposed. As I have formulated moral nominalism, the normativity of proper functioning is not construed nominalistically. It is given a realist interpretation. Whether human mental capacities are functioning properly is a matter of objective normative fact. Proper functioning is thus the same in all human communities. But the normative and evaluative concepts that are available to people making judgments of political morality will differ from polity to polity. Different kinds of claims will be acknowledged, and different ways of organizing political cooperation will be found acceptable by reasonable people.

These differences have a historical explanation. They are the result of the past operation of conceptual-cum-social processes of the sort described in the previous chapter. Although the world is increasingly interconnected, this was less true in the past. There were sharper local differences in the normative and evaluative concepts employed in thinking about how to organize political cooperation, and these differences have left traces in the sets of concepts available now in different polities. In addition, the histories of different polities have been marked by different exogenous changes in the social environment of the sort that can prompt conceptual transformation, for example, changes produced by infectious diseases or by conquest. As was noted in the previous chapter, the history of moral normativity forms a part of the overall historical process.

It would nevertheless be misleading to regard moral nominalism as a species of moral relativism. Relativism, as it is usually understood, is the view that what is morally right in one society or culture is different from what is morally right in another society or culture. The rightness at issue

here is to be understood as fundamental. Some absolutist views have the consequence that what is right in one society or culture can be wrong in another. An absolutist view might, for example, contain a principle, putatively timeless and universal, directing agents to follow local custom in some respects. For a properly relativist view, however, the fundamental principles of moral right and wrong are different for the members of different groups. Relativist views are often grounded in an anti-realist meta-ethical theory which holds that what an agent has moral reason to do depends on the attitudes he or she happens to have, with attitudes then being understood as determined socially. Thus it can be expected that all the residents of a particular community will have roughly the same attitudes, and acknowledge the same reasons for action.

Moral nominalism is not relativist in this sense. Its immediate consequence is that the zone of reasonable disagreement will be different in different polities. But there may nevertheless be quite a bit of overlap between the zones characteristic of two different polities. More important, although the concepts generally employed in political judgment will differ somewhat from polity to polity, the concepts in the possession of a particular human being are not determined by ineluctable social forces. Through travel, or various media of communication, a member of a polity may acquire concepts familiar in another polity but unfamiliar in her own.[1] If these concepts can be employed in competently reasoned judgments about how political cooperation in her polity morally ought to be organized, the judgments will constitute an addition to the zone of reasonable disagreement in that polity.

The view such an individual develops will doubtless be marginal in the sense explained earlier, at least initially. If there is a dominant reasonable view in her polity, it will usually draw on concepts that have been familiar for some time in that polity. But as we have seen, dominance does not determine what is right. Those holding marginal reasonable views may have no alternative but to act in accordance with the dominant view if they wish

---

[1] In *Meaning and the Moral Sciences* (London: Routledge & Kegan Paul, 1979) p. 56, Hilary Putnam speaks of "the universal intercommunicability of human cultures." Philip Pettit's concept of "commonability" is also relevant here. "Commonability is a property of rules [a person] follows: it requires them to be such that if there are others, and if they try to identify the rules she follows as rules they can follow themselves, then it is possible they will succeed: it is possible that they will knowledgeably identify the rules in that way" (*The Common Mind: An Essay on Psychology, Society, and Politics* (Oxford: Oxford University Press, 1993), p. 181). Pettit thinks that the commonability of rules shows that the capacity for thought is socially constituted. This is not my view. Commonability is rather a consequence of the fact that the proper functioning of human mental capacities, considered as a normative attribute, is the same everywhere.

to participate in the larger life of the polity. But they can still reasonably reject the existing way of organizing political cooperation (while those holding the dominant view can reasonably reject this rejection).

I propose, then, to speak not of relativism but of localism. Moral nominalism has the consequence that there will be local variation in the zones of reasonable disagreement marking different polities, and thus in political morality itself. Similarly, there will be local variation in the views that are dominant in different polities. Indeed, different views could be dominant in two polities even though the zone of reasonable disagreement is the same in both. But since any properly functioning human can, given the right conditions, acquire any normative or evaluative concept, the judgments of political morality that can correctly be made in a given polity are not socially or culturally circumscribed in the way that relativism typically supposes.[2]

The most interesting question about the localism that I have described concerns what it implies for the moral appraisal of polities other than one's own. The answer to this question has a number of different aspects. Before turning to them, however, it will be useful to explore in a bit more detail the contrast between relativism, as it is usually understood, and what I have called localism.

RELATIVISM AND LOCALISM

The most familiar contemporary version of relativism, in philosophical circles at least, is that proposed by Gilbert Harman.[3] A key feature of this view is a distinction between two kinds of moral ought-judgments. Harman understands ought-judgments as reporting the existence of sufficient reason for accepting some statement or directive. One kind of ought-judgment uses the "ought" of evaluation, as in "There ought to be less poverty in the world." Here the language of ought is employed to make a value judgment, to say that it would be a good thing morally if there were less poverty in the world. The reasons alluded to are reasons for approving a reduction in poverty.

---

[2] In *Fieldwork in Familiar Places* (Cambridge, MA: Harvard University Press, 1997), ch. 1, Michelle Moody-Adams describes a view that she calls "descriptive cultural relativism." Among its problematic features, she says, are the claims "that cultures are internally integrated wholes, that cultures are fundamentally self-contained and isolable sets of practices and beliefs, and that cultural influence on belief and action must be understood deterministically" (p. 21).

[3] Gilbert Harman, "Moral Relativism Defended," *The Philosophical Review* 84 (1975), pp. 3–33.

The second kind of moral ought-judgment involves what Harman calls the "inner ought." An inner ought-judgment is a particular kind of judgment that an agent ought to do something. It has two features. It implies, (1) that the agent has sufficient reason to do that thing, and (2) that the speaker endorses these reasons. Harman regards reasons for action as provided by motivational attitudes. His developed view is that these attitudes are intentions to keep an agreement provided that others do so as well. An intention is understood as a disposition to behave in a certain way, and the agreement in question is simply a de facto coincidence of such dispositions (the dispositions are "in agreement"). What are usually called moral conventions can be understood as agreements of this sort.

Because inner ought-judgments presuppose agreement in attitude between the speaker and the agent, the "ought" of evaluation and the inner "ought" can part company. Cases can arise in which, although we can use the "ought" of evaluation to say that a certain action ought to be performed (meaning that we have good reason, given our attitudes, to approve its performance), we nevertheless cannot use the inner "ought" to say that the agent in question ought to perform this action (where the implication is that he has sufficient reason to perform it).

For example, consider the judgment, "The Saudis ought to allow freedom of religion." In making this judgment, we might be employing the "ought" of evaluation to report the existence of reasons for approving this result. On Harman's view, these reasons would be provided by our Western motivational attitudes. But we cannot appropriately use the sentence to express an inner ought-judgment to the effect that the Saudis – that is, the men comprising the Saudi ruling elite – have sufficient reason to allow freedom of religion. The requisite agreement in attitude does not exist. We can condemn, from our perspective, the way political cooperation is organized in Saudi Arabia, but we cannot claim that what the rulers are doing is wrong, where this means that it is wrong of them to do it. A judgment of that sort is in order only when we can suppose that the agents of whom we are speaking share our attitudes and these attitudes give them sufficient reason to perform the specified action.

It is not necessary for our purposes to consider how Harman defends his moral relativism. Our goal is simply to compare the localism associated with moral nominalism with traditional relativism. It will be useful, however, to note one complication that is mentioned by Harman.[4] The set of attitudes shared by the members of a social group may be incoherent in certain

---

[4] Ibid., pp. 17–18.

respects. Some of the attitudes may conflict with others. Harman's example is a society where slavery is an established institution, accepted by everyone, including the slaves. The members of such a society may nevertheless share an attitude to the effect that autonomy is to be respected. If the exposure of this incoherence would transform the existing attitudes in the direction of an unambiguous rejection of slavery, we can say that slavery is impermissible in that society – that it is wrong of the people there to hold slaves – even though the institution of slavery is solidly established.

The agreement in attitude that, on Harman's view, is presupposed when we make an inner ought-judgment need not, then, be an agreement in actual attitudes. It is enough that there would be an agreement in attitude within the society in question, and between the members of the society and outsiders undertaking the moral appraisal of it, if the relevant attitudes were made coherent. Still, what it is right or wrong to do in a given society is ultimately determined by the attitudes found there, or to be more precise, by those that figure in the agreements in intention that Harman posits.

How does the localism associated with moral nominalism differ from Harman's view? In the first place, Harman's view has the consequence that, given the attitudes operative in a group, there is a single correct answer to the question of what the members of that group have sufficient moral reason to do. They have sufficient reason to do what they would be motivated to do if their shared attitudes were made coherent. But localism provides for reasonable disagreement about what constitutes the morally appropriate way of organizing political cooperation. In place of shared attitudes, localism speaks of a set of socially available normative and evaluative concepts. But the employment of these concepts in a new situation is affected by an individual's personal history of judgment. As a result, different members of a polity may interpret the concepts differently or give the associated reasons different weights when they conflict.

A second point concerns the possibility of a contrast between what morality requires and established social convention. As was noted earlier, a social convention can be understood as a kind of agreement in motivational attitude found within a group. The existence of such a convention has the consequence that the members of the group perform actions of the same type in circumstances of the same type. Part of what many people find objectionable about moral relativism is that it seems to entail that whatever behavior is conventional in a particular group will be morally acceptable, or even required, in that group. But, we usually think, moral reasoning, properly understood, should provide a critical perspective on existing conventions.

As we have seen, Harman's relativism is able to accommodate some critical perspective on the conventions actually in place in a given society. But the standard of moral rightness is still provided, ultimately, by social conventions. His view is just that the relevant conventions are not the existing social conventions in the form they actually take, but the existing conventions in the form they would take after they were subjected to a process of mutual adjustment designed to fashion them into a coherent whole. As a result, there is no possibility of fundamental criticism of the entire body of existing social conventions.

Moral nominalism provides for greater critical leverage on existing arrangements. The zone of reasonable disagreement is understood counter-factually. It is constituted by the set of judgments about how various aspects of political cooperation ought to be organized that the members of a polity would make if they were reasoning competently with the socially available concepts. Competent reasoning with normative and evaluative concepts has a motivational aspect. Whether a new situation catches the extrapolative dispositions associated with a particular concept depends, in part, on the motivation experienced in that situation. In the political case, this motiva-tion is provided by the disposition to participate in a process of mutual concession when others are similarly disposed. This disposition will be possessed by all properly functioning humans, and it underlies the sense of fairness. The operative concepts provide ways of packaging this disposi-tion as particular judgments of political morality, judgments concerning what would constitute a fair way of organizing some aspect of political cooperation. The concepts, and thus the resulting sense of fairness, can differ from polity to polity. But the motivational disposition constrains the judgments that can be made. Consequently, these judgments may fail to support the social conventions that are actually in place. If, for example, the conventions are shaped by the coercive actions of a subgroup pursuing its own interests, the overall pattern of concessions specified by the conven-tions will probably not find support in the motivational dispositions of a properly functioning cooperator.

We must bear in mind here the observations of the previous chapter. As we saw there, the conceptual-cum-social process posited by moral nominal-ism reciprocally alters both the set of available concepts and the general social situation. Thus it will usually be possible for competent reasoners employing the available concepts to make judgments endorsing the basic structure of social cooperation found in their polity. But this need not always be the case. The conceptual-cum-social process envisaged by moral nominalism presupposes the proper functioning of both of the capacities

engaged, the linguistic and the motivational. So where existing social arrangements cannot be regarded as giving expression to the disposition to participate in a process of mutual concession that will be experienced by properly functioning cooperators, the widespread acceptance of these arrangements will not testify to their reasonableness.

Our example in the previous chapter concerned the acceptance of slavery. But there may be other social arrangements that cannot be fitted to the dispositions of cooperatively disposed people as these are informed by the available concepts (that is, by those of the available concepts that are capable of giving form to this motivational matter). Moral nominalism can, then, make a place for criticism of existing conventions that goes beyond the observation that they form an incoherent set. It should also be mentioned that even when it is possible for properly functioning cooperators to accept the existing basic structure, the available concepts may allow competently reasoned judgments that reject this structure. These judgments will typically be marginal, but they will still fall within the zone of reasonable disagreement. The localism implied by moral nominalism can thus provide for radical rejection of the status quo.

Finally, relativism and localism bring with them different ways of understanding the evolution of political morality, the transition from one way of understanding moral rightness in the political sphere to another. Harman's theory allows for the possibility of moral change prompted by environmental change. A changing environment could cause changes in the operative attitudes, thus changing the form that the agreements in intention found within a polity would take if the relevant attitudes were made coherent. But the normative notion of coherence itself has nothing to say about the appropriateness or inappropriateness of the initial changes in attitude created by changes in the environment, and no other normative notion takes up the slack. How attitudes change when the environment does is simply a matter of brute causal fact.

For moral nominalism, by contrast, the transitions involved in the evolution of political morality are under full normative guidance. In a properly functioning human, moral change results from an exercise of judgment that engages both the human linguistic capacity and the human cooperative capacity. The disposition to make and seek concessions that will be possessed by all properly functioning humans is given new conceptualized form as new cases arise that resist routine extrapolation from previous practice. And since the devising of new conceptual forms is a manifestation of the proper functioning of the human linguistic capacity, it has a normative dimension. As was described in the previous chapter, social change may

introduce into this process an element of force that is not the force of the better argument. But in properly functioning humans, the response to this force will be normatively guided.[5]

BORDERS AND MIGRATION

We can now turn to the moral appraisal of other polities. The first case to consider is that in which the people doing the appraising are themselves involved in a cooperative endeavor with the members of the polity being appraised. This case is straightforwardly accommodated within moral nominalism. According to moral nominalism, judgments of political morality use socially available concepts to give conceptually articulated structure to cooperative motivation. But cooperative motivation is most readily elicited when an opportunity to participate in a cooperative endeavor actually presents itself.

Actual cooperation that brings with it the moral appraisal of another polity takes two principal forms. One is cooperation in border areas, where people who are members of different polities must establish a commonly accepted framework of interaction. The other is cooperation within a territory where the long-time residents have been joined by newcomers who have brought with them expectations concerning the organization of political cooperation that were formed in their home countries. In the contemporary world, situations of this latter sort arise in connection with immigration to an existing polity.

In cases of both kinds, we confront a new dimension of reasonable disagreement. The characterization of reasonable disagreement in chapter 3 envisaged judgments that draw on a common set of normative and evaluative concepts. The judgments disagree because the members of the polity, proceeding within different judgmental histories, interpret these concepts differently or attach different weights to the reasons marked by the concepts. By contrast, the disagreements that characterize political

---

[5] In *Fear of Knowledge: Against Relativism and Constructivism* (Oxford: Clarendon Press, 2006), ch. 3, Paul Boghossian attributes to Nelson Goodman a view he calls "cookie-cutter constructivism." According to this view, concepts are tools for carving up some sort of basic stuff. The moral nominalism I have proposed is similar. Facts of political morality are constructed by the imposition of conceptualized form on the motivational matter provided by the disposition, which will be experienced by all properly functioning humans, to make or seek concessions in cooperative contexts when others are similarly disposed. Boghossian argues (p. 47) that if constructivist views are to avoid inconsistency, they must be relativistic. I believe that, by virtue of the localism it implies, moral nominalism satisfies this requirement, although as I have explained, it takes a realist view of the normativity of proper functioning.

cooperation in border areas, or following immigration, often arise from the fact that the parties are drawing on different sets of normative and evaluative concepts. As we saw in chapter 3, even when all parties are taking their concepts from a single set, there can be disagreements grounded in the fact that some decline to employ certain of these concepts. I mentioned the example of Oscar Wilde, who said that "blasphemous" was not one of his words. But within a single political tradition this phenomenon plays a relatively small role. It looms larger when the parties to a disagreement are drawing their concepts from different political traditions.

In this case, the parties, even if cooperatively disposed, will have different senses of fairness, both narrow and broad. They will judge appropriate different patterns of concession. Since all groups seeking to establish political cooperation face similar problems, it is to be expected that the concepts of political morality found in different polities will be similar in some respects. But there will also be differences, which will be more marked the more the histories of the polities in question differ. We need, then, to consider in greater detail how disagreement among people whose judgments of political morality draw on different sets of concepts can count as reasonable.

Disagreement is reasonable only if the conflicting judgments are competently reasoned. But this requirement has an aspect that we have not previously needed to mention. Where disagreement is reasonable, each party rejects the positions taken by the other parties. But the rejection of an opposing view can be reasonable – can manifest competent reasoning – only if that view is understood. Further, since we are speaking of the rejection of a view, it must be possible to understand a view without accepting it. These requirements can be met if the parties to the disagreement have an accurate appreciation of how political cooperation would be structured if the different views in play were implemented.

Achieving this sort of understanding is relatively unproblematic when the opposing positions are based on different interpretations of shared concepts, or the assignment of different weights to reasons marked by shared concepts. But when the parties to a political disagreement draw their normative and evaluative concepts from different political traditions, mutual understanding presupposes an effort by the parties to familiarize themselves, to some extent, at least, with the alien concepts. So we must add a requirement to this effect to the counterfactual specification of the zone of reasonable disagreement. It consists of the judgments that would be made if the parties were reasoning competently. But competent reasoning about how to organize political cooperation presupposes an understanding of how it

would be organized if the proposals of the other participants were put into effect, and this requires some grasp of the concepts in which these proposals are formulated – enough to appreciate, in broad outline at least, what would be involved in organizing cooperation in the way proposed. For example, if the non-Muslim members of a Western polity are reasonably to reject, or accept, a proposal to allow certain aspects of the cooperation that takes place in the polity to be governed by *Sharia* law, they must understand in broad outline what would be involved.

The parties to the kinds of disagreements we are now considering will, then, be adding new concepts to the concepts they initially possess. It is likely, however, that the new concepts will undergo some transformation in the process. The extrapolative dispositions associated with the new concepts will have to be integrated with the dispositions associated with the concepts a given individual already possesses. This will typically alter somewhat the content of the new concepts, as they are employed by those who have effected the integration. But this is to be expected when properly function-ing humans, proceeding within different political traditions, confront one another in cooperative contexts. Giving one's own twist to concepts asso-ciated with a different tradition of political cooperation is an unavoidable aspect of competent reasoning in these circumstances. The resulting dis-agreements are thus reasonable, although like all reasonable disagreements, they will be marked by the fact that the parties usually do not regard the positions they reject as competently reasoned.

Now let us turn to some particular cases of this general phenomenon. The simplest is immigration, legal or illegal, to a polity where political cooperation is organized in a way the immigrants judge to be inappropriate, in whole or in part. The example just given will serve here as well. The newcomers might judge political cooperation in the polity where they now reside to be inappropriately organized because certain interactions are not governed by *Sharia* law. In this case, established decision-making proce-dures will be available to resolve reasonable disagreement, at least if the immigrants regard the procedures as legitimate. But the phenomenon of dominance may still play a role. The immigrants may confront a dominant view, enacted into law, to which they must conform if they want to participate in the larger life of the polity. Indeed, even if no view is dominant within the population of long-time residents, the different views held by the long-time residents may share certain features that are alien to the political traditions of the newcomers, with the result that the immigrants confront what is, from their perspective, a dominant view. This could be the case even if the long-time residents have acquired the requisite

familiarity with the concepts of the newcomers. They may nevertheless decline to employ these concepts in judgments of political morality, or use the associated words in ways the newcomers regard as incorrect.

Since a dominant view is not usually the only reasonable view of a given issue that can be taken within a polity, competently reasoning newcomers may still be able to reject the way political cooperation is organized. On the assumptions we are making, they will likewise have become familiar with the concepts of the long-time residents, but, again, they may decline to employ these concepts or interpret them in ways the long-time residents regard as incorrect. Still, as we saw in chapter 4, confrontation with actions that are regarded as morally wrong can, over time, have the effect of forcing competent reasoners, with a force that is not the force of the better argument, to make accommodating changes in their conceptual materials. Where there has been immigration, the immigrants are likely to be forced to make more such changes than the long-time residents, at least if the immigrant population is smaller than the population of long-time residents. Simply by virtue of the difference in numbers, the immigrants will confront more situations that force conceptual change. Aware of this fact, newcomers may try to avoid contact with the larger society so as to maintain their commitment to their traditional way of life. But if reasonable people will be disposed to participate in a cooperative effort to establish a common framework of interaction in the place where they live, it can be argued that withdrawal is an unreasonable course of action. Of course, if the influx of immigrants is large enough, the view that long-time residents hold of the appropriate way of organizing political cooperation may cease to be dominant.

Similar points can be made about the case where the newcomers do not regard as reasonable the established procedures for resolving political disagreement, voting by the method of majority rule, for example. They may still have to work through these procedures if they want to have some influence on the way political cooperation is organized, and this, too, could have the effect of changing their minds about what is reasonable. I have been focusing on reasonable disagreement between long-time residents and newcomers, but, of course, the question of how political cooperation should be organized will admit of reasonable disagreement within each group as well. My goal in the foregoing discussion has simply been to highlight some aspects of reasonable disagreement that are peculiar to political cooperation between long-time residents and newcomers.

Reasonable disagreement of the sort we are now considering becomes more pronounced when we move from immigration of the sort familiar in

the modern world to the migrations of peoples that characterized much of the past – for example, the migrations associated with the collapse of the Roman Empire. These migrations were often not to, or from, a state in the modern sense, a social form in which a single locus of decision-making exercises effective control over all the residents of a particular, relatively extensive territory. Political cooperation might rather have taken place within groups, such as tribes or clans, whose membership was defined by something other than residence in a particular territory.

In this latter case, the long-time residents would not have been able to assign the newcomers a position within the political structures already in existence in the territories experiencing the influx. But once the newcomers had arrived, the question of how to shape interaction among the different groups would have arisen, and, in properly functioning humans, would have prompted a process of mutual concession. This in turn would have led to the emergence of a zone of reasonable disagreement geared to the new situation. Formal political decision-making procedures capable of selecting a cooperative scheme for all the people involved might ultimately have been instituted. But even in the absence of such procedures, the conceptual-cum-social process would have reshaped the thinking of the members of the different groups.

The same general story can be told about political cooperation in border lands. Members of contiguous polities who live near a border will typically interact with their opposite numbers. If they are functioning properly, and as a result are cooperatively disposed, they will seek to establish some jointly understood way of structuring this interaction. Establishing a formal decision-making procedure might be tantamount to secession from the two original polities. But short of this, we could find a social process of shared deliberation, involving attempts at mutual understanding, and also conceptual change created by practical confrontation with people acting on different views. The result could be the emergence of a zone of reasonable disagreement different from that found in either of the "home" polities. Similarly, a dominant understanding of the appropriate way of structuring interaction that differs from the dominant view in either of the home polities might emerge in the border area.

We are ultimately concerned in this chapter with the implications of moral nominalism, and the localism associated with it, for the appraisal of the way political cooperation is organized in polities other than one's own. In the cases considered in this section, the appraisers have actual social contact with the polity being appraised. They are newcomers appraising the way political cooperation is organized in a polity to which they have moved,

they are long-time residents appraising a form of political organization that newcomers have, in a certain sense, brought with them, or they are residents of a border area appraising the way the people on the other side of the border organize political cooperation. In all these cases, appraisal can involve the rejection of alien ways of organizing political cooperation. But it would be inappropriate to give this phenomenon a relativistic construal, a construal according to which what is right for "them" is different from what is right for "us." Since the appraisers are attempting to live with the people they are appraising, what we should expect, if the relevant capacities are functioning properly, is the construction, and elaboration over time, of a new zone of reasonable disagreement. In general, moral nominalism substitutes reasonable disagreement for relativism.

APPRAISAL WITHOUT CONTACT

In an important discussion of relativism, Bernard Williams makes a distinction between a real confrontation with an alien social system and a notional confrontation.[6] The confrontation is real if the alien system is a real possibility for us; it is notional if the alien system is not a real possibility for us. One of Williams's examples of a social system that is not a real possibility for us is the system of medieval Japan. Williams suggests that judgments appraising an alien social system are in order only if the system is a real possibility for the people making the judgments. When this is not the case, we have what Williams calls the relativism of distance, a non-judgmental attitude toward an alien social system.

Williams's view is controversial, but we do not need to explore the controversy.[7] For our purposes here, the important point is that a distinction similar to the one that Williams makes has a place when we approach the moral appraisal of other polities within the framework of moral nominalism. According to moral nominalism, competently reasoned judgments of political morality are made by using socially available normative and evaluative concepts to give structure to the disposition, which will be possessed by all properly functioning humans, to make and seek concessions in a cooperative context. This means that we can make a moral judgment about an alien system of political cooperation only if we can somehow place ourselves in that system of political cooperation, thereby activating the

---

[6] Bernard Williams, *Ethics and the Limits of Philosophy* (Cambridge, MA: Harvard University Press, 1985), ch. 9.

[7] For critical discussion, see Moody-Adams, *Fieldwork in Familiar Places*, ch. 2.

cooperative dispositions that provide the "matter" to which socially available normative and evaluative concepts give form.

For Williams, asking whether an alien social system is a real possibility for us is asking whether we could transform our system into that system. This would entail replacing our concepts with those of the other system. But replacing our concepts is not something we can do in the way we can, for example, take off our clothes and then put on new ones. Replacement, when it comes to concepts, is a matter of transformation. In the previous section, I spoke of integrating unfamiliar concepts with one's own. Having done this, one might eventually remove the concepts one formerly employed. But since the content of the imported concepts will undergo a transformation in the course of the process of integration, the concepts that remain when we remove from the mix our original concepts (or their later versions) will not be exactly the same as those employed in the alien system from which the integrated concepts were imported. The question whether an alien system is a real possibility for us becomes, then, the question whether a process of transformation of the sort just described could take place. This will depend on whether, in properly functioning cooperators, the initial attempt to integrate the alien concepts, and the subsequent attempt to remove the original concepts, would succeed or fail.

For the purposes of appraising the system of political cooperation in another society, however, the important question is not whether we could adopt that system. We have to be able to place ourselves in the social system we are evaluating, but this is not to be understood as our bringing that system to where we are. It is rather a matter of our going to where it is. The question we now confront is how people who are not immigrants, but rather residents of some other polity, can in the relevant sense, one that involves the activation of human cooperative dispositions, go to the polity being appraised.

The first point to note is that some features of the system of political cooperation in place in another society may lend themselves to negative appraisal independently of the conceptual standpoint of the appraiser. As has been mentioned, it is plausible that the moral impermissibility of chattel slavery is a priori in the sense that the associated judgments do not depend on the availability of historically generated normative or evaluative concepts, such as the concept of autonomy. Chattel slavery involves, in essence, cooperation by a subset of the total population of a polity to deny social acknowledgment to any claims that might be made by the people held as slaves, despite the fact that they are clearly participants in the overall system of social cooperation in place in the polity. Thus chattel slavery is a morally

impermissible way of organizing political cooperation even if some of the normative and evaluative concepts available in the polity provide a basis for judgments supporting it.

There may be other a priori principles of political morality. Williams has suggested one. In his book *Truth and Truthfulness*, he says that the unmediated use of coercion to establish social control – that is, coercion unmediated by a sound justification – is universally an injustice.[8] He also argues that this principle may enable liberals to show the members of hierarchical societies that there is good reason for rejecting those arrangements. Liberals may be able to demonstrate to the members of hierarchical societies that the instruction they have received concerning what gives legitimacy to the existing arrangements is, in effect, a form of coercion. It should be noted, however, that even if a demonstration of this sort is successful, it does not follow that the people receiving it will have been given a reason to establish a liberal society. After they see that the instruction they have received is tantamount to coercion, they must still come to some conclusion about the form that political cooperation ought to be given, and this will depend on the judgments they can make with the normative and evaluative concepts that remain available to them. I say more about this later.

These observations lead to a more general point. All ways of understanding how political cooperation ought to be organized that are compatible with the proper functioning of human cooperative capacities will acknowledge claims that the members of the polity can make against one another and against the polity as a whole. In this sense, narrow fairness is a moral universal. But the fact that all properly functioning participants in a system of political cooperation will possess a sense of fairness does not mean that what is correctly judged fair will be the same in every polity. The cooperative dispositions that underlie the sense of fairness are structured by judgments employing socially available concepts, especially concepts that can be employed in making claims, and the sets of concepts available to the members of different polities will be different in certain respects. The claims that the members of a polity can make will thus vary somewhat from polity to polity. Similar points apply to broad fairness. The concepts available in different polities may identify different social states of affairs as morally important. Every way of understanding the appropriate organization of political cooperation will specify a pattern of concessions among the members of the polity. But where the concepts are different, the patterns will be different.

---

[8] Bernard Williams, *Truth and Truthfulness* (Princeton: Princeton University Press, 2002), ch. 9.

With the stage thus set, we can consider how, within the framework of moral nominalism and the localism it generates, the moral appraisal of a polity in which the appraiser is not living is to be understood. As an example, we might consider the appraisal by citizens of the United States of a polity that does not provide the sort of legal guarantees of freedom of religion found in the USA. As has been mentioned, such appraisal requires thinking one's way into a system of political cooperation that is not one's own. Moreover, this process of thinking one's way in must in some fashion involve the activation of the disposition to make and seek concessions that underlies judgments of political morality. Since most political questions admit of reasonable disagreement, the best one can expect is that the resulting judgments will find a place within the zone of reasonable disagreement in that polity.

This "thinking one's way in" is problematic, however. Whether one agrees or disagrees with the way political cooperation is organized in the society being appraised, one's reasoning can be competent only if one understands the positions that are taken within that polity. So the process of thinking one's way into another polity associated with making moral judgments about that polity must involve acquiring a familiarity with concepts available to the people actually living there. But the means of doing this available to outsiders, such as reading or watching documentary videos, will be imperfect. It might thus seem doubtful that any judgment criticizing or endorsing the way political cooperation is structured in a polity where the person making the judgment has never lived can be competently reasoned.

A further aspect of this problem should also be mentioned. Moral judgments guide action, and encounters with the actions performed by those holding a particular moral view play an important role in the appraisal of that view. These encounters may present one with features of the local form of life that cannot be accurately captured in speech. But someone who is attempting to appraise the system of political cooperation in place in a polity where he has not lived will not have encountered the actions peculiar to that system. This, too, raises questions about whether the political judgments made by an outsider can be competently reasoned.

The problem just described is reduced if the appraiser has proxies in the polity being appraised, local cooperators who have imported the concepts of the appraiser and integrated them with their original concepts in a way that preserves the proper functioning of their cooperative capacities in the local context. Thus a citizen of the United States who favors legal guarantees of freedom of religion of the sort found in the USA may have proxies in a polity

that restricts religious freedom in various ways. These might be members of that polity who, as a result of living for a time in the United States, have come to accept that fairness requires extensive legal guarantees of freedom of religion. When proxies of this sort are available, it will be possible for the external appraiser to have some confidence that his view of how political cooperation ought to be organized in the polity being appraised has a legitimate place there, despite the fact that he himself does not have a good understanding of the local situation. Of course, it does not follow that an external appraiser who has proxies in the polity being appraised can conclude that members of that polity who hold different views have fallen into moral error. The position staked out by the proxies, if it does indeed preserve the proper functioning of their cooperative capacities in the local context, will typically constitute just one of the positions falling within the zone of reasonable disagreement in that polity. This means that other members of that polity will be able reasonably to reject the judgments of the proxies.

In one sense, someone who has made no effort to acquire the conceptual apparatus of another polity can still make competently reasoned value judgments endorsing or rejecting the way political cooperation is organized there. It is enough that the pattern of concessions in place in that polity, as construed by the appraiser, is supported or condemned by judgments that are reasonable within the appraiser's home polity. Thus a citizen of the United States might find unacceptable another polity's imposition of restrictions on religious expression of a kind that would be legally impermissible in the USA. We can regard such judgments as employing what was earlier termed the "ought" of evaluation. They will assert that, from the standpoint of the appraiser, things are, or are not, as they ought to be. But the important question, when we set out to appraise another polity, is whether we can claim that the people actually living there have good reason to organize their affairs in the way we deem appropriate. In Harman's view, judgments to this effect must employ the "inner" ought, which presupposes agreement in attitude. As we have seen, moral nominalism does not work this way. But it still places limitations on judgments that purport to ascribe reasons for action to people living in other polities.

To repeat, an external appraiser can justifiably assert that there is sufficient reason for people in the polity being appraised to structure political cooperation in the way the appraiser deems appropriate if she has proxies there, local residents who have imported the appraiser's concepts and competently employ them, or some local version of them, to make judgments about how political cooperation ought to be organized in their polity. And given the points made in the previous section, other local people, if

their own reasoning is to be competent, must make an effort to acquire an understanding of the concepts the proxies have imported. But their personal histories of judgment may be such that they can competently reject the conclusions of the proxies, and thus of the external appraiser whose proxies they are. Reasoning competently with the socially available concepts, they may be able to conclude that certain restrictions on religious freedom are appropriate, that they are narrowly or broadly fair.

Further, the resulting disagreement may ultimately be resolved in a way that rejects the conclusions of the appraiser and her proxies. This might happen because an alternative reasonable view is dominant in the polity being appraised. But even if there is no dominant view, routine political decision making may enact into a law a view different from that held by the appraiser and her proxies. In general, democratic deliberation makes it more likely that whatever view is enacted is reasonable, is compatible with the proper functioning of human cooperative capacities as they have been shaped by the socially available concepts. But this need not be the view of the appraiser and her proxies. Also, as will be discussed in the next section, non-democratic decision-making procedures could be reasonable in the local context.

When the question of how political cooperation ought to be organized in the polity being appraised admits of reasonable disagreement, then, it may not be possible for an external appraiser to assert that the people there have sufficient reason to organize political cooperation in the way she favors, even if she has proxies in that polity. Still, conceptual change is ongoing and relations of dominance can be reversed. So an external appraiser can hope that people in the polity being appraised will eventually have sufficient reason to organize political cooperation in the way she favors. She may even attempt to make this happen. This is a delicate matter, however. Conceptual change usually requires more than argument. Argument constitutes an aspect of a larger process of conceptual-cum-social change precipitated in part by actions that people take on the basis of judgments of political morality that they regard as correct. External appraisers might urge their proxies to act. But active intervention by the appraisers themselves could run counter to their own convictions of political morality. They might, for example, value autonomy or national self-determination, and condemn paternalism.

WESTERN AND NON-WESTERN

In the previous section, we saw that even if an outsider has proxies in a particular polity, she may not be able to conclude that the members of the

polity have sufficient reason to structure political cooperation in the way she favors. This will be the case if the question of how to structure cooperation in that polity admits of reasonable disagreement, and most people in the polity hold a different reasonable view.

In many contexts, this point should be uncontroversial. Some people in France doubtless advocate the organization of economic cooperation there in accordance with the so-called Anglo-American model, so outsiders who favor this model have proxies in France. But it does not follow that most people in France have reason to embrace the model. The personal histories of judgment from which most competent French reasoners proceed may provide a basis for rejecting the Anglo-American model. Or to take another example, although partisans of American-style religious liberty may have proxies in France, the personal histories of judgment from which most French reasoners proceed may lead them to endorse an official secularism that prohibits certain forms of religious expression, such as the wearing of head-scarves by school girls, that would be protected in the United States.

In these cases, however, the disagreement is between two ways of structuring political cooperation in a liberal democracy. The point may look different when what is at issue is the appropriateness of establishing liberal democracy in the first place. A number of countries in the world today are not liberal democracies, or at least not fully functioning liberal democracies, if contemporary Western polities are taken as paradigms of full functioning. It is not uncommon to find Westerners judging that these polities ought to be liberal democracies, or that the values of liberal democracy ought to be more fully realized in them. If such judgments are echoed by competently reasoning proxies in the polities in question, these Westerners will be able to regard fully functioning liberal democracy as a reasonable option under local conditions. But it might be suggested that a stronger claim can be made. It might be suggested that no other option can be reasonable.

Here is an argument for that conclusion. Reasonable disagreement is competently reasoned disagreement, employing socially available concepts, concerning what would constitute an appropriate way of organizing political cooperation. Any way of organizing political cooperation brings with it a pattern of concessions, so reasonable disagreement is, in part, disagreement about what would be broadly fair. Where such disagreement exists, the question of fairness arises at a higher level, as the question of what would constitute a reasonable-as-fair way of resolving these first-order reasonable disagreements. But the decision procedures of liberal democracy provide the only possibility. Democratic procedures (that are themselves functioning properly) give everyone an opportunity to affect political outcomes, and

liberal rights provide protection against the tyranny of the majority. No other institutional form does as good a job of respecting the claims that people who reasonably disagree can make against each other or the polity as a whole. Reasonable disagreement, however, is a universal fact of political life. So all cooperatively disposed people reasoning competently about how to organize political life must acknowledge the appropriateness of liberal democracy. Or at least this is so once the concepts necessary to frame judgments supporting liberal democracy become available.

This argument can be questioned, however. Typically, where democracy is absent, we have despotism of some sort. Coercion replaces legitimate authority. Further, indoctrination may lead the members of the polity to accept an ideology that does not embody competent reasoning about what would be fair. This point was mentioned earlier in connection with Williams's observation about the injustice of unmediated coercion. But to sustain the argument that no one can reasonably reject liberal democracy, we need to do more than observe that political cooperation is not in fact reasonably organized in many non-democratic polities. We need to establish that no cooperatively disposed human, reasoning competently with the full set of locally available normative and evaluative concepts, could reject liberal democracy. Can this be done?

Doubts can be raised by considering one way someone might come to the conclusion that liberal democracy is not required. The argument for liberal democracy we are now considering is based on the claim that reasonable disagreement is a fact of political life. The zone of reasonable disagreement is defined counterfactually. It is constituted by the pattern of disagreement we would find if everyone in the polity were reasoning competently, and it may differ significantly from the pattern of disagreement we actually find. This would be especially likely in a polity with low levels of literacy or education. But then a mode of political organization that provides for the training of experts in the employment of the locally available normative and evaluative concepts, and specifies that political cooperation is to be organized as directed by these experts, might actually provide the best way of resolving reasonable disagreement. Reasonable disagreement in the polity could be equated with disagreement within the group of experts, and if everyone else was prepared to defer to the decisions of the experts, the procedures employed by the experts to resolve their disagreements would constitute an acceptable way of resolving reasonable disagreement in the polity as a whole.

There is also another consideration that is relevant to the alleged universal appropriateness of liberal democracy. In polities with high levels of literacy

and education, it is more likely that the positions actually taken by the members will fall within the zone of reasonable disagreement. But a significant number of the positions taken will still be unreasonable. They will reflect incompetently reasoned views about what would be narrowly or broadly fair, or fail to reflect thinking about fairness at all. Nevertheless, Western polities provide, with a few minor exceptions, for universal adult participation in political decision making. The basic reason for this is that the normative and evaluative concepts available in Western polities include some, such as the concept of autonomy in the political sense, that reflect the conviction that the way human life is to be lived, at both the individual and collective levels, is something for the people doing the living to decide. The justification of liberal democracy in a typical Western polity depends as much on this conviction as it does on a judgment to the effect that the institutions of liberal democracy provide the fairest way of resolving reasonable political disagreement.

But the idea that a good human life is one in which the people doing the living decide on a path through life is not the only alternative on offer in the world's cultures. We also find the idea that each person is dealt a certain lot in life and must accept it. This fatalistic view can be made more palatable by a conceptual apparatus that, while affirming human powerlessness in the face of larger forces, represents these forces in a humanly intelligible form. This is the route taken by many of the world's religions. Taking it need not mean abandoning fairness as a fundamental value of political cooperation. Religious concepts can ground claims that the members of a polity are able to make against each other or against the polity as a whole. They can thus provide a framework for thinking about narrow fairness. And where religious concepts identify social values that are regarded as capable, sometimes, of outweighing these claims, a place can be made for broad fairness as well.

If, however, the locally available concepts support a conception of the good life that emphasizes resignation rather than choice, the rejection of liberal democracy could be locally reasonable. This conclusion will receive added support if it is thought that only people who have received special training in the employment of the locally available normative and evaluative concepts, such as priests or mullahs, can be expected actually to hold locally reasonable views. As was described earlier, the mechanisms by which the experts resolve their disagreements could then suffice for the resolution of reasonable disagreement in the polity as a whole.

It might be objected that this way of obtaining the result that the members of a polity can reasonably reject liberal democracy is plausible only where there is unanimous support for the alternative. Once we add to

the mix people operating with other normative and evaluative concepts, for example, Western concepts that they have imported, the rejection of liberal democracy will again be unreasonable. Where unanimity is lacking, non-democratic institutions will be imposed on people who cannot regard them as justified.

This brings us to the heart of the issue of the universal appropriateness of liberal democracy. We have noted Williams's observation that unmediated coercion, coercion unmediated by a sound justification, is everywhere an injustice. Presumably, the justification must be one that has validity for those affected, if not in the sense that they accept it, at least in the sense that they would accept it if they were reasoning competently. But political decisions are almost always coercively enforced. So where the members of a polity reasonably disagree at the second level, disagree about the appropriate way of resolving reasonable disagreement, or the appropriate way of making political decisions generally, some injustice of the sort Williams identifies is unavoidable. Some people will be subjected to coercion that is, for them, unmediated by a sound justification. The only relevant question is how severe the injustice is, and this depends in the first instance on the number of people experiencing injustice. If the decision procedure being employed is accepted by most competent reasoners drawing on the locally available concepts, and especially if it has the support of a dominant reasonable view, there will be relatively little injustice. It is regrettable that there is any, but if the situation were reversed, and the procedure associated with a marginal view imposed, the injustice would be greater. To make the point more concrete, the advocates of theocracy will experience unavoidable injustice in a liberal democratic polity, and the advocates of liberal democracy will experience unavoidable injustice in a locally reasonable theocracy.

These observations give us a way of understanding despotism. We have despotism if and only if the injustice of unmediated coercion could be reduced by replacing the operative way of making and enforcing political decisions with another reasonable alternative available within the polity. If instituting any of the available alternatives would just make things worse, the actual arrangements cannot be deemed despotic even though some people are subjected to coercion unmediated by what, for them, is a sound justification. Typically, despotism will be accompanied by extensive coercion or indoctrination. Only in this way can political control be maintained in the face of large numbers of people who reasonably reject the operative way of making political decisions, or would if they were able to reason competently. But coercion and indoctrination do not constitute its defining feature.

Despotism is at its most extreme when the group in power is running the polity for its own private benefit or amusement. Here no reasonable view, no view that gives expression to the human disposition to make and seek concessions in cooperative contexts, will support the use to which coercion is being put. But we also have despotism when a small group is using coercion to enforce a locally reasonable view of the appropriate way of making political decisions against a larger group that reasonably rejects that view, or would reasonably reject that view but for indoctrination. Whether the injustice of unmediated coercion rises to the level of despotism, then, depends on the numbers. But since the question of the appropriate way of resolving reasonable disagreement itself admits of reasonable disagreement, we cannot conclude from the fact that despotism is ultimately a matter of numbers that every polity should be a liberal democracy employing the method of majority rule.[9]

There is one further line of argument that defenders of the universal validity of liberal democracy might try. On reflection, it might be said, competent reasoners will realize that the concepts available in any polity are human creations, the product of a historical process.[10] But this realization is incompatible with a fatalistic view of the human situation. Once we become reflectively aware that we create our concepts, and thus the moral worlds we inhabit, we will be on the alert for social forces that tend to undermine the proper functioning of the capacities engaged, and we will be prepared to remake the moral worlds in which we live so as to preserve the proper functioning of these capacities in a changing social environment. Reflective awareness of the actual source of our concepts thus brings with it what the critical theorists of the Frankfurt School call enlightenment and emancipation. And enlightenment and emancipation are incompatible with a fatalistic conception of the human situation.

---

[9] The indoctrination that accompanies despotism can change minds, but this must not be confused with the operation of the conceptual-cum-social process described in the previous chapter. In both cases, a force that is not the force of the better argument plays a role. But in the conceptual-cum-social process, the changing of minds is an aspect of the proper functioning of human conceptual and cooperative capacities. People change their minds because they find that the maintenance of proper functioning in an evolving social situation, which they are forced to confront, requires this. And these changes give rise to actions that further the evolutionary process. By contrast, when minds are changed by indoctrination (and there may be less genuine changing of minds than the enforced uniformity of expressed opinion suggests), the proper functioning of human conceptual and cooperative capacities is compromised.

[10] In *Ethics and the Limits of Philosophy*, ch. 9, Bernard Williams notes that the desire for reflective understanding of society, and of human activities generally, is more widespread and deeper in modern societies than in earlier societies. He mentions that this is one of the reasons that the social forms of the past are not a real option for us.

Again, however, it is not clear that the superiority of Western ideas is so easily established. On the view being proposed in the present book, what one becomes aware of when one engages in the kind of reflection described is the conceptual-cum-social process. Consciousness of this social dynamic puts people in a position to exert greater control over the social forms they occupy, but the result might still be general acceptance of a fatalistic understanding of the human situation. Since the conceptual-cum-social process will have been responsible for the emergence of the fatalistic view in the first place, it is not obvious that reflective awareness of the process would make continued acceptance of that view impossible.

There appears to be some support for this conclusion within critical theory itself. In his discussion of the Frankfurt School, Raymond Geuss describes two different approaches to critical theory, which he associates with Jürgen Habermas and Theodor Adorno.[11] In both cases, reflective awareness is achieved by bringing to bear principles identifying sound patterns of reasoning, which Geuss calls epistemic principles. For Habermas, these principles have universal validity. They are derived from the presuppositions of communicative action, which is a universal human activity, and they require a deliberative form of democracy. For Adorno, however, the epistemic principles are themselves historical products, local in character. Critical reflection is thus a matter of the elaboration of a particular historical tradition in a way that the tradition itself identifies as manifesting sound reasoning. Critical reflection that takes place within a local tradition is liberating in the sense that it brings reflective understanding into line with genuine normative constraints, and adapts this understanding to a changing social environment. But the constraints are local in character, local ways of elaborating the proper functioning of human mental capacities, and thus the social arrangements that survive critical reflection will display local variability as well.[12]

On the view Geuss ascribes to Adorno, critical reflection may not require the rejection of a fatalistic understanding of the human situation. People who are reflectively aware of their role in shaping the concepts they employ might still choose to give further development to a conceptual apparatus, constructed by previous generations, that represents humans as subject to forces they cannot control. They will seek to purge from this apparatus

---

[11] Raymond Geuss, *The Idea of a Critical Theory: Habermas and the Frankfurt School* (Cambridge: Cambridge University Press, 1981), pp. 61–69.

[12] Geuss suggests (ibid., pp. 66–67) that Habermas's view can be interpreted, in Adorno's terms, as the product of a local process of reflection carried out in the West.

conceptual elements that have not been reflectively fashioned. But the tradition being elaborated may call for this task to be entrusted to a trained elite.

Issues of this general sort are at the forefront of post-colonial theory, at least as it is presented by Robert Young.[13] Young describes the conceptual struggles of writers with roots in those parts of the world that experienced Western colonialism. These writers, Young says, have sought to reject modernity, which they think of as essentially Western, without falling back into a traditionalism that is not viable in the modern world, the world that modernity has, for better or worse, created. Young makes the interesting suggestion that the philosophy of "deconstruction" developed by Jacques Derrida, whose own roots were in Algeria, can contribute usefully to the post-colonial enterprise.[14] Deconstruction, on this reading, is a tool that enables the person employing it to free herself of Western ideas without at the same time invoking other Western ideas.

Derrida's project in *Of Grammatology* illustrates the strategy.[15] His goal there seems to be to establish that the Western metaphysical tradition, with its associated "logocentrism," lacks the inevitability it seems to possess. But the usual method by which we establish that something is not inevitable – namely, placing it in a larger context which reveals that there are alternatives to it – can itself be regarded as a component of the Western metaphysical tradition. Derrida's deconstruction of this tradition is intended to generate the conviction that it lacks inevitability without presenting a specific alternative to it. If successful, the project would clear the ground for the development of locally authentic conceptions of political morality in non-Western polities.[16]

THE FUTURE OF POLITICAL MORALITY

What does the discussion so far in this book imply about the future of political morality? The process of conceptual-cum-social change that I have described has no implicit end point. Future conceptions of political morality will be constrained by the fact that they must provide suitable

---

[13] Robert J. C. Young, *Postcolonialism: An Historical Introduction* (Oxford: Blackwell, 2001), esp. part IV.

[14] Ibid., ch. 28.

[15] Jacques Derrida, *Of Grammatology*, trans. G. C. Spivak (Baltimore: Johns Hopkins University Press, 1974), part I.

[16] It should be noted that on Derrida's view, there can be no rational requirement to collaborate with a project of deconstruction. Deconstruction constitutes at best an interpretive possibility that some people may, depending on psychological contingencies, find liberating.

packaging for human cooperative motivation. The concepts must be such that the associated extrapolative dispositions are caught by a form of motivation that will be experienced by all properly functioning humans, the disposition to make and seek concessions in the context of a cooperative endeavor when others are similarly disposed. As a result of this "catching," a particular conceptualized structure is imparted to the motivational disposition, a structure that can display local variations. But within the boundary set by human cooperative dispositions, moral change can go on indefinitely.

Since the process of conceptual-cum-social change has no implicit end point, it is senseless to speculate about the distant future of political morality. But there may be some basis for informed speculation about the near-term future in a global context. The recent past has witnessed the global propagation, if not the full global acceptance, of some Western moral ideas, notably the idea of universal human rights, the idea that all people, as human beings, have certain claims that they can make against the polities in which they reside and, indeed, against the entire human community. Is there some reason to expect this process of Westernization to continue, and in particular to bring about the global dominance of a conception of political morality supporting liberal democracy?

In the previous section, we saw that people in the West do not appear to have at their disposal a sound argument that can force all competent reasoners to conclude that liberal democracy is the only acceptable way of organizing political cooperation. Actually existing non-democratic arrangements are often despotic, in the sense described in the previous section, and it can be argued that democracy provides an effective check on despotism.[17] But competent reasoners in non-democratic polities, drawing on a locally available political tradition, may be able to reject liberal democracy. They may be able to argue that whatever democracy's virtues as an antidote to despotism, there is no reason in principle why a non-democratic polity has

---

[17] The checking of despotism is an important theme in republican political thought. Republican theory understands freedom as non-domination. According to Philip Pettit, people enjoy freedom as non-domination when they control the interference to which they are subject. See his *Republicanism: A Theory of Freedom and Government* (Oxford: Oxford University Press, 1999). In "The Indeterminacy of Republican Policy" (*Philosophy and Public Affairs* 33 [2005], pp. 67–93), I argue against Pettit's claim that determinate conclusions about policy can be derived from the concept of freedom as non-domination. Pettit has replied in "The Determinacy of Republican Policy: A Reply to McMahon" (*Philosophy and Public Affairs* 34 [2006], pp. 274–283). I continue the debate in "Nondomination and Normativity" (*Pacific Philosophical Quarterly* 88 [2007], pp. 319–327). Using the categories of the present book, what is at issue in this discussion can be put as follows. Can a competent reasoner make the maximization of non-domination, interpreted as de facto control over interference, the sole consideration giving conceptualized structure to the disposition, which will be possessed by all properly functioning humans, to make and seek concessions in cooperative contexts?

to be despotic, why, in a local context, it has to be marked by more unmediated coercion than liberal democracy.[18] Competently reasoning Westerners can still subject non-democratic arrangements to negative appraisal, especially if they have proxies in the polities in question. But under the scenario envisaged, other competent reasoners in these polities, drawing on locally available concepts, will be able to reject this negative appraisal.

As we saw in the previous chapter, however, people who competently judge that political cooperation ought to be structured in a certain way will often have opportunities to give that structure to some of the interactions in which they participate, even when an opposing view of the appropriate way of structuring political cooperation is dominant. Further, taking these opportunities can initiate a process of conceptual-cum-social change that effects a reversal of dominance. The earlier discussion of this phenomenon was focused on the case where the members of a polity share a set of normative and evaluative concepts. But such change can also take place within polities, which constitute the majority now, where some people are operating not only with traditional concepts but also with imported concepts. Is there some basis for supposing that the various processes of conceptual-cum-social change now underway in different parts of the world will result in the increasing Westernization of the conceptions of political morality found in the world?

When the conceptual-cum-social process alters the zone of reasonable disagreement, or the distribution of people within the zone, a force other than the force of the better argument has a role in changing people's minds. This was a feature of the process that resulted in the emergence of liberal democracy in the West. Political and economic revolution contributed importantly to this development. The events comprising these revolutions were brought about by people acting in a way they regarded as justified by the available normative and evaluative concepts, and these actions forced other people, as properly functioning cooperators, to make accommodating changes. It is possible that the Westernization of political morality on a global scale could be brought about by similar processes of revolution inside non-Western polities. But if Westernization is occurring today, other mechanisms seem to be doing most of the work.

The most important engine of change is global economic integration along broadly capitalist lines. Global economic integration is not a new

---

[18] It must be conceded, however, that verifying a claim that non-democratic arrangements are not, in a particular local context, despotic will be difficult in the absence of a vote by secret ballot.

phenomenon, but it seems to be accelerating. A polity's economic structure forms an important component of its overall system of political coopera-tion, and this structure will license claims that play a role in judgments of narrow and broad fairness. To the extent that a single economic structure is emerging all over the world, the range of options for organizing the remaining aspects of political cooperation will be reduced. The choice among these options will not be economically determined. It will be guided by judgments of narrow and broad fairness grounded in locally available concepts. But the resulting pattern of differences among the world's polities will have some of the character of variations on a common theme. And if the dominant capitalist structure can be regarded as having its home in the West, these will be variations on a Western theme. Moral worlds will still be made out of moral worlds, so political morality will be different in the different polities dealing with globalization. Precise replication of Western conceptions of political morality is not to be expected. But local concep-tions could increasingly take the form of locally appropriate reinterpreta-tions of Western ideas.

Local accommodation of the capitalist economic structures typical of Western polities need not by itself force the adoption of a conception of political morality that supports liberal democracy. But some other aspects of the process of globalization may point in the direction of liberal democ-racy. Global economic integration can be expected to bring about the accelerated importation of concepts from other polities, with Western concepts, especially, becoming increasingly familiar around the world. This could have the effect of altering the zone of reasonable disagreement in non-Western polities in such a way that there is increasing overlap with the zone in typical Western polities. Similarly, global economic integration could affect the way people are distributed within the zone found in a particular polity, increasing support for liberal democracy.[19]

It should also be mentioned that the social dynamic we have been examining can be supplemented with a logical dynamic. Western concep-tions of fairness, narrow and broad, constitute a resource that is available to non-Western polities in their dealings with the West. The members of non-Western polities can point out that Western moral principles require that

---

[19] A change of this sort would have a bearing on the viability of the post-colonial initiatives mentioned in the previous section. Whether they succeed in setting the polities for which they are designed on a locally authentic path will depend on the shape of the zone of reasonable disagreement in those polities, and the distribution of people within the zone. If the number of local residents operating with imported Western ideas is large, it may be difficult to establish the dominance of a conception that post-colonial theorists deem locally authentic.

they be treated in a certain way. This gives them a form of power, normative power, in their dealings with the West, and this normative power can be important given the de facto social power on the other side. But a central element of the normative dimension of thought and action – of reason – is a requirement that like cases be judged alike. So people who make claims against the West grounded in Western conceptions of fairness will experience logical pressure to act in accordance with those conceptions.

So far, we have been focusing on the Westernization of particular non-Western polities. The phenomenon of global economic integration suggests another possibility, however. The moral worldmaking that moral nominalism envisages could increasingly take place on a global scale. The worldwide cooperation presupposed by such a process of worldmaking could be cooperation among the world's polities, or it could be what might be called cosmopolitan cooperation among individuals with roots in different polities. Here, too, there will be a zone of reasonable disagreement, arising from the fact that the cooperators start from different conceptual traditions. As was explained earlier, political disagreements among people starting from different traditions will not be reasonable unless everyone involved understands, in broad outline, at least, what the others are proposing, and acquiring the concepts necessary for such understanding may be difficult for even the most intelligent and well-traveled cosmopolitan. But as the world's polities accommodate themselves to the process of global economic integration, the different local traditions may be brought closer together. This in turn may make possible a situation in which the concepts of political morality employed in all the world's polities become familiar throughout the world. Of course, even if this were the case, individual and social differences in judgmental history would still result in reasonable disagreement about the appropriate way to organize global political cooperation. This fact is relevant to the attempts, now gaining momentum, to develop theories of global justice. People proceeding within different traditions may reasonably disagree about what global justice requires.[20]

I have described some ways that the conceptions of political morality found in the world could, in the future, take on a Western character. Since my own moral convictions are Western, I could hardly view this development as a descent into unreasonableness, but it is not my intention here to advocate it.

---

[20] Some recent discussions of global justice are Thomas Nagel, "The Problem of Global Justice" (*Philosophy and Public Affairs* 33 [2005], pp. 113–147), Joshua Cohen and Charles Sabel, "Extra Republicam Nulla Justitia" (*Philosophy and Public Affairs* 34 [2006], pp. 147–175) and A. J. Julius, "Nagel's Atlas" (*Philosophy and Public Affairs* 34 [2006], pp. 176–192).

In the previous section, we explored the possibility that non-Western models of political cooperation could be locally reasonable given the available normative and evaluative concepts. But whether or not Western ideas emerge to global dominance, it seems clear that because of increasing global interaction, the moral worlds in which future human beings live, or at any rate the worlds of political morality, will be more similar than they are now, and markedly more similar than they were in the past.

CHAPTER 6

Morality and history

On the view I have proposed, the correctness of a judgment of political morality depends on the proper functioning of two different components of the human mental apparatus, the motivational disposition to make or seek concessions in cooperative contexts, and the extrapolative dispositions associated with the mastery of a socially provided set of normative and evaluative terms. The ultimate result is a body of cooperative motivation that has a particular, conceptually articulated structure. A properly functioning member of a polity will be able to employ the available terms to make valid claims against other members or against the polity as a whole. The available terms may also include some that identify certain social states of affairs as possessing a value that can sometimes justify the abridgment of claims. The understanding of appropriate concession embodied in a given member's judgments of political morality will constitute her sense of fairness.

In the previous chapter I argued that moral nominalism implies what I called localism. Different normative and evaluative concepts will be available to the members of different polities, with the result that judgments of political morality will differ somewhat from polity to polity. I explained this by noting that the set of available concepts is determined by an evolutionary process, and the histories of this process will be different in different polities. This has the consequence, however, that localism extends to the past. Since the concepts that were available in the past differ in various respects from those available in the present, the judgments of political morality that could have been made by competent reasoners in the past will differ from those that can be made by competent reasoners in the present.

Within the framework of moral nominalism, the fact that the concepts available in the past were different from those available now means that moral normativity itself was different in the past. The normativity of proper functioning was not different in the past. Moral nominalism construes this realistically. It is the same for all humans, and, assuming there has been no

evolution of the biological structures responsible for the relevant mental powers, it has taken the same form throughout human history. But the concepts employed in moral judgment have a history, and for moral nominalism, this means that moral normativity itself has a history. Moral worlds are made out of moral worlds, and past worlds were different from our present worlds.

I suggested at the end of the previous chapter that a process of convergence may be underway, in the sense that the zones of reasonable disagreement found in the world's polities may overlap more in the future than they do now. If, as is sometimes claimed, all present-day humans are descended from a single small African group, we can also say that the early history of moral normativity was a history of divergence. As the original group grew and split into the subgroups that populated different regions of the world, the conceptual-cum-social process unfolded within each of these subgroups. In this way, the normative and evaluative concepts, presumably relatively crude, employed by the first humans were elaborated into highly refined structures, different in different places. Since, on this picture, all subsequent moral worlds have had a common ancestor, some similarity among them is to be expected. Further, many of the groups following these divergent histories underwent similar social transformations, for example, those connected with the advent of agriculture and the emergence of towns. But there have also been striking differences in the moral worlds, especially the worlds of political morality, constructed.

Moral realists will concede that the moral concepts available in the past were different in some respects from those available now. But they will understand this as meaning that people at different times have represented, that is, have misrepresented, in different ways a body of timeless moral truths. It is compatible with moral realism that the history of moral thought has been a history of decay, that people in the past had a more accurate perception of the moral domain than we do now. Most moral realists, however, probably think that the history of moral thought has been one of progress, that people in the present have a more accurate perception of the timeless truths of morality than people in the past. Scientific realists attribute progress in our understanding of the natural world to the development of certain methods of scientific investigation, and some moral realists hold a similar view.[1]

---

[1] See, for example, Richard Boyd in "How to Be a Moral Realist," in G. Sayre-McCord, ed., *Essays on Moral Realism* (Ithaca: Cornell University Press, 1989), pp. 181–228. This sort of view was discussed in the final section of chapter 1.

Moral nominalism is compatible with the idea that there are some time-less truths of political morality. Some requirements of political morality appear to be directly implied by the proper functioning of human cooperative capacities. I have mentioned two possibilities. The first is a requirement that all those participating in a particular cooperative enterprise – all those performing tasks that benefit other participants – be recognized as possessing claims that can be made against the other participants or the enterprise as a whole. This has the consequence that chattel slavery is necessarily unfair. The second is the requirement implicit in Williams's observation that unmediated coercion is everywhere an injustice, although as we have seen, where there is reasonable disagreement about the appropriate way of making political decisions, some injustice of this sort will be unavoidable. It may also be the case that, as a matter of contingent fact, certain normative and evaluative concepts have been universally available throughout history. But the people of the past clearly operated with total sets of normative and evaluative concepts, especially concepts of political morality, that were different from our own. So the all-things-considered judgments of political morality that competent reasoners could have made in the past will differ in many respects from those that competent reasoners can make now.

The claim that moral normativity was different in the past is a claim about right and wrong, not about blame. Moral realists may be prepared to acknowledge that people in the past cannot be blamed for failing to organize political cooperation in the way that we now (realists suppose) know to be required by morality. If people in the past lacked the necessary concepts, they could not have made the requisite judgments. Moral nominalism can likewise make a distinction between wrongness and blame. Wrongness is determined by the judgments that properly functioning cooperators operating with the available concepts could have made. But the wrongness of certain past arrangements will not be blameworthy if it can be attributed to failures of proper functioning for which the agents were not responsible. The fundamental claim that moral nominalism makes about the past, however, is that what morality actually required in the past was different in some respects from what it requires now.

I described the mechanism of moral evolution in chapter 4. In this chapter I want to explore a few issues that arise in connection with the idea that moral normativity has a history. I first consider how we can know the past of moral normativity. Next, I take up the implications of moral nominalism for the enterprise of making moral judgments about the past, in particular, judgments that the practices and institutions of the past were

morally unacceptable. After discussing the issue in general terms, I turn to what is arguably the basic form of political cooperation in the recorded past, hierarchy, and consider the extent to which the hierarchical political structures of the past were open to moral criticism then. Of special interest will be the way the phenomenon of reasonable disagreement affects such judgments. I conclude with a brief examination of the possibility of rectifying the wrongs of the past, of correcting what, from our present point of view, appear to be the moral errors of the past. In general, the discussion in this chapter will focus on the Western past as it looks from the standpoint of the Western present.

HISTORICAL KNOWLEDGE

According to moral nominalism, political morality at a particular time and place in the past was constituted by the local zone of reasonable disagreement. This in turn was determined by the concepts that were available to the participants in political cooperation then and there. The zone consists of the judgments that properly functioning cooperators, drawing on the available concepts, could have made about the appropriate way to organize political cooperation. As we saw in chapter 3, disagreement is to be expected because the extrapolative dispositions possessed by someone who has mastered the use of a set of moral terms will be influenced by that individual's personal history of judgment with those terms.

The present configuration of the zone of reasonable disagreement in our polity is the product of a historical process in which earlier configurations evolved into later configurations. Knowledge of this historical process has two aspects. First, we must know the concepts of political morality that were available to properly functioning cooperators at various points in the past, and also the social and natural environment that obtained then. To the extent that we can acquire this knowledge we will be able, by a process of reenactment, to replicate the moral judgments that competent reasoners living then could have made.[2] Or at least this will be so if we ourselves are reasoning competently. Second, we must achieve some kind of rational comprehension of the process of evolution itself, some understanding of why it passed through the stages it did. We should remind ourselves of the

---

[2] The notion of reenactment is due to R. G. Collingwood. See the references cited in note 12 to chapter 2. The full understanding of a particular utterance requires knowledge of what the person producing it intended to accomplish, which in turn requires knowledge of the speaker's social world. In "Meaning and Understanding in the History of Ideas" (*History and Theory* 8 [1969], pp. 3–63), Quentin Skinner argues that attending to facts about intention is central to the correct method in the history of ideas.

scope of political morality. It consists of the normative considerations that govern political cooperation, but on the view we are taking here, there is more to political cooperation than the establishment of a government. It is cooperation to put in place a pattern of concessions within a particular polity. The concepts of political morality underwrite the claims that the members of a polity can make against one another and against the polity as a whole. They may also distinguish various social values that can compete with these claims, altering the pattern of concessions that is ultimately appropriate.

Written materials from the past can provide us with epistemic access to the normative and evaluative concepts employed by past people, and to the social and natural environment that obtained then. Of course, this presupposes that we can understand the languages employed. A mastery of the terms used in documents written in a dead language, or in an earlier form of a living language, cannot be acquired by encounters with examples of the correct use of these terms in the actual historical context. A history of translation of a past language into more recent languages, and ultimately into a contemporary language, provides an alternative route by which present people can acquire competence in a past language. The fact that there can be no encounters with examples of correct use in the original context makes it unlikely, however, that a present person will have precisely the same understanding of the correct use of a term used in a past document that native speakers of the language in question had. This problem will be especially pronounced in the case of normative and evaluative terms, the correct use of which, on the view I have proposed, involves making judgments that give form to motivational dispositions activated by encounters with particular situations.

Our grasp of the normative and evaluative concepts employed in past societies will, then, be imprecise. We can never fully recapture past moral worlds. But, especially where a copious supply of documents is available, we can still obtain an approximate understanding of these moral worlds. We can obtain an approximate understanding of the available concepts and the existing social and natural environment, and thus of the judgments that past people could have made if reasoning competently.

Some post-modern theorists of history have questioned the possibility of knowing the past.[3] But the relevant epistemic tool, testimony, functions in the same way in historical contexts as it does when we employ it to learn

---

[3] For an overview of historical post-modernism, see Alan Munslow, *Deconstructing History* (London: Routledge, 1997).

what is happening in the present at some location that is not accessible to our direct observation. Past documents function the same way, epistemically, as an email reporting the weather in London.[4] Further, inference to the best explanation can support conclusions about past societies that are not reported in the documents we have. Indeed, using this epistemic tool, we can come to know things about those societies that the people living in them did not know.[5] It is possible, then, to gain epistemic access to past social worlds. And when this knowledge is added to an understanding of the normative and evaluative concepts employed in the past, an understanding that we acquire in learning the languages of the past, we can gain epistemic access to past moral worlds.

Achieving an understanding of why the moral past turned into the moral present is a more complicated matter. The process of moral evolution is a process of conceptual-cum-social change. Social and conceptual changes reciprocally influence one another. Conceptual change is often a response to new social situations, but by making possible novel judgments that result in new kinds of action, conceptual change can bring about new social situations.

The fact that moral normativity evolves in this way means that we cannot describe the emergence of the moral present out of the moral past as a logical phenomenon, a process in which judgments about what is required in situations of various kinds give way to other judgments as the implications of the available concepts are grasped. Or at least this is so if logic is understood as constituted by the standard inferences associated with the proper functioning of human mental capacities. Hegel's logic is intended to capture the sorts of transitions we are discussing.[6] But the "inferences" involved are licensed by the Hegelian dialectic, and while it purports to trace a process that unfolds in something mental, this is not the mind of a human being.

---

[4] For a discussion of testimony, see Alvin I. Goldman, *Knowledge in a Social World* (Oxford: Clarendon Press, 1999), ch. 4. There is a survey of various epistemological theories of testimonial knowledge on pp. 126–130.

[5] See Gilbert Harman, "Inference to the Best Explanation," *The Philosophical Review* 74 (1965), pp. 88–95. An example is the inference that astronomers made from the detection of regular radio pulses from deep space to the existence of stars with strong magnetic fields that rotate very quickly, eventually named "pulsars." The existence of such stars provides the best explanation of the pulses, and this is sufficient warrant for supposing that they exist. Unlike standard induction (the inference from "every observed A has been an F" to "All A's are F's"), an inference to the best explanation can be made on the basis of a single observation.

[6] For an account of Hegel's logic, see Charles Taylor, *Hegel* (Cambridge: Cambridge University Press, 1975), part III.

Viewing the evolution of moral normativity as a conceptual-cum-social process means viewing it as a part of the historical process generally, and this process has a causal dimension. Earlier events and states of affairs cause later events and states of affairs. The rational comprehension of the evolution of moral normativity will, then, involve the comprehension of causal transitions. Such comprehension can sometimes be achieved by deducing the occurrence of events, or the obtaining of states of affairs, from general causal laws together with statements of initial conditions.[7] But for the most part, rational comprehension of a historical process is achieved by the construction of narratives. A well-constructed narrative presents the events it describes as connected in such a way that earlier events lead to later events. This is what enables us to follow what we regard as a story, in contrast to merely registering the sequence of events described by a chronicle.

A typical historical narrative presupposes an understanding of the general causal mechanisms responsible for human behavior in social contexts. It seeks to present the events of some time and place as unfolding in accordance with these mechanisms. The result is a story that "makes sense." But the comprehension of the historical process that a narrative provides is not entirely causal. A narrative has a beginning, a middle, and an end, and the end is not merely where the story stops. A typical narrative will not be teleological, presenting the events it describes as taking place in order to bring about the event or state of affairs with which it ends. But the rational comprehension of a historical process provided by a narrative will be influenced by where the narrative ends. The significance, in contrast to the cause, of the narrated events will be determined by where the narrative ends, and this will affect the overall understanding of what is narrated.[8]

We must not, however, lose sight of the fact that a historical narrative achieves rational comprehension of the events it narrates in part by presenting what comes earlier as causing what comes later. This means that a historical narrative proceeds on the assumption that the events it describes actually took place. Some post-modern theorists reject this idea. They regard historical narratives as textual substitutes or replacements for the

---

[7] For a defense of the role of such explanations in history, see Carl Hempel, "The Function of General Laws in History," *The Journal of Philosophy* 39 (1942), pp. 35–48.

[8] In "Narrative Explanation" (*The Philosophical Review* 112 [2003], pp. 1–25), J. David Velleman proposes that the significance of a story or narrative should be understood in terms of some emotional resolution it reliably produces in the audience. In *Metahistory: The Historical Imagination in Nineteenth Century Europe* (Baltimore: Johns Hopkins University Press, 1973), Hayden White distinguishes different literary forms that narratives can possess. He suggests that the choice of form – for example, the form of tragedy – can affect the significance that a sequence of events is perceived as having.

past, which is no longer available to us.[9] Historians, on this view, typically trade on the "reality effect," understood on the model of the effects by which painters or writers of novels convey realism, but there is no expectation that historical narratives will yield rational comprehension of actual events in the past, which are assumed to be hidden behind an opaque wall of texts.[10] To take this line is to give up on the possibility of rational comprehension of events in the past.

Bernard Williams has commented insightfully on historical narrative. He begins by noting that narrative explanation in history presupposes that we know many particular facts about the past. Sensitivity to the limitations of narrative is possible only for those who agree that the past is real and that we can gain epistemic access to it. He then says, "It is only because we can accept large numbers of facts about the past, many of them in themselves very boring, that we can confront the genuinely disturbing suggestion that historical understanding requires narrative, and narrative demands closure, and closure in history is always a fiction and often a lie."[11] Narratives have endings, but the historical process does not make stops. So when it comes to history, we confront the paradoxical situation that our principal way of achieving understanding inevitably misrepresents what we seek to understand.[12]

---

[9] One prominent exponent of a post-modernist approach to the past, F. R. Ankersmit, says, "we can never test our conclusions by comparing the elected text with 'the past' itself" ("Reply to Professor Zagorin," *History and Theory* 29 [October 1990], p. 281). And in another place, he says, "in the postmodernist view, evidence does not point towards the *past*, but towards other *interpretations* of the past ... for the modernist, the evidence is a tile that he picks up to see what is underneath it; for the postmodernist, on the other hand, it is a tile that he steps on in order to move on to other tiles" ("Historiography and Postmodernism," *History and Theory* 28 [May 1989], pp. 145–146).

[10] For the reality effect, see Roland Barthes, "Historical Discourse," in M. Lane, ed., *Structuralism: A Reader* (London: Jonathan Cape, 1970), pp. 145–155.

[11] Bernard Williams, "Philosophy and the Understanding of Ignorance," in his *Philosophy as a Humanistic Discipline* (Princeton: Princeton University Press, 2006), p. 172. For related discussion see Velleman's "Narrative Explanation." It is worth noting that a lie is a false assertion made with the intention to deceive.

[12] Historians often divide history into periods. Periodization is a narrative device. A period has a beginning, a middle, and an end. In *Truth and Truthfulness* (Princeton: Princeton University Press, 2002), ch. 10, Williams notes the possibility of a minimalist narrative, which is restricted to making sense of how things have reached any particular point in the story. In this case, the way the narrative ends does not serve to establish the significance of what has gone before. In *Narration and Knowledge* (New York: Columbia University Press, 1985), Arthur Danto argues that because actions and events can be redescribed in terms of their consequences, and the future is open-ended, the past is never closed. We can never have a complete and final understanding of what happened then. There is always the possibility that a new historical narrative will present some later event, possibly an event in our own future, as the end of a story that began in the past, thereby giving new significance to what happened in the past.

It is arguable that the best response to this problem is a collective effort to construct a number of different historical narratives. The events and states of affairs described must actually have occurred, and the way the earlier is represented as giving rise to the later must be causally plausible. But otherwise, more is better than less. Since different narratives will stop at different places, a multiplicity of narratives can convey some sense of the endlessness of history. A multiplicity can also do some justice to the fact that history is broad as well as endless. The collective construction of a set of historical narratives will be comparable to the fabrication of a rope, with each plausible narrative constituting one of the threads in that rope.

Since the conceptual-cum-social process that has given rise to our present moral world is part of the larger historical process, these general points about historical narrative apply to attempts to explain why the moral worlds of the Western past gave way to the moral world of the present – why, for example, liberal democracy emerged out of feudal arrangements. A number of different stories can be told, and each causally plausible one will give us partial insight. Of course, these stories may disagree on certain points, but when this happens, we can often suppose that we are presented with reasonable disagreement. As we saw in chapter 1, there can be reasonable disagreement concerning questions of fact, and this includes explanatory questions. Competent reasoners, working with a given body of evidence in a way that fully manifests their competence, can reach different conclusions.

Although there is no single correct way of narrating the emergence of our present moral world out of the moral worlds of the past, it is possible to make a couple of general observations about the history of moral norma-tivity. First, ways of organizing political cooperation that were reasonable in the past, in the sense that their acceptability fell within the zone of reasonable disagreement, can become unreasonable as the historical process unfolds. As the social environment changes, it may cease to be possible for competent reasoners to use the traditional concepts to give structure to their cooperative dispositions. The dispositions, as activated by encounters with the changing environment, may cease to be receptive to that particular conceptual form. Some examples will be discussed later. Within the frame-work of moral nominalism, an arrangement that will be rejected by all competent reasoners drawing on the socially available moral concepts is incontestably wrong. So another way of putting this point is to say that ways of organizing political cooperation that would be incontestably wrong now, at least in the West, may not have been wrong in the Western past.

Second, as was noted in the discussion of moral evolution at the end of chapter 4, the changes in the social environment that give rise to conceptual

change can be produced by actions that, at the time they occur, all reasonable members of the polity in question would judge morally unacceptable. Such actions might take the form of collective efforts by subgroups to impose a certain structure on social cooperation. The conceptual changes that competent reasoners produce in response to the actions of unreasonable people will manifest the proper functioning of human mental capacities in the existing social environment. But the story of these changes will be the story of competent responses to moral incompetence. Moral worlds are made out of moral worlds, but the transitions can be prompted by moral failure of various kinds. The history of moral normativity thus has some of the character of a history of the judgments about where to go next made by somebody who has a tendency to get lost.

JUDGING THE PAST

According to a familiar saying, "The past is a foreign country. They do things differently there."[13] Further, as we have seen, the localism that is implied by moral nominalism extends to the past. Right and wrong are different there. I have noted that within the framework of moral nominalism, certain ways of structuring political cooperation can be regarded as wrong a priori. But in general, for moral nominalism, moral normativity is conditioned by the available concepts, and the concepts of political morality available in the Western past were clearly different in important respects from those available now. Most importantly, the concepts available in the Western past included some suitable for justifying hierarchical ways of structuring political cooperation. The observations in chapter 5 about the appraisal of other contemporary polities are, then, germane to the enterprise of making moral judgments about the past.

In that chapter it was noted that the appraisal of other contemporary polities can take different forms. But when it comes to the past, only one of these is relevant, what I called appraisal without contact. We cannot travel

---

[13] L. P. Hartley, *The Go-Between* (New York: Knopf, 1954), p. 3. The view expressed in this quote is characteristic of the modern conception of history, which is generally held to have emerged at the end of the eighteenth century. According to this conception, history produces new forms of human life that are fundamentally different from past forms. The ancient view, by contrast, was that human life is always the same, and that the study of history does not familiarize us with different forms of life, but rather provides us with lessons that, because human life is always the same, can be applied to present problems. For discussion, see Alex Callinicos, *Theories and Narratives: Reflections on the Philosophy of History* (Durham: Duke University Press, 1995), pp. 54–65. A somewhat different perspective on the modern conception of history is provided by Joyce Appleby, Lynn Hunt, and Margaret Jacob in *Telling the Truth about History* (New York: Norton, 1994), ch. 2.

to past societies, so the appraisal of the polities of the past is like the appraisal of a contemporary polity by someone who has never been there. The first point to bear in mind about appraisal without contact is that we need to make a distinction between judgments employing the "ought" of evaluation and judgments employing the "ought" that ascribes reasons for action to the people whose conduct we are appraising.

Judgments of political morality are judgments about how political cooperation ought to be organized, and for moral nominalism, such judgments presuppose cooperative motivation. So to employ the "ought" of evaluation, we must be able to inject ourselves in imagination into the past polity we want to evaluate, thereby securing the activation of our cooperative dispositions by the situation that obtained there, to the extent that we can know what it was. A judgment employing the "ought" of evaluation will use our present concepts of political morality to give structure to this motivation. It might, for example, judge the hierarchical political structures common in the Western past to have been morally unacceptable because they were not democratic, or because they violated the autonomy of the vast majority of the members of past polities.

As we saw in chapter 5, however, the important question in the case of appraisal without contact is what the people actually living in the polity in question have sufficient reason to do. The discussion of this point in the previous chapter employed the notion of a proxy. A proxy, as described there, is someone who, through travel, the use of various media of communication, or encounters with traveling Westerners, has become familiar with contemporary Western political concepts and given them a central place in his political thinking. It is unlikely that the imported concepts will completely supplant local concepts in the proxy's thinking. Nevertheless, the existence of proxies of the right sort makes it possible for a Westerner to judge that political cooperation in a contemporary non-Western polity ought to be organized more or less as it is in the West, where the ought-judgment records the fact that some competent reasoners actually living in that polity could make that judgment.

Parallel points apply to judgments to the effect that the people of the Western past acted wrongly in organizing political cooperation as they did. The most straightforward way of showing that they failed to do what there was good reason for them to do is to identify proxies in those polities. The two cases, making judgments about contemporary non-Western polities and making judgments about our own Western past, are not completely analogous, however. Proxies in contemporary polities are people who have traveled to the West, or learned about it in some other way. But as has been

mentioned, there is no possibility of travel, or communication, between the past and the present. If we have proxies in past polities, this must be because the concepts that give content to our present political judgments were available in the Western past, if not in exactly the form they possess now, in an earlier form. This idea is not implausible. To take just one example, despite the subordination of women in the past, feminism has a long history. In many past polities, there were people who saw no reason why a woman could not make the same claims as a man (at her level in the hierarchical structures of the time), and these people may have been reasoning competently with the locally available concepts.

To the extent that we have proxies in the polities of the Western past, then, we will be able to say that organizing political cooperation in those polities in the way it is now organized in the modern West was a reasonable option under local conditions. In particular, we will be able to say that the rejection of the forms of hierarchy that distinguish the Western past from the Western present was a reasonable option. What the proxies would have judged an appropriate replacement for the hierarchical structures will, however, depend on the precise content of the concepts that were available then and there, so it may be different in some respects from what we would try to create if we could somehow be transported to the past.

We must not, however, overlook the phenomenon of reasonable disagreement. The existence of proxies in the polities of the Western past enables us to say that political views similar to our own had a legitimate place in those polities. Or to be more precise, we can say this if the proxies were reasoning competently – displaying the proper functioning of the relevant mental capacities – and their view would have survived deliberation, conducted in good faith, with the other members of those polities. But opposing views may also have been reasonable in the polities of the Western past, may also have given expression to competent reasoning employing the available concepts. A reasonable member of a past polity may have been able to judge various forms of hierarchy appropriate, for example. The doctrine of the divine corporation was mentioned in chapter 4, and there may have been other ways that a competent reasoner, armed with the locally available concepts, could have endorsed hierarchy. In addition, as we have seen, declining to make use of some of the available concepts can be compatible with reasonableness. The personal histories of some people may be such that they find it appropriate to exclude from their repertoires certain concepts in the socially available set. So the failure of other members of the polities of the Western past to employ the concepts employed by our proxies need not entail that these other members were

unreasonable. The most we can realistically hope is that views analogous to those commonly held in modern Western polities fell within the zone of reasonable disagreement in the polities of the Western past.

The fact that views similar to our own fell within the zone of reasonable disagreement in the past does not mean that the zone has stayed the same throughout Western history. Some of the judgments that are reasonable now may have no counterparts in the Western past. Similarly, many of the judgments that a reasonable member of a past polity could have made may no longer be reasonable. In particular, in modern social settings, it may not be possible for a properly functioning cooperator to make use of certain components of the conceptual apparatus that supported the forms of hierarchy characteristic of the Western past. Human cooperative dispositions, as they are activated by the circumstances of modern life, may not be receptive to those concepts.

In considering the history of moral normativity, we must also take into account the phenomenon of dominance. Recall that to qualify as dominant, it is not enough that a view be widely accepted in a particular polity. It must also be reasonable. In holding it, the members of the polity must be reasoning competently with the available concepts and within the framework of their experience.[14] Nevertheless, there is some reason to suppose that moral views alien to our modern Western sensibilities could have satisfied these conditions. As was noted in chapter 4, one and the same conceptual-cum-social process is typically responsible both for the available moral concepts and the basic structure of political cooperation. It does not follow that competent reasoners will endorse the status quo in its entirety. The existing institutions and practices may be judged morally defective in various respects. But where there is a dominant view, the same process will have produced both that view and the basic structure. So the judgments licensed by the dominant view will typically endorse the basic structure. Moral criticism will then consist of observations to the effect that existing arrangements do not reflect the ideal form of this structure.

In the discussion of localism in the previous chapter, it was noted that even if people in non-Western polities have no reason to organize political

---

[14] As was mentioned in chapter 5, note 10, Bernard Williams has suggested that the desire for reflective understanding of society, and of human activities generally, is more prominent in modern societies than in earlier societies, and that this is one reason the social forms of the past are not a real option for us. If the people of the past were less reflective than they are now, the practice of making judgments about how political cooperation ought to be organized was presumably less well established than it is now. But we can still employ the idea of what the people of the past would have accepted if they had been reasoning competently with the available concepts and within the framework of their own experience.

cooperation in the way it is organized in the West, we in the West can still undertake to bring about conceptual change, or a reversal of dominance, in non-Western polities. This presents us with another disanalogy between the moral appraisal of other contemporary polities and the appraisal of past polities. We cannot intervene in the past to produce conceptual change or a reversal of dominance. It might be argued, however, that in the case of the Western past, such actions would be superfluous because the very reversal of dominance that we would have tried to produce has actually taken place. Hierarchy has given way to the forms of egalitarianism characteristic of modern Western moral thinking. This raises the possibility of a different route to the moral criticism of the past. Since a reversal of dominance has taken place, we can charge the people living before the reversal with a failure to appreciate the potential of the conceptual materials available to them. We can say that had they been more astute, the reversal would have occurred earlier.

On the account of the history of morality that we have been exploring, this line of criticism fails. As we saw in the previous section, the evolution of moral normativity cannot be regarded as a logical process. It is a conceptual-cum-social process, in which conceptual and social change reciprocally condition one another. Moral normativity at a given place and time is constituted by the zone of reasonable disagreement there and then, and a reversal of dominance, a change in the distribution of people within the zone, is explained in the same way as the evolution of the zone. If a formerly marginal view becomes dominant, this is because, as the conceptual-cum-social process unfolds, more people find themselves in situations that make adopting that view reasonable. The people of the Western past, however, had not yet lived through the changes, industrialization, for example, that brought into existence the modern moral world. Thus they had no basis, as competent reasoners, for duplicating this evolutionary process in their own reasoning. They could not have given themselves our understanding of political morality simply by subjecting the positions they held to rational elaboration. Moreover, even if some had been prescient enough to antici-pate what would come, they would have had no reason to abandon the views they held at the time. The actual unfolding of the conceptual-cum-social process changes what people have sufficient reason to do, but the mere foreseeing of the future does not. Absent the social changes, the conceptual changes are inappropriate.[15]

---

[15] In *Fieldwork in Familiar Places* (Cambridge, MA: Harvard University Press, 1997), ch. 2, Michelle Moody-Adams appears to argue that we can criticize past societies for failing to live up to our

To sum up this discussion, there are two ways of approaching the moral appraisal of the past. We can use our imaginations to inject ourselves, armed with our present moral concepts, into the past polity we are concerned with, and make the judgments about it that we would make if its practices and institutions were suddenly to appear in our own polity. Thus, we might judge unacceptable the absence of democracy. Because we will not have a clear understanding of what was involved in living within those practices and institutions, these judgments will not be as sound as those we would make if the institutions and practices actually did appear in our own polity. But otherwise, this way of making moral judgments about the past is relatively easy.

It is also, however, anachronistic. If the moral appraisal of the past is to be historically sound, it must proceed on the basis of what the people living then had sufficient reason to do. We can say that they acted wrongly in organizing political cooperation as they did only if they acted against reasons they themselves had. Certain kinds of moral realism may yield the result that the people of the past had the same reasons we have, but under moral nominalism this cannot be taken for granted. If they had different concepts, they had different reasons. It seems, in fact, that earlier forms of many of our contemporary concepts of political morality were available on the margins of the polities of the Western past. So it is plausible that competent reasoners living at the time could have made judgments rejecting, in fundamental respects, the social practices and institutions that existed then. But it is also likely that judgments rejecting this rejection were reasonable in the past, and the views expressed by these judgments may have been held by the vast majority of people living then.

To the extent that forerunners of modern Western views were marginal in the Western past, we can regard the emergence of our modern moral world as involving a reversal of dominance. To repeat, to count as dominant, in the sense in which I am employing the term, it is not enough that a view is held by most members of a polity. It must also be reasonable. It must be supportable by competent reasoning employing the available normative

standards if we can reinterpret their moral thinking in our own terms. This may be relatively easy if we can find proxies in a particular past society. But the view of the proxies may have been marginal in the society in question, in which case most people in that society would not have had sufficient reason to live as we do. If there was in fact a reversal of dominance, there will be a sense in which the past contained the seeds of the present. But this does not mean that past people, through reinterpretation of their conceptual materials, could have thought their way to our present understandings of political morality. Reinterpretation is, broadly speaking, a logical process, while the reversal of dominance is not a purely logical process. It is a conceptual-cum-social process that depends importantly on the alteration of the social environment by concrete action.

and evaluative concepts. A reversal of dominance is effected by the conceptual-cum-social process described in chapter 4. Narrating a reversal of dominance is a delicate matter. It is not enough to tell the causal story of a change in view. It must be made plausible that the new judgments whose emergence and diffusion are being described were reasonable in the evolving social context. A certain amount of rational reconstruction of the thinking of past people will thus be required. For present purposes, however, the important point is that we may not be able to attribute to widespread unreasonableness in the Western past the fact that political cooperation then took a form alien to modern Western moral sensibilities.[16]

HIERARCHY

In the previous section, I suggested that the hierarchical organization of political cooperation that was common in the Western past may have been morally acceptable then. Or to be more precise, although various features of the institutions and practices of the Western past were doubtless morally unacceptable then, this unacceptability is to be understood as consisting in deviation from an ideal that was itself hierarchical. On the view I have proposed, a way of organizing political cooperation is morally acceptable when it can be endorsed by reasonable members of the polity in question, operating with the available concepts. In this section, I explore in greater detail the possibility that hierarchy was morally acceptable in the Western past.

First, it will be useful to say a bit more about how hierarchy is to be understood. In its basic form, I shall suppose, a hierarchical mode of political cooperation has the following features. First, it is cooperation to maintain a framework of social statuses. The statuses are defined by the

---

[16] In note 24 of chapter 2, I considered the possibility of obtaining a principle of fairness valid for all human beings simply by reflecting on the disposition to make and seek concessions that will be possessed by all properly functioning humans. I argued that this is not in fact possible because a process of mutual concession can have a determinate outcome only if the disposition to make and seek concessions is given a conceptualized structure, and the concepts available in different polities will yield different structures. These concepts are generated by the conceptual-cum-social process as it evolves over time. It should be mentioned that the understanding possessed by the cooperators of the relative strength of the reasons justifying concession will also be a historical product. On the account I have provided, the strength of these reasons, for a given cooperator, is determined by the strength of the disposition to make and seek concessions when it is packaged by the corresponding concepts (and the capacities engaged are functioning properly). But so understood, strength depends both on the place in the overall conceptual scheme of the concepts doing the packaging, and on the nature of the social situations which activate the disposition. Both will change as the conceptual-cum-social process unfolds, with the result that understandings of relative strength that previously made sense to members of a polity may cease to do so.

rights to direct, and the obligations to obey, associated with them. Higher status individuals have rights to direct more people in more ways, and obligations to obey fewer people in fewer ways, than lower status individuals. Second, status is largely fixed by birth. There will be exceptions, but on the whole, the members of a hierarchically structured polity are simply born into a particular position in the hierarchy and occupy it for life. We need not suppose that those in higher positions routinely direct the actions of those in lower positions. There will typically be a complex code of behavior enjoining actions by inferiors that accommodate superiors in various ways, and the existence of this code may be the most visible manifestation of hierarchy. In general, the social function of explicit direction by superiors is to alter established behavior when circumstances warrant this. So in a stable social environment, explicit direction will play a smaller role in maintaining political cooperation.

In modern Western polities, by contrast, political cooperation proceeds on the assumption that everyone has a single status, that of a self-directing agent. Political cooperation proceeds on the assumption that everyone is, in this sense, autonomous. To the extent that some members have rights to direct other people, or obligations to obey other people, these rights and obligations result from choices that members make. This does not mean that in modern Western polities, government is authorized by the consent of the governed. The view that the right to direct that governments possess is created by the consent of the governed is open to serious objections.[17] It is preferable to approach the legitimacy of government as was done in chapter 4, through the idea that a properly functioning human will be disposed to cooperate in the creation of a political society, a society in which interaction is coordinated by established authority. This way of understanding legitimacy is applicable to the hierarchical polities of the Western past as well as to contemporary polities. We can say that political authority was legitimately exercised in the past if cooperatively disposed people, reasoning competently with the available normative and evaluative concepts, would in general have found it appropriate to cooperate in the maintenance of the political structures that existed then.

Now let us turn to the question of the reasonableness of hierarchy. T. M. Scanlon has discussed a position he calls parametric universalism. This is the view that there are universal moral principles, but what they imply about how people should behave – for our purposes, about how political

---

[17] See A. John Simmons, *Moral Principles and Political Obligations* (Princeton: Princeton University Press, 1978), chs. 3 and 4.

cooperation should be organized – varies depending on local conditions.[18] This gives us one way of approaching the idea that hierarchy was reasonable in the past, but no longer is. A mode of political organization that is wrong in one context may be right in another because various empirical facts that are relevant to the organization of political cooperation are different in the two contexts. Thus it could be argued that there are certain timeless and universal features of good political organization, but that in the Western past, when illiteracy was common, few people were educated, and communication was poor, democratic polities would not have possessed these features. Rather it was necessary to concentrate political power in a small elite. This was true even in the cities and towns of the Western past, which are often regarded as the incubators of democracy. Democratic rights were restricted to, or skewed in favor of, an urban elite. Parametric universalism allows us to deem these arrangements reasonable at the time.

Within parametric universalism, there is no distinction between the "ought" of evaluation and the "ought" that ascribes reasons for action. Since the fundamental moral principles are timeless, our present understanding of them, if correct, is valid for the people of the past as well. Moral nominalism, by contrast, requires the distinction, at least if we assume that moral normativity has evolved. As I have said, there may be some timeless and universal features of good political organization, such as the non-existence of chattel slavery. But in general, the features of good political organization are determined by the normative and evaluative concepts available at a particular time and place. To the extent that judgments of political morality are determined by something timeless and universal, this is the normativity of proper functioning, which underlies the disposition to make and seek concessions in cooperative contexts when others are similarly disposed, and guides the employment of the socially available concepts in judgments that give structure to this disposition. For parametric universalism, differences in how political cooperation ought to be organized at a particular time and place are *derived* from timeless, universal principles together with information about local conditions. For moral nominalism, by contrast, such differences are rather the *product* of a historical process, the conceptual-cum-social process, that shapes in different ways a form of motivation that will be experienced by all properly functioning humans.

Parametric universalism is a realist view, and realist views, I have argued, cannot provide an adequate account of reasonable disagreement. I shall, then, proceed on the assumption that moral nominalism provides a better

---

[18] T. M. Scanlon, *What We Owe to Each Other* (Cambridge, MA: Harvard University Press, 1998), ch. 8.

way of understanding how hierarchy could have been reasonable in the Western past. It is also worth noting that if parametric universalism is the right approach to the question of what was reasonable in the past, it presumably is also the right approach to the question of what is reasonable in other contemporary polities. But in this case, parametric universalism seems far-fetched. It is hard to regard the differences among the political concepts that we find in the world today, the different kinds of claims and social values that are acknowledged, as explained by features of the local context that influence what is necessary to realize certain timeless and universal principles of good political organization. It is more plausible to attribute these differences to the fact that different historically generated concepts are being employed to give form to the general disposition to make and seek concessions in cooperative contexts. But if moral nominalism does a better job of explaining the differences among present polities, it presumably also does a better job of explaining the differences between the present and the past.

For moral nominalism, conceptual change constitutes a part of a larger conceptual-cum-social process in which conceptual change and social change reciprocally condition one another. This appears to create the possibility that the endorsement of hierarchy in the Western past could have been a dominant view in our sense, a reasonable view held by most of the members of past polities. The conclusion might seem problematic, however. In general, right is to be distinguished from force, normative power from causal power, and the essence of normative power is that it displaces causal power in the structuring of human affairs. Indeed, the displacement of brute causal power by normative power, of force by right, can be regarded as the essence of the human phenomenon. The distinctive feature of our form of life is that we live in a world of "oughts."

A picture of this sort underlies Rousseau's argument in *On the Social Contract*.[19] Rousseau regards the social contract as effecting a transition from a form of life that lacks a normative dimension to one that possesses a normative dimension. The view I am proposing also envisages a transition of this sort, but not one produced by agreement. Rather in the course of the natural history of the human race, a line was crossed. In chapter 2, I mentioned Thomas Nagel's view that when a certain level of biological complexity is reached, rationality – that is, thought that has a conscious normative dimension – becomes possible. But although the distinctive

---

[19] Jean-Jacques Rousseau, *On the Social Contract*, in Jean-Jacques Rousseau, *The Basic Political Writings*, trans. D. Cress (Indianapolis: Hackett, 1987).

feature of our form of life is that we live in a world of "oughts," the proper order of things can be subverted. Normative thought can be corrupted or displaced by causal power, and, it might be held, this is especially likely to have happened when we find the general acceptance of hierarchical social arrangements.[20]

The subordination of the normative to the non-normative is a feature of a number of philosophical theories of the social domain. The Marxian model is the most familiar.[21] According to this model, social reality accommodates itself to the level of development of the forces of production, and part of this process of accommodation is the generation of a form of consciousness that is consonant with the existing economic structure. Most political thought is thus ideology, a body of opinion that supports the existing structure because it has that function. A different picture is provided by Michel Foucault. According to him, knowledge, or justified belief, and power are two different modes of presentation of one underlying reality. In his book *The Order of Things*, Foucault describes a historical process in which earlier forms of thought, which he calls "epistemes," give way to later forms.[22] But these transitions are in no way normatively guided. Thus thought is conditioned by something that lies beyond normativity.

The theory that I have proposed is not properly grouped with views of this sort. Moral nominalism is not a debunking theory that strips the domain of right of its claim to function as a constraint on power. It takes a realist view of the proper functioning of the human mental apparatus, and as I explained in chapter 4, it is generally optimistic that the apparatus functions properly. Individual failures of proper functioning are common, but on the whole, the conceptual-cum-social process that shapes the evolution both of moral concepts and of basic social structures will supply the members of a polity with moral concepts genuinely attuned to their social environment, concepts suitable for guiding the management and modification of existing social structures. The assumption that, overall, human cooperative and conceptual capacities function properly receives support from the fact, which ought to occasion more surprise than it does, that social organization exists at all.

---

[20] As was mentioned in the previous chapter, Williams has argued that liberals may be able to show members of contemporary hierarchical societies that the instruction they have received concerning what gives legitimacy to existing arrangements is just a form of coercion.

[21] See for example, Karl Marx, "Preface to A Critique of Political Economy," in David McLellen, ed., *Karl Marx: Selected Writings* (Oxford: Oxford University Press, 2000), pp. 424–428.

[22] Michel Foucault, *The Order of Things: An Archaeology of the Human Sciences* (New York: Vintage Books, 1994).

Moral nominalism, then, provides a basis for supposing that the conceptual apparatus of hierarchy characteristic of the polities of the past was capable of giving form to the cooperative dispositions of the properly functioning members of those polities. As was noted in chapter 4, the presence of concepts that are unsuitable for this role cannot be ruled out, and they may have influenced the way political cooperation was in fact organized. But the operation of the conceptual-cum-social process makes it likely that reasonable members of these polities, although rejecting any features of political cooperation produced by people acting on unsuitable concepts, would have remained broadly supportive of hierarchy. Similarly, we cannot rule out the possibility that some of the political arrangements of the past were despotic, in the sense explained in the previous chapter. Powerful subgroups may have succeeded in imposing political decision-making procedures that would have been rejected by most reasonable members of the polities in question. But the operation of the conceptual-cum-social process again makes it likely that this rejection would have been effected on the basis of judgments that were broadly supportive of hierarchical forms of political organization.

It appears, then, that the antecedent operation of the conceptual-cum-social process, which produced both the available concepts and the overall social environment that the people of the time confronted, could have made judgments supporting hierarchical social arrangements feasible for competently reasoning members of the polities of the Western past. The boundaries of the zone of reasonable disagreement are never completely clear, and the boundaries of the zone in a past polity may be especially unclear to us in the present. Still, if we make the assumption that, on the whole, human conceptual and cooperative capacities function properly, the central place occupied by the conceptual apparatus of hierarchy in the political thinking of the peoples of the Western past provides some reason for supposing that acceptance of hierarchy was a reasonable position in those polities – indeed, a dominant position, a position that most members of these polities, reasoning competently with the available concepts, would have endorsed.[23] As has been mentioned, the past acceptance of a hierarchical ideal is

---

[23] In general, the proper functioning of the disposition to make and seek concessions when others are similar disposed, which underlies competent reasoning about questions of political morality, presupposes contact with the thinking of the similarly disposed others envisaged by the disposition. Modern media of communication were not available in the hierarchical polities of the past, but people who were not members of ruling elites still had ways of making known their views about the appropriate way of organizing political cooperation. So there is some basis for regarding all segments of society as participating in the fashioning of the conceptual apparatus that was available in those polities.

compatible with the rejection, on the basis of that ideal, of many particular aspects of the way political cooperation was actually organized.

The claim that judgments supporting hierarchy were reasonable in the Western past receives further support from the fact that in important respects, hierarchy is still with us. Political morality, at the most basic level, is the morality of authority and property. Hierarchy, as I defined it above, is a way of structuring authority relations. The reversal of dominance that has created the modern West has involved the replacement of the idea that some people have, simply by the nature of things, the right to direct other people by the idea that everyone is, simply by the nature of things, a self-directing agent. Property, understood merely as ownership, can also give rise to hierarchy, however. Ownership does not bring with it a right to direct the actions of other people, but it can create directive power, the ability to get people to do certain things by telling them to do these things. This is especially true of the ownership of productive resources. The owner of productive property has an ability to reward or punish certain other people, the employees. As a result, employees have a reason to comply with the directives issued by the owner. So private ownership of productive property introduces an element of hierarchy into modern life.

The moral acceptability of this property-based form of hierarchy is something about which reasonable people in the present can disagree. Competent reasoners, drawing on the political concepts of the modern West, can conclude that the form of hierarchy associated with private ownership of productive property is just as objectionable as that associated with the possession by some people of a personal right to direct the actions of other people. But the political concepts of the modern West also provide a basis for judgments to the effect that property-based hierarchies are acceptable, that they are narrowly or broadly fair, and this view is dominant, to varying degrees, in Western polities.[24]

Directive power requires a normative license. Where it lacks such a license, we could have despotism. It might be thought that in the case of directive power exercised by private owners of productive resources, at least, such a license could be provided by the consent of the governed, the employees. Elsewhere, however, I have argued that in a modern capitalist economy, where the actions of large corporations have a significant impact on the public good, the directive power possessed by the owners of productive property requires the same sort of license as the directive power

---

[24] Many Western polities have competitive socialist parties, but as far as I am aware, they no longer campaign on a platform of eliminating private ownership of all major productive resources.

possessed by modern governments, a license grounded in the fact that the exercise of this power facilitates cooperation to promote the public good.[25] Cooperation-facilitating authority can be exercised democratically, but it need not always be exercised in this way. Where it is not exercised democratically, we will have a form of hierarchy.

As long as we confine ourselves to political authority narrowly construed, the authority of governments, the idea that hierarchical modes of political organization were morally acceptable in the Western past is unlikely to excite much controversy now. In the West, the battle for democratic government has been won, so we do not have to worry that people will infer from the reasonableness of monarchy or aristocracy in the past that it would be reasonable in the present. But the subordination of women to men was also a feature of the Western past, and to a certain extent, it is still with us. As a result people are likely to be less sanguine about the sexual hierarchies of the past. Admitting their reasonableness could be taken as an endorsement of sexual hierarchy in the present. What should we say about the possible reasonableness of sexual hierarchy in the past? In addressing this question, we must bear in mind that we are talking about political morality. We are not concerned with whether the physical abuse of women was morally wrong in the past. That can be taken for granted. We are concerned with the reasonableness of certain relations of authority and property.

Within the framework of moral nominalism, two observations about the sexual hierarchies of the past are in order. First, if the endorsement of sexual hierarchy, and in particular patriarchy, was a dominant reasonable view in the Western past, this is because a conceptual-cum-social process manifesting the proper functioning of human conceptual and cooperative capacities produced the requisite concepts and secured their wide employment. Presumably this is to be understood as something that took place in the distant past. In the early history of Western peoples, conceptual structures capable of licensing patriarchy emerged in a way that manifested the proper functioning of human conceptual and cooperative capacities in the existing conditions. We also need to suppose that subsequent changes in the social circumstances of Western life provided most competent reasoners with no basis for abandoning this view.

The conceptual-cum-social process that we are envisaging must be understood as encompassing the judgments and actions of women. The past endorsement of sexual hierarchy can be regarded as a dominant

---

[25] I argue for this conclusion in "The Public Authority of the Managers of Private Corporations," forthcoming in G. Brenkert and T. Beauchamp, eds., *The Oxford Handbook of Business Ethics*.

reasonable view, a reasonable view held by most of the members of a past polity, only if it could have been endorsed by a large number of competently reasoning women operating with the available conceptual resources. If the endorsement of sexual hierarchy in the Western past cannot be understood as possessing this status, we must take seriously the possibility that its maintenance constituted a form of despotism. We should note here, once again, that the reasonableness of hierarchy as an ideal is compatible with the unreasonableness of particular aspects of existing hierarchical practices and institutions.

The second observation we need to make concerns the emergence to dominance in Western polities of the modern view that all humans have a single status, that of a self-directing agent. After this change, people reasoning competently on the basis of the available conceptual materials could not have endorsed the subordination of women. This means that the relatively recent recognition of the equality of women in Western polities is not to be attributed to the evolution of the zone of reasonable disagreement. Rather it is to be attributed to the slow recognition by the members of Western polities that the subordination of women was contrary to a view of the appropriate way of organizing political cooperation that had for some time been dominant.

It might be suggested that the recognition of the wrongness of slavery, culminating in its abolition in Western polities, can be explained the same way. With the emergence to dominance of the view that all humans have a single status, that of a self-directing agent, it became impossible for people reasoning competently with the socially available concepts to accept slavery. The emergence to dominance of the idea that all humans have the status of self-directing agents may have made it easier for the members of Western polities to see that slavery was wrong. When people were understood as occupying various positions in a hierarchical social system, it was doubtless harder to discern the distinctive wrongness of slavery. But within the framework of moral nominalism, the wrongness of slavery is not tied to the morality of autonomy. Chattel slavery is wrong a priori. Regardless of the available concepts, no form of political cooperation can be reasonable that involves denying to some of the participants any recognition at all as sources of claims.

RECTIFYING PAST WRONGS

Demands for the rectification of what present people regard as past injustice – for reparations or apologies – are a feature of contemporary moral life.

What does the view that moral normativity has a history, that what is wrong now may not have been wrong in the past, imply about the appropriateness of these demands? The general lesson, I believe, is that we should focus on the rectification of present wrongs. This is so even in the case of slavery, which according to moral nominalism was unquestionably wrong in the past. I discuss reparations in this section and apology in the next.

Rectification is always the rectification of past wrongs, although the wrong may be only minutes in the past. In the standard case involving individuals, the perpetrator and the victim are both still alive at the time rectification takes place. The demands for reparations that are the concern of this section are different in several respects. In the first place, they typically involve collective agents. A collective agent can remain in existence longer than a human being can. Thus a historical wrong that occurred before any person now alive was born may still have taken place during the "lifetime" of a collective agent. But the actions of a collective agent are the actions of the humans cooperating to maintain it. So in the case of a wrong perpetrated by a presently existing collective agent before any people now alive were born, the demand for reparations has the following basic form. Because of a wrong perpetrated by some past people against other past people, some present people should transfer resources to other present people. Within the framework of moral nominalism, we need to distinguish two kinds of cases, those where the wrongness of the past actions or arrangements did not admit of reasonable disagreement at the time in question, and those where it did.

The creation and maintenance of the institution of chattel slavery provides the most straightforward example of the first kind of case. The claim that reparations are required for this historical wrong in the United States is the claim that because of the history of slavery in the United States, the present population of the United States, acting collectively through the government, should transfer resources to a subset of the present population. There are, however, two different ways that the history of slavery can be understood as requiring this action. Both involve inheritance. On the first, the people enslaved in the past had a claim against the United States at the time they lived, and this claim has been inherited by their descendants, while the obligation to pay it has been inherited by the people now comprising the United States. On the second, what has been inherited is not a set of claims that certain past people had, but the injustice that gave rise to these claims. It has been passed down. There has been some modification, but it is still identifiably a later stage of the same injustice. We thus confront a present injustice that is a legacy of a past injustice, a

present injustice that has a historical explanation. The moral requirement facing present people in this second case is a requirement to do what is necessary to eliminate the present injustice.

There are some reasons for thinking the second approach is more workable. It avoids the problems created by the fact that the United States, as a collective agent, came into existence only at the end of the eighteenth century, while the first slaves arrived in the territories that became the United States much earlier. Further, it enables us to sidestep the thorny issues, grounded in the philosophy of personal identity, connected with the fact that the present descendants of the people enslaved in the past would not have existed, as the particular people they are, if their ancestors had not been enslaved.[26]

There are also reasons for thinking that the second approach better reflects our moral intuitions about reparations for acknowledged wrongs perpetrated by collective agents in the distant past. This can be brought out by considering how "natural" rectification – the restoration of equality between the relevant populations by impersonal social forces operating over time – affects the claim for reparations. We do not hear any calls today for reparations for ancient slavery. Nor are the people of Belgium and the Netherlands seeking reparations from Spain for what the Duke of Alba did in the sixteenth century. And the people of Spain are not demanding reparations (from whom?) for the Moorish invasion of the Iberian Peninsula and the period of Umayyad rule that followed. The reason appears to be that no present injustice is seen as explained by these actions. But the current situation would be irrelevant if the demand for reparations were grounded in the inheritance of claims. If claims are inheritable, then no matter what their current condition of life, the descendants of the victims have a right to receive resources from the descendants of the perpetrators. If Bill Gates has an ancestor who was a victim of injustice, he has a right to be even richer than he is. So the fact that moral intuition does not support the call for reparations where there has been natural rectification of wrongs in the distant past suggests that when this call possesses intuitive force, what we are focusing on is not past injustice, but present injustice that has a historical explanation. What is owed will then be determined by what is required to correct the present injustice.

More interesting for our purposes are cases where, in considering the question of rectification, we have to take account of the fact that moral normativity has a history. On the view I have proposed, moral normativity,

---

[26] For discussion of this issue, see George Sher, "Transgenerational Compensation," *Philosophy and Public Affairs* 33 (2005), pp. 181–200.

at a given place and time, is constituted by the zone of reasonable disagreement there and then. I have suggested that the boundaries of the zone of reasonable disagreement can never be determined with precision, and the epistemic challenge is even greater when we are concerned with the past. But we can construct an example that will at least illustrate the issues we confront when the relevant parts of political morality have evolved over time. This example concerns the cultural deprivation associated with efforts by Europeans to convert the indigenous peoples of the Americas to Christianity. Cultural deprivation raises moral issues when it compromises the ability of the victims to lead meaningful lives. The discussion that follows may not be completely accurate historically, but it will give us a way of exploring how the evolution of moral normativity can affect the issue of rectification.

Cultural change is a fact of the human condition. From the standpoint of modern Western ideas, it is acceptable only when it is autonomously produced by the people whose culture has been changed. When we think of cultural deprivation in connection with the actions of people of European descent in the Americas, one example that might come to mind is the destruction of the culture of the Plains Indians in the nineteenth century. This culture was itself a relatively recent innovation, being made possible by the introduction of the horse to the Americas by the Spanish. Yet no one thinks of the advent of this horse-based culture, and the attendant destruction of the form of life that preceded it, as a further cultural wrong perpetrated by Europeans in the Americas. The reason is that the change was effected autonomously by the people whose way of life was transformed.

This point is important because recent scholarship seems to have replaced the idea that Europeans converted the indigenous peoples to Christianity with the view that a complex process of intercultural exchange took place.[27]

---

[27] "It is now broadly recognized that the interaction of Christianity with native American religions in the colonial era (and indeed subsequently) was characterized by reciprocal, albeit asymmetrical, exchange, rather than the unilateral imposition of an uncompromising, all-conquering and all-transforming monotheism." Nicholas Griffiths, "Introduction," in N. Griffiths and F. Cervantes, eds., *Spiritual Encounters: Interaction between Christianity and Native Religions in Colonial America* (Lincoln: University of Nebraska Press, 1999), p. 1. See also Fernando Cervantes, "Epilogue, the Middle Ground," in the same volume, pp. 276–285. In a similar vein, in *Facing East from Indian Country: A Native History of Early America* (Cambridge, MA: Harvard University Press, 2001), pp. 79–90, Daniel Richter notes that for the indigenous peoples of eastern North America, acceptance of Christianity need not have involved a surrender of indigenous culture. Indigenous spiritual life, he says, was accustomed to accommodating new spiritual powers, and the adoption of Christianity by some indigenous people can be viewed as a form of diplomacy. It cemented ties, in a way traditional within those cultures, with people, missionaries, who had the status for the indigenous peoples of ambassadors of the newcomers.

To the extent that this is so, it becomes difficult to speak of cultural deprivation. Still, the idea that the introduction of Christianity into the Americas involved cultural deprivation is not completely misguided. This is especially true in the areas under Spanish control, where various forms of coercion were employed to suppress "idolatry" – that is, traditional forms of spiritual life.[28] The actions in question form a relatively small part of the overall story, and they may not have succeeded in fully eliminating indigenous forms of spirituality. But they clearly deprived the indigenous peoples affected of important cultural resources.[29]

We can begin by considering how these actions might have looked from the standpoint of European moral normativity. The Spanish established political control in the Americas by conquest. Modern Western moral normativity condemns this, but it was the universal practice in the past, no less in pre-Columbian America than elsewhere. Further, there is evidence that in the past, Western moral normativity regarded the establishment of political control by conquest as legitimate.[30] So let us suppose that competent sixteenth-century Europeans, operating with the concepts available to them, could have judged the conquest of the Americas morally acceptable. Where the establishment of political control is morally acceptable, so is the making of laws, and the use of coercion to enforce those laws. This means that the Spanish could have judged the use of coercion to enforce their laws morally acceptable as well.[31]

---

[28] See Iris Gareis, "Repression and Cultural Change: The 'Extirpation of Idolatry' in Colonial Peru," in Griffiths and Cervantes, eds., *Spiritual Encounters*, pp. 230–254.

[29] After noting the resilience of indigenous forms of spirituality in one region of Peru, Gareis says:

> The institutionalized extirpation campaigns weakened the indigenous religions of the Huarochiri nevertheless. In particular, the great religious ceremonies celebrated in pre-Columbian times in honour of the local deities could no longer be performed. These ceremonies had been in former times at the core of ethnic solidarity, since all the villages gathered for the celebration and were united in worshipping the most important deities of the region … The fact that indigenous religious activities could only be carried out secretly and in privacy soon dispossessed the native religions of their former social functions. ("Repression and Cultural Change," p. 241)

> As she later puts it, "Thus, the persecution weakened the native religions at the sociopolitical level" (p. 243).

[30] For example, Thomas Hobbes, writing in the seventeenth century, distinguishes between commonwealth by institution and commonwealth by acquisition. Commonwealth by acquisition involves the authorization as sovereign of someone who has established effective control by force. See Thomas Hobbes, *Leviathan*, ed. E. Curley (Indianapolis: Hackett, 1994), ch. 20.

[31] In chapter 5, I proposed a definition of despotism. This definition was grounded in Williams's idea that coercion unmediated by a sound justification is everywhere an injustice. I argued that where there is reasonable disagreement about the appropriate way of making decisions that resolve first-order reasonable disagreements, some injustice of this sort is unavoidable, and I suggested that what political morality requires is its minimization. We have despotism if the number of competently reasoning

The next question we face is whether competent Europeans could also have judged acceptable the particular policy we are now focusing on, the suppression of indigenous forms of spirituality. On the picture we have been exploring, the concepts available to competent reasoners in the Western past made possible the endorsement of hierarchical ways of organizing political cooperation. But political control cannot be achieved solely by coercion. Various supporting norms must be internalized. Further, a single society requires a single set of norms. Prior to the rise of literacy and general primary education, socialization to a religion was one of the main ways that Western polities secured the internalization of these norms. These observations suggest that the Spanish, working within the framework of Western political morality that existed at the time, could reasonably have supposed that the imposition of Christianity was both required and acceptable.[32] Some competent European reasoners, employing the concepts available to them, may have been able to reject this judgment. But such views were marginal. Thus we cannot expect them to have guided the thinking of the relevant collective agents, Spain or the Catholic Church.

members of the relevant population who would favor the replacement of the existing political decision-making procedure by a particular known alternative exceeds the number supporting that procedure.

Williams may have identified an a priori requirement of political morality. If so, the establishment of political control by conquest can be morally acceptable only if it does not result in despotism. This condition could be met in a number of ways. For example, conquest could bring peace out of war, as envisaged by Hobbes, or the conquerors could be perceived as liberators by various groups within the conquered population. But it is enough that no single alternative to the regime established by conquest would be regarded as preferable by more people in the affected population, reasoning competently with the available concepts (including any acquired from the conquerors). One important reason for this could be that the establishment of political control by conquest has been the historical norm, and thus local political thought is accommodating of it. Of course, arrangements that are not despotic initially can become despotic as political thinking evolves, although since despotism is partly a matter of numbers, changes in the composition of the relevant population must also be taken into account.

Exploring global history from this angle would be an interesting exercise. I am in no position to speculate about what the result would be in the case of the Spanish conquest of the Americas, about whether it involved despotism in the sense I have proposed. For present purposes, which are merely illustrative, I shall assume that it did not – that no alternative procedure for resolving political disagreement within the population subject to Spanish control would have been preferred by more members of that population, reasoning competently with the concepts available to them. This is compatible with the possibility that even those who accepted Spanish political control could have judged unreasonable various particular policies adopted by the Spanish.

[32] There appears to be some reason to suppose that the Spanish saw things this way. "[Viceroy of Peru Francisco de] Toledo's efforts to extend inquisitorial jurisdiction over the indigenous population were perhaps not originally motivated by his concern for the Christianization of the Amerindians, but may well have been designed as a means of strengthening the power of the crown. The Spanish Inquisition was one of the pillars of modern absolutism in Spain and could be used as a political tool. One of its purposes was to keep the subjects under religious and ideological control" (Gareis, "Repression and Cultural Change," p. 232).

I am not sure that anyone has enough information about the political morality of the peoples of pre-Columbian America to reach definite conclusions about how competent indigenous reasoners, employing the concepts available to them, would have regarded the suppression of traditional forms of spirituality. But it will be enough for present purposes to posit a pre-Columbian form of political morality in light of which these actions were wrong. Let us, then, imagine that the indigenous people attached fundamental importance to maintaining the integrity of their social groups.[33] And let us suppose that the preservation of traditional forms of spirituality was necessary for the maintenance of social integrity. If, from the indigenous standpoint, preventing actions that were required to maintain social integrity constituted an injustice, competent indigenous reasoners could have regarded the Spanish as perpetrating an injustice.

As I have said, I do not claim that this account is completely accurate, historically. My goal here is simply to provide an illustration of the way the evolution of moral normativity can affect the project of rectification in the present. If we suppose that moral normativity in the two past populations had the forms described, what are implications for rectification in the present?

Let us focus first on the inheritance of claims to compensation. We are assuming that from the standpoint of Western political morality, as it existed at the time, the imposition of Christianity per se was not wrong. I have also noted that where the establishment of political control is morally acceptable, so is the use of coercion to enforce the law. It seems clear, however, that the suppression of idolatry was accompanied by actions that went beyond what was required to enforce the law, actions such as murder, assault, and theft. Let us suppose that competent Europeans operating with the available concepts would have judged actions of these kinds morally wrong, and that Western moral normativity, in the form it possessed at that time, required compensating the victims of such wrongs. If, as we are now assuming, claims to compensation are inheritable, it follows that Western moral normativity must acknowledge some sort of requirement of compensation in the present. But Western moral normativity has evolved in such a

---

[33] Some support for this as a picture of indigenous moral normativity can be derived from what is known about indigenous views of property. According to Richter (*Facing East from Indian Country*, pp. 54–55), the indigenous peoples of eastern North America had the concept of personal property, but viewed it as involving only rights to use, so that unused items became available for use by others. European understandings of property, by contrast, gave pride of place to the right to control an item, which means that an owner had a right to prevent access by others to an unused item. The indigenous understanding seems better to reflect the idea that preservation of the integrity of the social unit is the overriding concern.

way that the suppression of indigenous spirituality, per se, now appears to constitute an additional wrong accompanying the conquest because it effected cultural change in a way that violated autonomy. What is the significance of this for the issue of rectification? Can claims for compensation, so to speak, grow as moral normativity evolves to regard particular actions as wrong for a further reason? Can they become claims to receive greater compensation?

It is difficult to see how they can. Making the descendants of the perpetrators pay additional compensation because what their ancestors did would be wrong for a further reason now seems to amount to punishing them (the present descendants) for a wrong they did not commit. Indeed, from the standpoint of Western political morality, it can be denied that anyone committed these wrongs. The actions in question were endorsed by a moral view that was, we are supposing, reasonable in the community of the agents at the time the actions were performed. Taking the perpetrators to be collective agents does not alter this conclusion. So, on the assumptions we have been making, the descendants of the perpetrators, or the current members of the perpetrating collective agents, can reasonably reject the claim that they should pay compensation for the violations of autonomy associated with the suppression of indigenous forms of spirituality.

How do things look from the standpoint of indigenous moral normativity? To answer this question, we must supplement our hypothesis regarding the content of indigenous political morality with one about its subsequent history. One possibility is that indigenous political morality evolved, by the mechanism I have posited, which can involve adaptation to social change, into a local variant of modern Western political morality that does not give fundamental importance to the maintenance of the integrity of the indigenous group. Assimilation into the larger population and adoption of its cultural forms is regarded as acceptable. The other important possibility is that the concepts employed by the descendants continue to provide a basis for the conclusion that the maintenance of group integrity is morally required, and this is the dominant position among the descendants. Let us consider these possibilities in turn.

On the first, it appears that the descendants of the original victims cannot be understood as possessing an inherited claim to compensation. As time passed, maintaining the integrity of the group ceased to be required. So from the standpoint of the indigenous understanding of moral normativity, the wrong simply disappeared. The inheritance of rights to compensation and obligations to pay it is a matter of the reconstituting of these rights and obligations in each succeeding generation. But this depends on whether

moral normativity still provides a conceptual package in which the claims can be wrapped. If this ceases to be the case, the rights to compensation and obligations to pay it generated by previous wrongdoing cease to exist.[34] By contrast, if indigenous moral normativity, while evolving, retained its emphasis on the preservation of the integrity of the group, the concepts necessary to reconstitute in succeeding generations the rights and obligations created by the original events could well have survived the evolutionary process.

This latter possibility presents us with a further issue, however. We must consider what, given that the right to compensation has survived, would now be owed. In general, the appropriate response to a wrong is restoration of the status quo ante. One must literally undo the original injury, or else transfer to the victim resources sufficient to place him or her on the same "indifference curve." It is arguable that no amount of money can make up for the loss of an element of one's culture that contributes in an important way to the meaningfulness of one's life. So let us suppose that the appropriate response in the case of the first generation was the literal restoration of the status quo ante, acceptance of indigenous forms of spirituality and assistance in reestablishing them. Where conversion actually took place, however, succeeding generations have consisted primarily of believing Christians who, it seems plausible to suppose, would reject the restoration of the status quo ante. Given this, it is unclear what, in the way of rectification, the survival of the original rights and obligations should be understood as entailing.

What does all this imply about how relations between the two present populations, the descendants of the agents of suppression and the descendants of the victims, should be structured? The former group might be understood as the present population of Spain, or as the part of the population of various Latin American countries that is of European descent. The conclusion of the above reasoning seems to be that even if the present descendants of the original victims have a basis, within their own moral framework, for claiming compensation, the present descendants of the agents have a parallel basis, within their moral framework, for denying

---

[34] As another example of this phenomenon, internal to Western culture, we might consider a violation of a code of honor that created a claim to compensation, perhaps in the form of participation in a duel. Suppose the compensation was not provided. The present descendants of the party that failed to observe the requirements of the code would doubtless find bizarre the idea that they had inherited an obligation to provide the necessary compensation to the present descendants of the victim of the breach. Such codes of honor play no role in modern Western life. But the inheritance of the obligation might have been accepted in the immediately following generation.

that they have an obligation to pay it. If the suppression of indigenous forms of spirituality was something that competent Europeans living at the time the actions took place were able to judge morally acceptable, the agents responsible could have denied that they had an obligation to pay compensation. And if the original agents had no obligation to pay, there is nothing for their descendants to inherit.

On the assumptions we have been making, then, the question whether compensation is required in the present will admit of reasonable disagreement. Members of the two present populations, the descendants of the agents and the descendants of the victims, can reasonably take opposing positions. To the extent that these disagreements arise within a particular polity, established mechanisms for resolving political disagreement, such as voting, can be employed to reach a decision about what to do.

We have been exploring the inheritance of claims to compensation for actions performed in the distant past. I have suggested, however, that when we find it plausible that resources should be transferred in the present because of actions performed in the distant past, this intuition is not best understood as grounded in a judgment that claims to compensation have been inherited. It is best understood as grounded in a judgment that an earlier injustice has been inherited. The injustice is still experienced, in some form, by the present descendants of the original victims. Given that the question whether the suppression of indigenous forms of spirituality, per se, constituted an injustice in the sixteenth and seventeenth centuries admitted of reasonable disagreement then, the case we are now considering is somewhat different from that of slavery. But it is arguable that the past actions in question, whatever their moral status when they were performed, have given rise to a present injustice of the relevant kind. The historical processes set in motion by the establishment of European political control of the Americas have created a situation in which it is difficult for indigenous cultures to sustain themselves, and to the extent that this makes it difficult for people to live meaningful lives, the result is a present injustice. It may be that all present members of the relevant polities, reasoning competently, would agree about the existence of this moral problem and about what needs to be done to address it. But even if these issues, too, admit of reasonable disagreement, the zone of disagreement will be different from that associated with the suggestion that claims to compensation have been inherited, and the distribution of opinion within the zone may be more favorable to rectification of some sort.[35]

---

[35] In *Multicultural Citizenship* (Oxford: Clarendon Press, 1995), Will Kymlicka argues that a liberal polity will accord extensive self-governance rights to incorporated indigenous groups.

APOLOGY

Now let us turn to apology. The rectification of some wrongs can be accomplished by an apology, and the idea that the leaders of present collective agents should apologize for the actions performed by these agents in the past (that is, by past members of these agents acting in their capacity as members) is gaining currency. The Pope, for example, has asked forgiveness for the way Catholics treated Jews and Muslims in the past. How are we to understand this phenomenon? Here again, the wrongness of the actions in question may be something that admitted of reasonable disagreement at the time they were performed. But when it comes to apology, present moral ideas assume greater importance.

There is something odd about the suggestion that present people who are not themselves wrongdoers of the particular kind at issue should apologize to present people they have not wronged in the specified way. The fact that it is the present leaders of collective agents, acting in their official capacity, who are expected to make the apologies reduces some of this oddness. Still, it does not render the phenomenon of apology completely unproblematic. Such apologies are typically made not to other collective agents that have existed for a long time, but to present people belonging to certain groups. And where the wrongs are in the distant past, we cannot say that the people to whom the apologies are made are the same people the collective agent wronged.

A different fact about group membership enables us, I think, to put the phenomenon of apology in proper perspective. The members of a collective agent at any particular point in time will usually identify with its past actions. Its history is, in a certain sense, their history. This can be a source of pride in the case of a collective agent that has an illustrious history or of shame when a collective agent has blemishes in its past. Thus, if the present members of a collective agent regard past actions by that agent as having been morally wrong, they will want to distance themselves from these actions. Present standards will loom large here. Even if the moral status of the actions in question admitted of reasonable disagreement when they were performed, the fact that the actions would be judged straightforwardly wrong by present standards can give rise to a desire for dissociation.

These points can be strengthened. Because it is in general true that people identify with the history of the collective agents to which they belong, there will be a presumption that they endorse the past actions of these agents unless they explicitly dissociate themselves from those actions.[36] The

---

[36] For a discussion of some issues germane to this point see the account of the collective self in Philip Pettit's *A Theory of Freedom: From the Psychology to the Politics of Agency* (Oxford: Oxford University

phenomenon of apology for the past actions of collective agents is, I think, best seen in this light. Strictly speaking, "apology" is the wrong word. What is required is rather an official repudiation, a repudiation by someone acting in an official capacity for the collective agent as a whole, of the past actions in question. This will remove the presumption that the present members endorse the actions.

An official repudiation of the sort described will be grounded in requirements governing present interaction. Just as the present members of a collective agent can be expected to identify with its earlier incarnations, the present members of the groups that suffered the treatment in question can be expected to identify with the earlier members of those groups. So the presumption that the present members of a collective agent endorse the past actions performed by that agent translates into a presumptive insult to the present descendants of the victims of those actions. In such a situation, the moral requirement of civility requires repudiation of the offensive actions, and this can be most effectively accomplished if the repudiation is official. Official repudiation removes the presumptive insult and affirms the moral and social equality of all the present people involved, the present members of the collective agent and the present descendants of the victims.

It may be helpful to say a bit more about the distinction between repudiating a past misdeed and apologizing for it. One apologizes to those personally affected by a misdeed. Repudiation, by contrast, is a way of assuring other moral agents, who have a general interest in the maintenance of the moral order, that one understands that one acted wrongly. The words "I'm sorry" may be employed in both cases, but the speech acts are different. One can be personally affected by something done to someone with whom one has a personal relationship, so apology to those who have such a relationship with the victim may be in order. But it is doubtful that merely identifying with the victims of a past misdeed constitutes a relationship of the requisite sort. If it did, a humanitarian who identified with the whole human race would be owed an apology for the past misdeeds of all the world's collective agents. As was noted earlier, past misdeeds can leave a legacy of injustice in the present. In that case, the victims of the present injustice will presumably be owed more than an apology. But it will be owed for something done to them, not something that was done to their ancestors.

Press, 2001), ch. 5. If Pettit is right, the repudiation, by the members of the present cohort of a collective agent, of some past actions performed by that agent – their refusal to endorse these actions – reduces the collective agent's present fitness to be held responsible for these actions.

CONCLUSION

This chapter has explored a number of philosophical issues that arise in connection with the idea, implied by moral nominalism, that moral normativity has a history. One conclusion we can draw from the discussion is that, when it comes to political morality, there is an important sense in which much of the past lies beyond present moral appraisal. We may have proxies in a past polity who could, as competent reasoners, have made criticisms of the existing institutions and practices similar to those we would make if, somehow, we could be transported to the past. But it will often be the case that the past people who, through their cooperative efforts, actually maintained the forms of political organization we are considering could have reasonably rejected these criticisms. Moral judgment is such an integral part of human life that coming to appreciate the justified indifference of the past to our present moral concerns can have the effect of divorcing the present from the past. But this loss may bring with it a compensating gain if it helps us to focus on our own moral moment.

Works cited

Anderson, Elizabeth, "What is the Point of Equality?" *Ethics* 109 (1999), pp. 287–337.

Ankersmit, F. R., "Historiography and Postmodernism," *History and Theory* 28 (May 1989), pp. 137–153.

"Reply to Professor Zagorin," *History and Theory* 29 (October 1990), pp. 275–296.

Appleby, Joyce, Lynn Hunt, and Margaret Jacob, *Telling the Truth about History* (New York: Norton, 1994).

Barthes, Roland, "Historical Discourse," in M. Lane, ed., *Structuralism: A Reader* (London: Jonathan Cape, 1970), pp. 145–155.

Blackburn, Simon, *Ruling Passions* (Oxford: Clarendon Press, 1998).

Boghossian, Paul, *Fear of Knowledge: Against Relativism and Constructivism* (Oxford: Clarendon Press, 2006).

Boyd, Richard, "How to Be a Moral Realist," in G. Sayre-McCord, ed., *Essays on Moral Realism* (Ithaca: Cornell University Press, 1989), pp. 181–228.

Brandom, Robert B., *Articulating Reasons: An Introduction to Inferentialism* (Cambridge, MA: Harvard University Press, 2000).

Brenner, Robert, "The Rises and Declines of Serfdom in Medieval and Early Modern Europe," in M. L. Bush, ed., *Serfdom and Slavery: Studies in Legal Bondage* (London: Longman, 1996), pp. 247–276.

Bush, Michael, "Serfdom in Medieval and Modern Europe: A Comparison," in M. L. Bush, ed., *Serfdom and Slavery: Studies in Legal Bondage* (London: Longman, 1996), pp. 199–224.

Callinicos, Alex, *Theories and Narratives: Reflections on the Philosophy of History* (Durham: Duke University Press, 1995).

Cervantes, Fernando, "Epilogue, the Middle Ground," in N. Griffiths and F. Cervantes, eds., *Spiritual Encounters: Interaction between Christianity and Native Religions in Colonial America* (Lincoln: University of Nebraska Press, 1999), pp. 276–285.

Chang, Ruth, "All Things Considered," *Philosophical Perspectives* 18 (2004), pp. 1–22.

Christensen, David, "Epistemology of Disagreement: The Good News," *The Philosophical Review* 116 (2007), pp. 187–217.

Cohen, G. A., "On the Currency of Egalitarian Justice," *Ethics* 99 (1989), pp. 906–944.

"Where the Action Is: On the Site of Distributive Justice," *Philosophy and Public Affairs* 26 (1997), pp. 3–30.

Cohen, Joshua, "Deliberation and Democratic Legitimacy," in J. Bohman and W. Rehg, eds., *Deliberative Democracy: Essays on Reason and Politics* (Cambridge, MA: MIT Press, 1997), pp. 67–91.

Cohen, Joshua and Charles Sabel, "Extra Republicam Nulla Justitia," *Philosophy and Public Affairs* 34 (2006), pp. 147–175.

Collingwood, R. G., *The Idea of History* (Oxford: Clarendon Press, 1946).

Daniels, Norman, "Wide Reflective Equilibrium and Theory Acceptance in Ethics," *The Journal of Philosophy* 76 (1979), pp. 256–282.

Danto, Arthur, *Narration and Knowledge* (New York: Columbia University Press, 1985).

Davies, Wendy, "On Servile Status in the Early Middle Ages," in M. L. Bush, ed., *Serfdom and Slavery: Studies in Legal Bondage* (London: Longman, 1996), pp. 225–246.

Derrida, Jacques, *Of Grammatology*, trans. G. C. Spivak (Baltimore: Johns Hopkins University Press, 1974).

Fodor, Jerry, *Concepts: Where Cognitive Science Went Wrong* (Oxford: Clarendon Press, 1998).

Foucault, Michel, *The Order of Things: An Archaeology of the Human Sciences* (New York: Vintage Books, 1994).

Gareis, Iris, "Repression and Cultural Change: The 'Extirpation of Idolatry' in Colonial Peru," in N. Griffiths and F. Cervantes, eds., *Spiritual Encounters: Interaction between Christianity and Native Religions in Colonial America* (Lincoln: University of Nebraska Press, 1999), pp. 230–254.

Geuss, Raymond, *The Idea of a Critical Theory: Habermas and the Frankfurt School* (Cambridge: Cambridge University Press, 1981).

Gibbard, Allan, *Thinking How to Live* (Cambridge, MA: Harvard University Press, 2003).

Goldman, Alvin I., *Knowledge in a Social World* (Oxford: Clarendon Press, 1999).

Goodin, Robert, *Reflective Democracy* (Oxford: Oxford University Press, 2003).

Goodman, Nelson, *Ways of Worldmaking* (Indianapolis: Hackett, 1978).

Griffiths, Nicholas, "Introduction," in N. Griffiths and F. Cervantes, eds., *Spiritual Encounters: Interaction between Christianity and Native Religions in Colonial America* (Lincoln: University of Nebraska Press, 1999).

Gutmann, Amy and Thompson, Dennis, *Democracy and Disagreement* (Cambridge, MA: Harvard University Press, 1996).

Why Deliberative Democracy? (Princeton: Princeton University Press, 2004).

Habermas, Jürgen, *The Theory of Communicative Action*, vol. I, trans. Thomas McCarthy (Boston: Beacon, 1984).

"Discourse Ethics: Notes on a Program of Philosophical Justification," in *Moral Consciousness and Communicative Action*, trans. C. Lenhardt and S. W. Nicholsen (Cambridge, MA: MIT Press, 1990), pp. 43–115.

Harman, Gilbert, "Inference to the Best Explanation," *The Philosophical Review* 74 (1965), pp. 88–95.

"Moral Relativism Defended," *The Philosophical Review* 84 (1975), pp. 3–33.

Hartley, L. P., *The Go-Between* (New York: Knopf, 1954).

Hempel, Carl, "The Function of General Laws in History," *The Journal of Philosophy* 39 (1942), pp. 35–48.

Hobbes, Thomas, *Leviathan*, ed. E. Curley (Indianapolis: Hackett, 1994).

Horgan, Terry and Mark Timmons, "Cognitivist Expressivism," in T. Horgan and M. Timmons, eds., *Metaethics After Moore* (Oxford: Clarendon Press, 2006).

Hurley, S. L., *Natural Reasons: Personality and Polity* (Oxford: Oxford University Press, 1989).

Justice, Luck, and Knowledge (Cambridge, MA: Harvard University Press, 2004).

Julius, A. J., "Nagel's Atlas," *Philosophy and Public Affairs* 34 (2006), pp. 176–192.

Kelly, Thomas, "The Epistemic Significance of Disagreement," in T. Gendler and J. Hawthorne, eds., *Oxford Studies in Epistemology*, vol. I (New York: Oxford University Press, 2006), pp. 167–196.

Korsgaard, Christine M., *The Sources of Normativity* (Cambridge: Cambridge University Press, 1996).

Kripke, Saul A., *Wittgenstein on Rules and Private Language* (Cambridge, MA: Harvard University Press, 1982).

Kymlicka, Will, *Multicultural Citizenship* (Oxford: Clarendon Press, 1995).

Larmore, Charles, "Pluralism and Reasonable Disagreement," in *The Morals of Modernity* (Cambridge: Cambridge University Press, 1996), pp. 152–174.

Locke, John, *The Second Treatise of Government*, ed. C. B. MacPherson (Indianapolis: Hackett, 1980).

Mackie, J. L., *Ethics: Inventing Right and Wrong* (Harmondsworth: Penguin, 1977).

Martin, Rex, *Historical Explanation* (Ithaca: Cornell University Press, 1977).

Marx, Karl, "Preface to A Critique of Political Economy," in *Karl Marx: Selected Writings*, ed. David McLellen (Oxford: Oxford University Press, 2000), pp. 424–428.

McDowell, John, "Non-Cognitivism and Rule-Following," in *Mind, Value, and Reality* (Cambridge, MA: Harvard University Press, 1998), pp. 198–218.

"Values and Secondary Qualities," in *Mind, Value, and Reality* (Cambridge, MA: Harvard University Press, 1998), pp. 131–150.

McMahon, Christopher, *Collective Rationality and Collective Reasoning* (New York: Cambridge University Press, 2001).

"Why There is No Issue Between Habermas and Rawls," *The Journal of Philosophy* 99 (2002), pp. 111–129.

"The Indeterminacy of Republican Policy," *Philosophy and Public Affairs* 33 (2005), pp. 67–93.

"Nondomination and Normativity," *Pacific Philosophical Quarterly* 88 (2007), pp. 319–327.

"The Public Authority of the Managers of Private Corporations," forthcoming in G. Brenkert and T. Beauchamp, eds., *The Oxford Handbook of Business Ethics*.

Mill, John Stuart, *Utilitarianism*, ed. G. Sher (Indianapolis: Hackett, 2002).

On Liberty, ed. David Bromwich and George Kateb (New Haven: Yale University Press, 2003).

Millikan, Ruth Garrett, "Truth Rules, Hoverflies, and the Kripke–Wittgenstein Paradox," *The Philosophical Review* 99 (1990), pp. 323–353.

Moody-Adams, Michelle, *Fieldwork in Familiar Places* (Cambridge, MA: Harvard University Press, 1997).

Munslow, Alan, *Deconstructing History* (London: Routledge, 1997).

Nagel, Thomas, *The Last Word* (Oxford: Oxford University Press, 1997).
   "The Problem of Global Justice," *Philosophy and Public Affairs* 33 (2005), pp. 113–147.

Patterson, Orlando, *Slavery and Social Death: A Comparative Study* (Cambridge, MA: Harvard University Press, 1982).

Peacocke, Christopher, *The Realm of Reason* (Oxford: Clarendon Press, 2004).

Pettit, Philip, *The Common Mind: An Essay on Psychology, Society, and Politics* (Oxford: Oxford University Press, 1993).
   Republicanism: A Theory of Freedom and Government (Oxford: Oxford University Press, 1999).
   A Theory of Freedom: From the Psychology to the Politics of Agency (Oxford: Oxford University Press, 2001).
   "The Determinacy of Republican Policy: A Reply to McMahon," *Philosophy and Public Affairs* 34 (2006), pp. 274–283.
   "When to Defer to Majority Testimony – and When Not to," *Analysis* 66 (2007), pp. 179–187.

Plantinga, Alvin, *Warrant and Proper Function* (Oxford: Oxford University Press, 1993).

Putnam, Hilary, *Meaning and the Moral Sciences* (London: Routledge & Kegan Paul, 1979).

Quine, Willard Van Orman, "Two Dogmas of Empiricism," *The Philosophical Review* 60 (1951), pp. 20–43.

Rabb, Theodore K., *The Last Days of the Renaissance and the March to Modernity* (New York: Basic Books, 2006).

Rawls, John, *A Theory of Justice* (Cambridge, MA: Harvard University Press, 1971).
   Political Liberalism (New York: Columbia University Press, 1993).

Richardson, Henry S., *Democratic Autonomy* (Oxford: Oxford University Press, 2002).

Richter, Daniel, *Facing East from Indian Country: A Native History of Early America* (Cambridge, MA: Harvard University Press, 2001).

Rorty, Richard, *Contingency, Irony, and Solidarity* (Cambridge: Cambridge University Press, 1989).

Rousseau, Jean-Jacques, *On the Social Contract*, in Jean-Jacques Rousseau, *The Basic Political Writings*, trans. D. Cress (Indianapolis: Hackett, 1987).

Scanlon, T. M., *What We Owe to Each Other* (Cambridge, MA: Harvard University Press, 1998).

Schneewind, J. B., "The Divine Corporation and the History of Ethics," in R. Rorty, J. B. Schneewind, and Q. Skinner, eds., *Philosophy in History* (Cambridge: Cambridge University Press, 1984), pp. 173–191.

Shafer-Landau, Russ, *Moral Realism: A Defence* (Oxford: Clarendon Press, 2003).

Sher, George, "Transgenerational Compensation," *Philosophy and Public Affairs* 33 (2005), pp. 181–200.

Simmons, A. John, *Moral Principles and Political Obligations* (Princeton: Princeton University Press, 1978).

Skinner, Quentin, "Meaning and Understanding in the History of Ideas," *History and Theory* 8 (1969), pp. 3–63.

Smith, Michael, *The Moral Problem* (Oxford: Blackwell, 1994).

Sturgeon, Nicholas, "Moral Explanations," in G. Sayre-McCord, ed., *Essays on Moral Realism* (Ithaca: Cornell University Press, 1989), pp. 229–255.

Sunstein, Cass, *Legal Reasoning and Political Conflict* (New York: Oxford University Press, 1996).

Taylor, Charles, *Hegel* (Cambridge: Cambridge University Press, 1975).

Timmons, Mark, *Morality Without Foundations: A Defense of Ethical Contextualism* (New York: Oxford University Press, 2004).

Turley, David, *Slavery* (Oxford: Blackwell, 2000).

Van Roojen, Mark, "Knowing Enough to Disagree: A New Response to the Moral Twin Earth Argument," in Russ Shafer-Landau, ed., *Oxford Studies in Metaethics* (New York: Oxford University Press, 2006), pp. 161–193.

Velleman, J. David, "Narrative Explanation," *The Philosophical Review* 112 (2003), pp. 1–25.

Waldron, Jeremy, "Justice Revisited," *The Times Literary Supplement*, no. 4707, June 18, 1993, pp. 5–6.

"Rawls's *Political Liberalism*," in *Law and Disagreement* (Oxford: Oxford University Press, 1999), pp. 149–163.

Wedgwood, Ralph, "Conceptual Role Semantics for Moral Terms," *The Philosophical Review* 110 (2001), pp. 1–30.

"The Meaning of 'Ought'," in Russ Shafer-Landau, ed., *Oxford Studies in Metaethics* (New York: Oxford University Press, 2006).

Wertheimer, Alan, "Internal Disagreements: Deliberation and Abortion," in Stephen Macedo, ed., *Deliberative Politics: Essays on Democracy and Disagreement* (New York: Oxford University Press, 1999), pp. 170–183.

White, Hayden, *Metahistory: The Historical Imagination in Nineteenth Century Europe* (Baltimore: Johns Hopkins University Press, 1973).

Wikipedia, "Assisted Living," http://en.wikipedia.org/wiki/Assisted_living

Williams, Bernard, *Ethics and the Limits of Philosophy* (Cambridge, MA: Harvard University Press, 1985).

Truth and Truthfulness (Princeton: Princeton University Press, 2002).

"Internal and External Reasons," in *Moral Luck* (Cambridge: Cambridge University Press, 1981), pp. 101–113.

"Philosophy and the Understanding of Ignorance," in *Philosophy as a Humanistic Discipline* (Princeton: Princeton University Press, 2006).

Young, Robert J. C., *Postcolonialism: An Historical Introduction* (Oxford: Blackwell, 2001).

Index